Revised Edition

VOLUME AND OPEN INTEREST

Classic Trading Strategies for 24-Hour Markets

KENNETH H. SHALEEN

IRWIN
Professional Publishing®
Chicago • London • Singapore

Times Mirror
Higher Education Group

Library of Congress Cataloging-in-Publication Data

Shaleen, Kenneth H.
    Volume and open interest / Kenneth H. Shaleen. — Rev. ed.
        p.   cm.
    Includes bibliographical references and index.
    ISBN 0-7863-0988-1
        1. Futures market—United States.   2. Investment analysis.
    I. Title.
    HG6024.U6S48   1997
    332.64'5—dc20   96–22373

Printed in the United States of America
1 2 3 4 5 6 7 8 9 0 DOC 3 2 1 0 9 8 7

CONTENTS

FOREWORD TO THE FIRST EDITION

This book will relate the three variables of price change, volume level, and open interest fluctuation. The result will produce the direction of the major price trend and a reading of that trend's strength. In many examples, a classical bar charting price pattern will exist. The basic ramifications of these formations will be highlighted, but this book is not intended to be a comprehensive study of price pattern recognition.

A technical approach to the analysis of any organized market uses volume as an important input. The futures exchanges produce an additional vital statistic—open interest. The technical form that best lends itself to analysis of volume and open interest is the daily high-low-close bar chart of a futures contract. Consequently, bar charts will be used to illustrate the concepts.

Daily bar charting is heavily relied upon in "position" trading as opposed to shorter term techniques (point & figure, five-minute bar charts, etc.) utilized by traders. Volume and open interest changes should be important to all categories of market participants: short-term traders, foreign-exchange dealers, hedgers, and position traders.

FOREWORD TO THE SECOND EDITION

The phenomenal increase in an individual trader's ability to marshal the computational power of the personal computer has led to a proliferation of mathematical approaches to technical analysis. The first 140 years of wheat futures trading on the Chicago Board of Trade evolved with charts showing only volume and open interest plotted below prices. Now, the burgeoning of technical-analysis tools is held back (or slowed) only by the marketing cycle of the software vendors. One consequence of this increased use of mathematical tools is the demand for physical space on the screen or hard copy printout. This has occurred at the expense of volume and interest data.

Purveyors of the new analytical models do realize that a plot of volume and open interest must be included somewhere in the technical "toolbox." It's there. But the sensitivity of the scales on most default screens is abominable. The ability to zoom in or increase the sensitivity—to see nuances in volume and open interest changes—is a must.

Another reason that analysis of volume and open interest has been receiving less attention is the increasing complexity of the futures day. When does it start? When does it stop? Sources of data, such as the Internet, were not in use when the first edition of *Volume and Open Interest* was written. How should all this data be organized?

All of these considerations add up to push the study of volume and open interest into the smallest niche of futures technical analysis that it has ever occupied.

The basic application of the theory has not changed. The first 13 chapters of the original edition have been tweaked when necessary and additional examples added. I've addressed many of the new considerations in Chapter 14, "24-Hour Markets," and Chapter 15, "The Data."

I welcome and embrace the technological advances in computing power, and I applaud the move toward 24-hour futures trading. Indeed, that is the *raison´ d´etre* for this edition of *Volume and Open Interest*.

Ken Shaleen
Chicago
March 7, 1996

CATALOG OF CHARTS

CHAPTER

1

RATIONALE

The fundamentals of supply and demand make a market move higher or lower in the long run. In the short run (which can be hours, days, or even weeks depending on the time scale used), a market can go in the exact opposite direction of the larger fundamental picture. This is because many decisions are psychological judgments—based upon hopes, fears, greed, moods, and the like.

Volume and open interest can identify how traders are reacting to changing conditions. Analyzing volume and open interest changes results in a determination of which contingent, the longs or shorts, is the "strong hand." The position of the strong hand is the direction of the major price trend. The strong hands are deemed the "smart money." Interpretation of volume and open interest changes are an attempt to identify the smart money and determine what this contingent of successful traders is thinking.

Critics of technical analysis have a myriad of reasons. One comment often made is: The underlying cash, or spot, market is the dominant market; therefore, why should the futures market, a derivative, be analyzed? This is a valid question and merits a response.

The difference between a cash market price and a futures price is the "basis." The more stable this relationship, the easier the analytical task of determining the health of a price trend. For a clear explanation of this link, refer to Appendix C—"Basis."

There is no question that the cash, or spot, market is much larger in total turnover than the corresponding futures contract. Accurate statistics are difficult, if not impossible, to obtain in an over-the-counter market. For instance, what was the turnover (volume) in spot dollar–mark dealing in the U.S. interbank market yesterday? Since data availability is not timely, an exact answer is not possible. However, turnover figures are important inputs to a technical approach. Certain additional questions:—Were new positions opened? Was it liquidation? Was the price rally short covering?—also cannot be answered sufficiently.

Futures markets, on the other hand, generate exact high-low-close price data as well as open interest statistics that a trader can use effectively. A futures contract that has achieved a critical mass becomes a microcosm—diminutive but analogous to the large (interbank) system. Thus, futures clearinghouse statistics can be used as a surrogate without cash, or spot, market data. For example, if it was a high turnover day in interbank dollar–mark dealing in North American spot and forward transactions, it will be reflected in increased trading activity in the deutschemark (DM) futures pit on the International Monetary Market (IMM) in Chicago. If positions are being retained or rolled in the interbank market, no matter whether there are speculative or legitimate corporate hedges, this phenomenon also should be occurring in futures.

The premise is that changes in futures open interest reflect what is occurring in the larger cash market.

This premise is central to the analysis of any futures market chart and is the entire focus of this book.

CHAPTER

2

VOLUME

Volume (turnover) is simply the number of futures contracts traded during each trading session. A contract is consummated only when *both* sides of the trade agree to the price and quantity. At the end of a trading session, the total number of contracts bought equals the total number of contracts sold. Therefore the following equality always prevails:

Buy volume = Sell volume = Total volume

Published volume figures represent one side only. The phrase "more buyers than sellers" (or vice versa) is never true with respect to volume (or open interest) statistics. A more representative phrase to explain the rise in prices during a *particular* trading session might be "more *potential* buyers than sellers."

For example, if total volume (in all months) of deutschemark futures on the IMM was 35,000, what would that mean? It means that *35,000 contracts were bought,* which equals the *35,000 contracts sold,* and this is the *35,000 total contract* figure that is reported—*one side only.* Each contract represents 125,000 DM. If an extended result is desired, the number of trades is simply multiplied by the contract size.

SIGNIFICANCE OF VOLUME

Volume is a measure of *urgency.* It is the result of the need for traders and investors to "do something," and nothing creates more urgency in a market than a losing position. Since any useful chart analysis determines what the *losers* are doing, the technician will want to monitor this sense of urgency (i.e., volume), thereby assessing the health and strength of the prevailing price trend (up, down, or sideways).

The specific volume number is not important. It is necessary to classify the trading session's volume into one of three categories: low, average, or high. A discussion of how to determine these parameters is found in Chapter 6. The following sections in this chapter explore the relationship between price and volume. This analysis will demonstrate the importance of volume interpretation in formulating successful trading strategies.

IDEAL HEALTHY PRICE UPTREND

The ideal situation for a healthy bull market occurs when volume moves up as the bull market expands. A strong price uptrend is characterized by greater volume on days when prices close higher than on days when prices settle lower. Specifically:

Price up – Volume up

Price down – Volume down

Prices do not continually go up every trading session—even in the most bullish environment. There are always adverse price moves (sell-offs) against the direction of the major trend. Much can be learned about the overall health of the bull market by monitoring volume on these periodic and inevitable sell-offs.

If there was no urgency created in a market on a price sell-off, what type of

F I G U R E   2–1

Ideal Bull Market
Price versus Volume Interaction

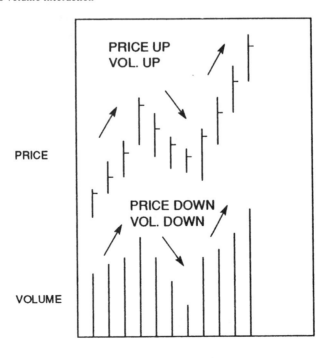

volume would be expected on the price-down day? It would decline. Although a lower close than the previous trading session was detrimental to the longs, no urgency was created. Such a proverbial "low-volume sell-off" is actually a bullish indicator. It tells the technician that the direction of the *major* price trend remains upward. The theoretically ideal relationship of price versus volume in a healthy bull market is found in Figure 2–1. An actual example of a healthy price uptrend can be seen in the November 1976 soybean chart shown in Figure 2–2.

Monitoring volume to identify price moves as countertrend is important. Low volume on price-down days is telling the astute trader that there is no urgency on the part of the longs to close out their positions. The prevailing major price uptrend should continue. This configuration of price and volume created the old adage "Don't sell a quiet market after a fall." A low-volume sell-off is actually a very bullish situation. The Plywood chart in Figure 2–3 illustrates this concept.

FIGURE 2–2

Healthy Price Uptrend

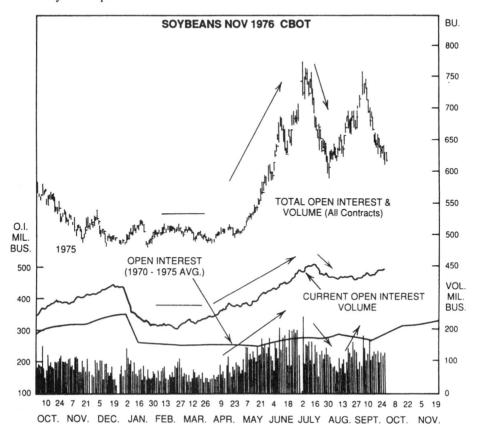

Volume: Increases on price-up days
        Decreases on price sell-offs

F I G U R E   2–3

Don't Sell a Quiet Market After a Fall

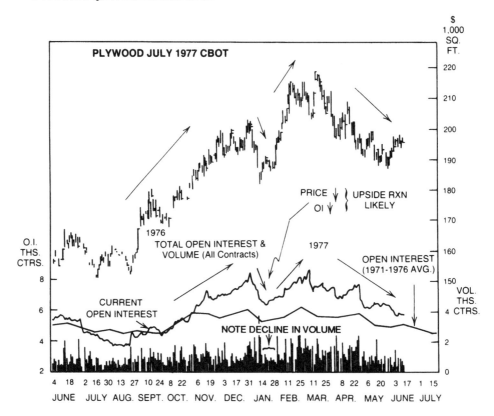

IDEAL HEALTHY PRICE DOWNTREND

The ideal situation for a healthy bear market is for a volume to increase as prices move lower. A strong price downtrend is characterized by expanding volume decreasing volume on price-up days.

Examine the chart in Figure 2–4, where the overall price trend is obviously down. Analyze a day in which quotes close lower than in the previous trading session. An increase in turnover associated with a price decline is the sign of a healthy bear market. Specifically:

Price down – Volume up

Price up – Volume down

Even in a long-term bear market, prices will not continually decline. Adverse moves against the direction of the major trend will result in price rallies— some lasting several days or, erratically, more than several weeks. If no urgency develops for the shorts to cover their positions, what should happen to volume? It should decline: this is the proverbial low-volume rally. A low-volume rally is

FIGURE 2-4

Ideal Bear Market
Price versus Volume Interaction

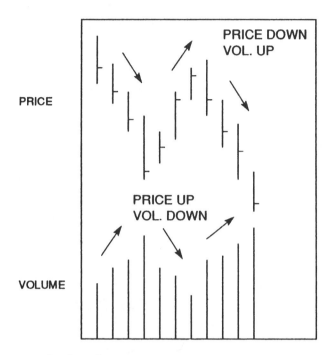

Volume: Increases on price-down days
        Decreases on price rallies

bearish. This price-versus-volume action signals to the technician that the direction of the major price trend remains downward. The price would be expected to keel over and begin moving down again. Then volume, ideally, would start to pick up. The ideal relationship of price versus volume in a healthy bear market is depicted in Figure 2–4; an actual example is found on the September 1984 T-bond chart shown in Figure 2–5.

A low-volume rally in a bear market is to be expected and will confirm that the downtrend is still intact. Hence: "Don't buy a quiet market after a rise." Figure 2–6 illustrates this situation on the November 1976 feeder cattle chart.

BLOWOFF VOLUME—A WARNING SIGNAL

This is one amplification of the ideal price-versus-volume configuration that is of paramount importance and should not be overlooked. Losing positions, especially speculative ones (as opposed to legitimate hedges), often create conditions that lead to excessive volume. The urgent need to close out losing positions produces "blowoff volume." This is a surge in the turnover to an extraordinary high level.

F I G U R E   2–5

Healthy Price Downtrend

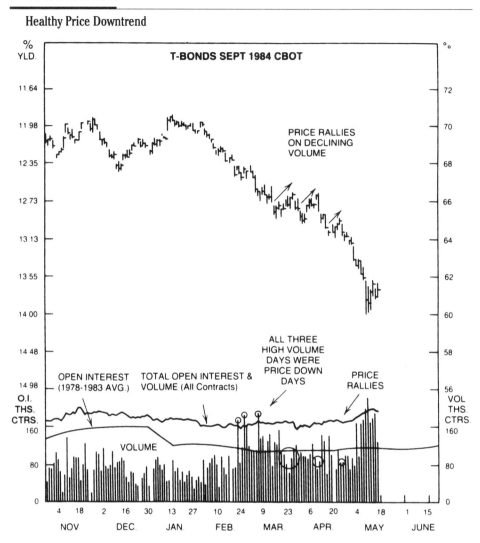

Volume of extremely high magnitude is a warning signal that the price trend is in the process of exhausting itself.

Prices often move violently in the opposite direction after such blowoff volume. Figure 2–7 illustrates the theoretical relationships between blowoff volume and price activity.

A Caveat

One caveat is in order: extremely high volume is the warning signal that indicates at least a *temporary* trend change. This signal does not have to coincide with the exact extreme-price day. Often blowoff volume will occur one trading session before the ultimate high or low price posting.

F I G U R E   2–6

Don't Buy a Quiet Market After a Rise

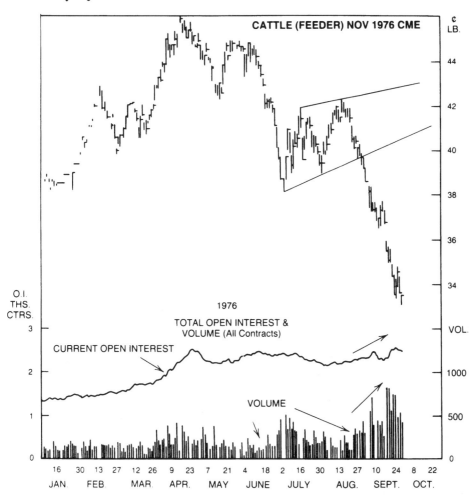

The Bull Case

Blowoff volume can best be understood in the context of specific markets. For instance, in a bull market, volume suddenly explodes. This volume surge can happen during trading sessions in which quotes close up, down, or unchanged. When posting the volume bar on the chart, it will stick out like the proverbial "sore thumb." The question then arises: Was any urgency created during that session's trading? Obviously, yes. Something occurred that, in more cases than not, placed the short sellers in considerable difficulty. The shorts, "buying in" their bearish positions, caused the turnover to explode. Whether short covering was truly responsible can be ascertained from the change in open interest.

It is also possible that the blowoff volume was created by a panic to "do something" as in a "flight to quality" (into short-term interest rate instruments).

FIGURE 2-7

Theoretical Examples of Blowoff Volume

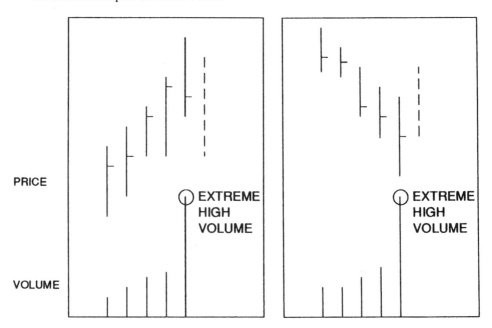

This can be seen in the December 1989 T-bill chart in Figure 2–8. Volume exploded as T-bill prices surged following the "Friday the 13th" U.S. stock market drop in October 1989. If the rally was net short covering, open interest should decline. In the T-bill example, open interest declined *after* the initial flight to quality. (See Chapter 3, "Open Interest.")

Blowoff volume signals the market top *or* the start of a correction in a bull market. The warning signal usually precedes a reaction of significant magnitude such that nervous longs may take evasive action by retreating to the sidelines. Aggressive traders may even try to pick a top by initiating new short sales. For ideas on *when* the actual volume (or a good estimate) is available, see the section "How/When to Obtain the Data" in Chapter 15.

THE BEAR CASE

Blowoff volume also provides a major clue to exhausting behavior in a bear market. Horrendously high volume following a series of declining prices would alert the technician to expect at least some price rally attempt. A price reversal occurs because many traders with speculative long positions do not use protective sell-stop loss orders. A big price-down day may occur, which would knock out many undercapitalized bulls, generating extremely high turnover.

FIGURE 2–8

Blowoff Volume

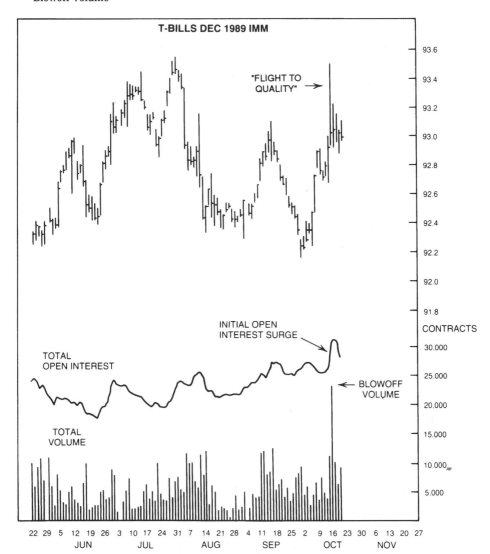

Many times the ultimate price low may be posted one trading session later than the blowoff volume signal. This is particularly true of the T-bond futures. A cursory check of the climactic endings to bear markets on many T-bond futures charts will reinforce this concept. The reason is the margin clerk. "Marking positions to the market" after the close makes it painfully clear that the long trader is "long and wrong." This prompts orders to sell at any price, creating the lower low in the next trading session.

Figure 2–9 exhibits this phenomenon on the March 1985 T-bond chart. Vol-

F I G U R E   2-9

Blowoff Volume

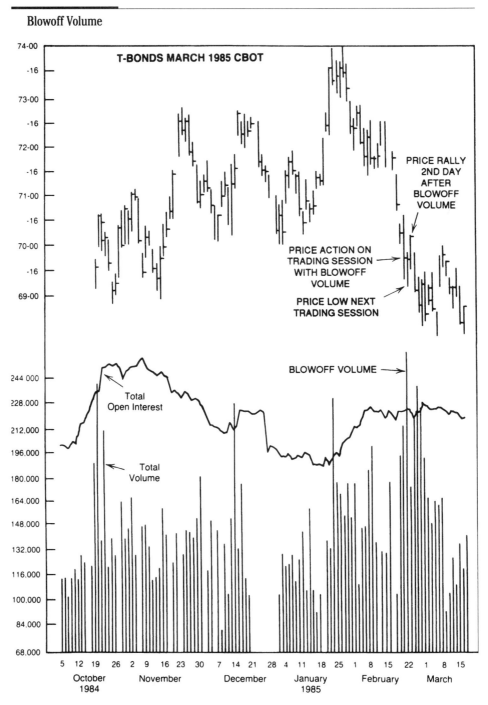

ume on February 22, a Friday, surged to 262,900 contracts. At the time, it was a
new all-time record for any futures contract on any exchange. Quotes bounced
upward for one trading session and then the price downtrend resumed.

HIGH VOLUME VERSUS BLOWOFF VOLUME

Technicians realize that high volume is a desired attribute on a breakout initiating a new price thrust, especially to the upside. Confusion between volume that is simply high and volume that is of blowoff proportion is inevitable. The "location" of the trading session in question can often provide a clue to provide the answer:

1. Breakout volume occurs at the *beginning* of a price move, often on the penetration of a trendline.
2. Blowoff volume, typically, is found *after* an extensive price move has occurred.

Thus, a graphic interpretation that includes price pattern recognition and trendline analysis is required. This is an art, not a science, but so is the setting of volume parameters in the first place!

To illustrate where to expect breakout volume versus blowoff volume on a chart, examine the two January 1990 energy charts in Figures 2–10 and 2–11. In Figure 2–10, the high-volume day in question occurred as quotes were breaking a trendline on the chart. This is an example of the desired high volume on an upside breakout. Figure 2–11 also contains a high volume trading session. Note that prices were in new high ground after a sustained price uptrend. This volume signal would be classified as blowoff volume. The interim price high illustrated in Figure 2–11 was set one trading session later with the one-day key reversal high-price posting. Refer to Chapter 13 for more information concerning key reversals.

Consistency of the Data

When comparing volume readings on a chart, you would assume that the volume has been calculated in a consistent manner, but this is not always the case. The Chicago Mercantile Exchange changed its method of calculating volume on days of options expirations or futures deliveries. This makes the job of the technician slightly more involved on those particular trading sessions. An in-depth look at this idiosyncrasy is contained in Chapter 15, "The Data."

TIC VOLUME

Technicians accessing real-time, open-outcry futures bar charts with less than one full day (clearing cycle) for each bar cannot obtain actual volume figures. There is a delay between the trade and when the exchange clearinghouse releases the figure. Tic volume is plotted at the bottom of these charts.

Quote vendors have developed software to monitor tic volume. Each price change within the period, without regard to the volume transacted at the price, increases the tic volume. Although this is not ideal, it does provide a surrogate for volume. Figure 2–12 is an example of a 30-minute bar chart with tic volume.

U.S. equity traders do have the benefit of online volume; it is printed on the "tape." As futures dealing becomes more electronic, technicians will have access to online volume.

Most users of intraday charts have a very short-term trading horizon. They

F I G U R E   2–10

Breakout Volume

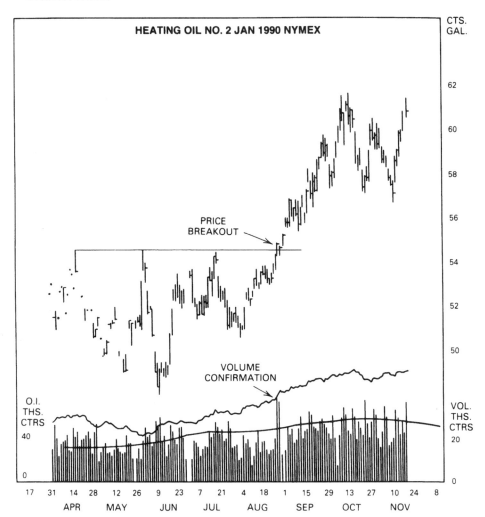

are usually out of all positions by the close. They are nimble traders who are only looking for quick price moves, and are not hindered by the absence of actual volume.

POINT & FIGURE CHARTS

A point and figure chart with its series of Xs and Os represents price changes that are independent of time. Very responsive point & figure charts are used by exchange floor scalpers and foreign-exchange dealers making two-way markets (stating both a bid and offered price.) Combining volume with this type of chart is impossible.

   If the point & figure chart is designed to observe very short-term time hori-

FIGURE 2–11

Blowoff Volume

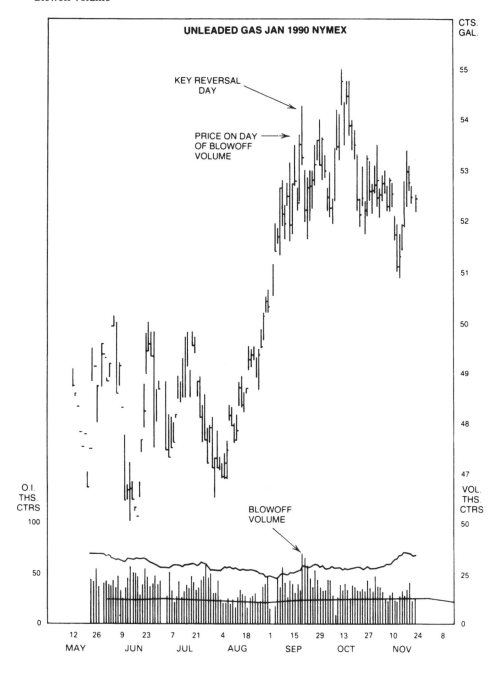

zons, the absence of volume is analogous to the trader using a five-minute bar chart. In this situation, quick reflexes in dealing are more important than an analysis of volume.

F I G U R E 2–12

Three Days of 30-Minute Bars with Tic Volume

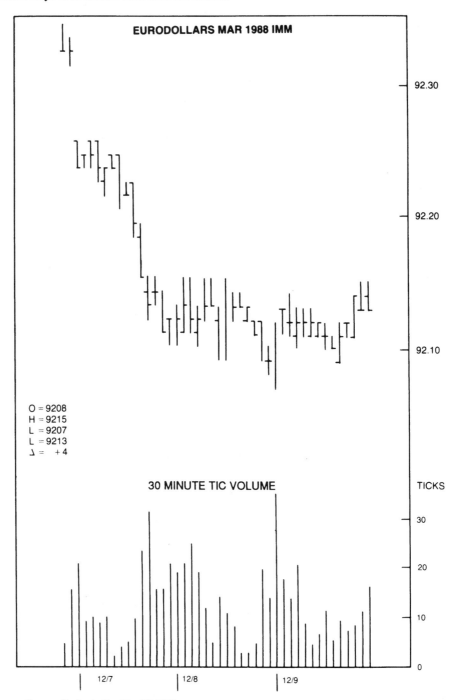

Source: Commodity Quote-Graphics TQ-2020.

A point & figure chartist can blacken in the square that represents the last trade of the "day." Then a date can be posted at the bottom of the chart. Obviously, no regular distance interval will exist between the dates on the chart. But this procedure will allow the chartist to cross-reference the point and figure chart to a specific date.

If volume statistics for the particular market being charted exist, some volume analysis would be possible via cross-referencing. Additionally, if the point & figure chart is of a CBOT future, Liquidity Data Bank™ statistics will be available. This important source of volume information is covered in detail in Chapter 11, "Support and Resistance."

CONVENTION

The typical chart convention plots volume as a vertical bar on the bottom of a chart; this is standard industry practice for any organized exchange. Suggestions to construct a chart and select responsive volume scales are found in Chapter 7.

In grain and oilseed futures trading, volume (and open interest) figures are often expressed in thousands of bushels rather than contracts. Each grain contract on the Chicago Board of Trade (CBOT) represents 5,000 bushels. Either figure (bushels or contracts) can be plotted on the volume scale as long as the methodology is consistent and the graph properly labeled.

3

OPEN INTEREST

Open interest (OI) is the summation of all unclosed purchases *or* sales at the end of a trading session. Confusion concerning the definition of open interest can be avoided by remembering this simple equality:

$$\text{Long OI} = \text{Short OI} = \text{Total OI}$$

Futures trading is a zero-sum game: for every dollar in there is a dollar out. Admittedly, the exchange clearinghouse and member firms scoop a little off the top, but for every open position in a futures market there has to be an opposite position. At the end of each trading session, the long open interest, by definition, must equal the short open interest. Published open interest figures are similar to those for volume in that what is reported by the clearinghouse to the public, press, and quote vendors is one side only.

An open interest scale is constructed at the bottom of each daily high-low-close futures bar chart. A dot marking the level of total open contracts at the end of each trading session is posted directly under the price activity. Connecting the daily postings yields a graphic portrayal of the changes in open interest. The *change* in open interest, not the absolute magnitude of open interest, is what is technically important.

Gold futures can be used as an example: Assume 180,000 contracts are reported as the total number of open positions. This 180,000 figure does not reveal how many separate entities are involved. What *is* known with certainty is that 180,000 long positions (each representing a 100-oz. contract) and 180,000 short positions are outstanding and yet to be offset or fulfilled via the delivery process.

HOW OPEN INTEREST CHANGES

Open interest changes from one trading session to the next; these fluctuations fall into one of three categories: (1) increase, (2) decrease, or (3) no change. Each of the three situations will be examined in the following example. For this illustration, it does not matter whether prices moved up or down. What is necessary is that a significant price change occurred. While no specific definition of what constitutes *significant* will be given, it is safe to assume that the definition begins at more-than-five minimum tics. The technical ramifications of these changes will be apparent later in this chapter, when the ideal healthy price uptrends or downtrends are discussed in detail.

Example

Prior day's total open interest = 180,000

Answer the question: Who is getting in or out of the market?

Case One: Open Interest Increases

Total open interest now at 183,000; a change of +3,000.

3,000 new long contracts.
3,000 new short contracts.

Case Two: Open Interest Decreases

Total open interest now at 178,000; a change of –2,000 .

2,000 long contracts sold out.
2,000 short contracts bought back.

Case Three: Open Interest Unchanged

Total open interest now at 180,000; unchanged.

In this situation, the trader would not know exactly what changing of positions was occurring.

In Case One, new positions on both sides are increased. In Case Two, both sides are liquidating. In Case Three, it is not obvious what changes in the makeup of participants is taking place.

Case Three would be an unlikely occurrence in a market with this magnitude of open interest. To illustrate the concept, an additional piece of information can be introduced into this scenario that would not be available to the analyst. If it was known that one new position (whether long or short) was placed, what else had to happen during the trading session? There had to be one liquidation.

Unchanged open interest means that the same number of participants (in terms of contracts) are in the market. There may have been some changing of positions. Old losing positions may have been meeting margin calls. New positions may have been initiated, balancing liquidated losing positions. What is important is that fuel is available to sustain the price trend.

SIGNIFICANCE OF OPEN INTEREST

For every profit dollar in futures trading there must be a loss dollar. Open interest is a reflection of this very important concept. If a futures trader makes a correct market judgment, where do the funds come from to pay off his or her winning position? The funds come from the loser. This may sound harsh, but it is a fact of life in every futures market. A technician should be very interested in what the losers are doing. The change in open interest is the key to this puzzle. The analysis of open interest changes is important for at least three reasons:

Open Interest Provides Fuel to Sustain a Price Move

The analogy of fuel to the market is like that of fuel to a fire. If the fuel is removed from a fire, the fire will go out. If fuel is removed from a price trend, the trend will change. Fuel in a futures market is provided by the losing positions. When open interest declines, fuel is being removed and the prevailing price trend is running on borrowed time. For a healthy, strong price trend (either up or down) to continue, open interest ideally should increase, or at least not decline. This is so important a concept that *remembering the word fuel as a surrogate for open interest will place a trader ahead of 80 percent of all futures traders worldwide!*

Open Interest Indicates the Existence of a Difference of Opinion

There is nothing that creates a market more than a difference of opinion. This is reflected in a willingness to take an open position and hence an increase in open interest.

Economists state that any marketplace searches for an equilibrium price— the intersection of the supply and demand curve at a price that clears the market. What if a futures market was *at* the theoretical equilibrium and the entire dealing world knew it? What would be the level of open interest? Zero. There would be no need for hedgers to shift risk or speculators to put their hard-earned money on the line to outguess the market direction. But no one knows where equilibrium is; it is always shifting. Open interest measures the difference of opinion and, more importantly, how it is changing.

For instance, a borrower of funds tied to a floating interest rate (potential short hedger) knows that if rates rise, financial difficulty awaits in the form of higher costs. The borrower does not know which way rates are going, but wants to shift the risk of increasing rates. A speculator may think the market can be out-smarted and decides rates are going down. Both the borrower and speculator have a willingness to put on an open position.

Increasing open interest is the signal that profits will be available (from the loser) as fundamental supply-and-demand factors move interest rates toward a new equilibrium. What is important to understand is that the difference of opinion creates a market that can sustain a significant price move.

Open Interest Determines If the Losers are Being Replaced

Technicians do not care if a losing position is being financed by meeting margin calls and throwing more money at the market, or if a loser steps aside and new blood comes in to take the loser's place. What matters is that the funds are being posted at the clearinghouse. The losers are necessary to pay off the traders with the correct market judgment. When the losers decide that they "don't want to play the silly game anymore" and leave the market, open interest will decline. Obviously the losers pay the price for their misjudgment, but what is of importance to the technician is that declining open interest means the prevailing price trend has become very *unhealthy.*

IDEAL HEALTHY PRICE UPTREND

Figure 3–1 represents a healthy price uptrend that is expected to continue. Both the bulls and the bears are increasing their positions; open interest is increasing. The longs, however, are in control. The longs are the smart money.

The technician always attempts to monitor what the smart money is doing. In an uptrending market, this is obviously the bulls. If the longs are increasing their positions and the losers (shorts) are being replaced, open interest will be expanding. The price upmove is technically healthy.

When open interest increases along with price, existing longs may be adding to their profitable positions and/or new longs may be joining the bull bandwagon. The additional short sellers may be existing shorts adding to their losing positions and/or new short sellers entering the market. It does not matter which is occurring; both represent a healthy price uptrend.

Upon introduction to this concept, many students of technical analysis have difficulty believing there is a "strong hand." After all, aren't there an equal number of longs and shorts? The problem is being able to distinguish who is in con-

FIGURE   3–1

Ideal Bull Market
Price versus Open Interest Interaction

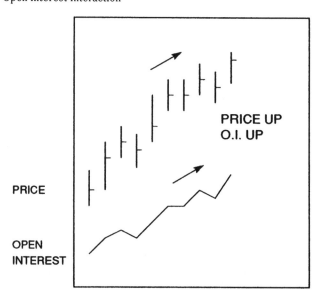

FIGURE   3–2

Healthy Bull Market

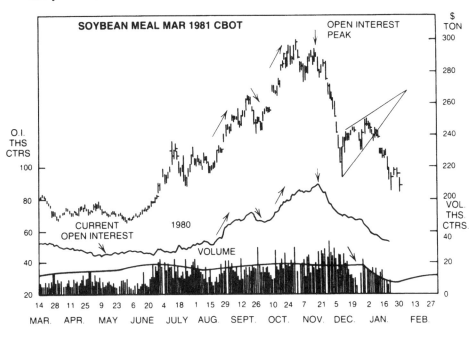

Open Interest: Increases on price updays
               Decreases on price sell-offs

trol. The direction of the price move determines which contingent is in control. Figure 3–2 shows the coincident nature of price and open interest during the inflation-driven agricultural markets of the early 1980s. The plywood chart in Chapter 2 (Figure 2–3) also displays coincident changes in price and open interest in a market that the public liked to trade from the long side.

Unhealthy Bull Market

The internal characteristics of the theoretical example shown in Figure 3–3 are very different from those in Figure 3–2. In Figure 3–3, price is increasing, but open interest is falling. The price uptrend here should *not* be expected to continue.

When open interest declines as prices increase, what are the longs doing? They are selling out their long positions, taking profits. What are the shorts doing? They are buying back, covering, or taking their losses.

Who has been correct in their market judgment all the way up? The longs. Who has been dead wrong all the way up? The shorts. The technician wants to side with the smart money.

The smart money is saying that prices have gone high enough. The losers are either so confused or do not have any money left (probably both) that they are throwing in the towel. The price upmove is coming from poor buying; this is a

FIGURE 3-3

Unhealthy Bull Market
Price versus Open Interest Interaction

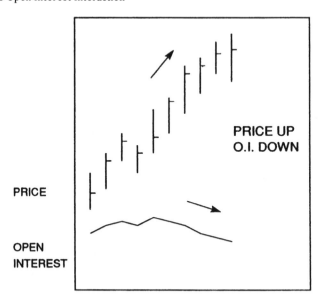

weak technical situation. The price uptrend is expected to reverse. The Kansas
City wheat chart in Figure 3–4 shows the early warning signal of open interest declining and the liquidation that occurred after a price run-up. This was the signal
that the bulls were no longer enamored with this market.

A Caveat

Before you assume the early-warning signal of open interest declining will always
indicate an impending price top, a caveat is appropriate. The signal of open interest declining prior to a price top does not occur all that often, perhaps only 15–20
percent of the time.

   Although the open interest decline may not flash the warning signal in a high
percentage of the price tops, it remains important. Failure to monitor open interest changes deprives a futures trader from obtaining vital insight as to what may
be occurring. Referring only to price does not portray what is/may be taking place
below the surface.

IDEAL HEALTHY PRICE DOWNTREND

The ideal healthy bear market is characterized by prices moving lower on increasing open interest. This is seen in the theoretical diagram in Figure 3–5.

   When prices settle lower than the previous close on increasing open interest,
the shorts are in control. The short sellers are pressing their winning positions.

FIGURE 3-4

Early-Warning Signal

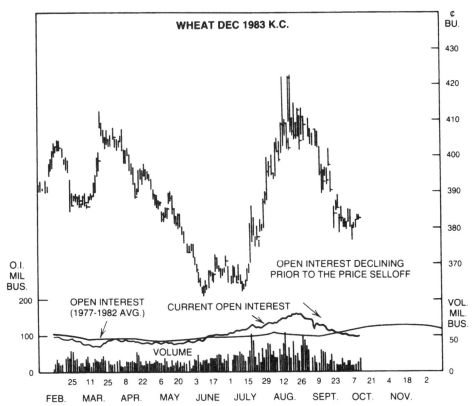

The longs are bottom picking and adding to losing positions. The bulls are "long and wrong"—making cannon fodder of themselves and providing fuel to sustain the price downtrend. This is seen in the latter stages of the bear market in corn illustrated in Figure 3–6.

The ideal healthy bear market of price down on increasing open interest would be expected to continue as long as open interest does not begin to decline. When the smart money (the shorts) decides to take profits, liquidation in total open interest will reflect this condition. Open interest declining would mean there is less conviction concerning the probable continuation of the price downtrend and less fuel to sustain the price downtrend. If total open interest begins declining as prices move lower, the early warning signal of an impending trend reversal is flashed. This situation is analogous to the declining open interest signal prior to a price top.

A Caveat

The ideal healthy bear market is found with far less frequency than the ideal healthy bull market. This is due to the idiosyncrasy of the "public" toward trading. They do not like a bear market and are reluctant to participate in one.

FIGURE 3–5

Ideal Healthy Price Downtrend
Price versus Open Interest Interaction

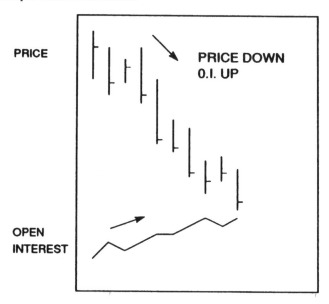

Even if a salesperson telephoned a potential client and explained that just as much money could be made on the way down and often in a shorter time period because markets tend to fall faster than they go up, the client's response would be, "Call me when it gets to the bottom and then I'll buy it." The public has a definite tendency to avoid a bear market!

The technical ramifications are such that a futures analyst is pleased if open interest is at least remaining flat during a bear market. In this situation, the losers are being replaced and the fuel is at least remaining constant.

A more likely bear market scenario is finding open interest declining. Declining price and declining open interest are classic characteristics of a liquidating market. This situation puts the prevailing price trend in a weak technical condition. *The bottom line is this: if traders wait to short a futures market only if open interest is expanding, they will not be on the short side very often.*

This is especially true of futures contracts that the public likes to trade from the long side. These include the traditional agricultural commodities (grains and livestock) and the metals. Figure 3–7 contains a theoretical graph of the normal interaction of price and open interest in a liquidating market. The rough rice chart in Figure 3–8 is a real-world example of what technicians normally see on the bottom of a futures chart following a large bull move in price.

Traders must think about idiosyncrasies peculiar to the specific markets they trade. A price top on a spot dollar–mark chart in interbank dealing would look like

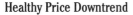

FIGURE 3–6

Healthy Price Downtrend

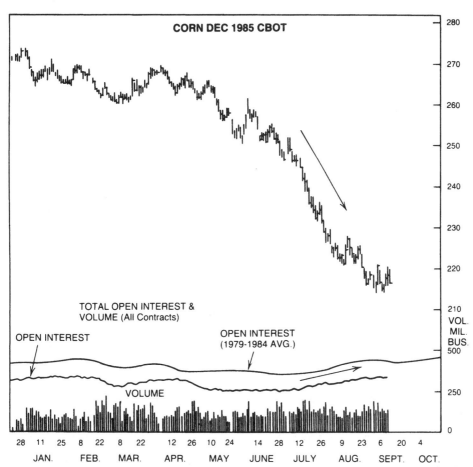

Open Interest: Increases on price downdays
                Decreases on price updays

a price bottom on a D-mark futures chart. The price scales used are the reciprocal of each other. These, and other specific traits, will be addressed for individual markets in Chapters 8 and 9. The problem of analyzing open interest on futures options is discussed in Chapter 7.

SIDEWAYS PRICE ACTIVITY

When prices are, in general, moving sideways in a choppy trading range, what use can be made of open interest changes? Relatively flat open interest along with sideways price activity is the most neutral condition; no predictive price implication exists.

F I G U R E   3–7

A Liquidating Market

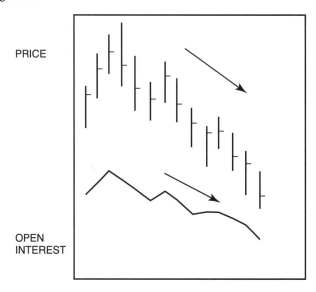

This does not mean that a trader should become complacent. More than likely, the direction of the next important price move will be signaled by a coincident increase in open interest. The IMM currency futures often exhibit this tendency. The December 1995 Japanese yen was in a healthy price downtrend in Figure 3–9 until the large price rally that occurred just as the nearby September future was expiring in the third week of September. The large decline in open interest due to the deliveries against the September future masked the short-covering nature of the rally. Important to learn from this chart is what happened after the amazingly flat open interest period during the month of October. The price breakout to the downside of a triangular trading range was accompanied by a coincident increase in open interest.

Therefore, after a period of flat open interest and erratic price action, an astute technician will realize that the next sustainable price move is highly likely to go hand in hand with a steady increase in open interest. A definite increase in open interest each trading session should help the trader maintain a directional bias. Traditional technical analysis such as trendline construction and support and resistance can be used to help the trader exit from a position when *price* dictates it.

Continuing the look at the December 1995 yen in Figure 3–9, note that after the short-covering price rally in early November, price and open interest again moved net sideways. Not shown on the chart is the fact that the yen future continued to slowly slide lower until late December 1995. Quotes then violated the lower boundary line of the large Descending Right Triangle (shown on the De-

F I G U R E   3–8

A Liquidating Market

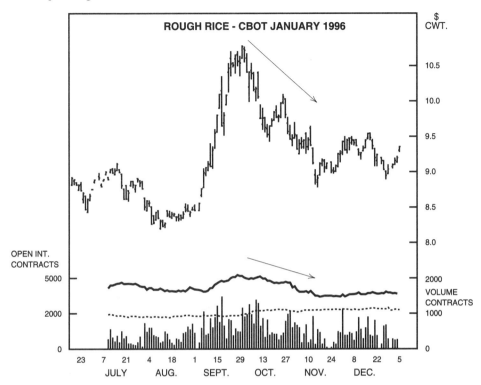

cember 1995 chart), and open interest began a sustained increase of over 25,000 contracts into mid-January 1996.

Price Steady, Open Interest Up

When open interest increases, new bulls are buying (opening new longs) from new bears who are selling (opening new shorts). This is an aggressive posture from both sides. Prices are not expected to remain stagnant. Once prices break out with a close outside a trading range, simply liquidating the losers should carry quotes a considerable distance. The technical signal created when open interest increases as price moves sideways is one of preparedness because a breakout is eminent.

There is a general rule of thumb for anticipating the probable extent of a price move that is often used by bar chartists: Once a breakout from a rectangular or triangular trading range has occurred, quotes are expected to move beyond the breakout level by a distance equal to the vertical height of the trading range.

FIGURE 3-9

Sideways Open Interest Followed by a Price Move and Increasing Open Interest

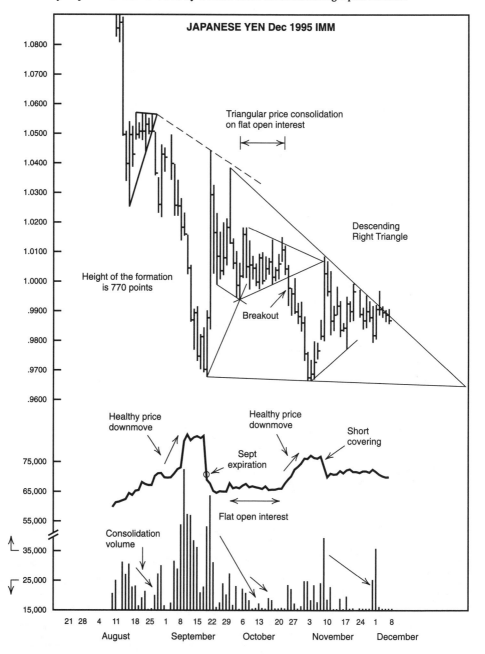

When open interest is building prior to the breakout, it is safe to assume that this height measuring objective is likely to be achieved. An example of this can be seen in Figure 14–3.

Price Steady, Open Interest Down

Open interest declining is the definition of a liquidating market. Together with sideways price movement on the chart, the picture is certainly far from dynamic. But the technician should not be lulled into a sense that nothing is happening. This condition is most often associated with a market trying to change direction.

If an upside breakout from sideways trading occurs, a technician must see increasing open interest. This is necessary to be comfortable in applying the traditional height measuring objective to obtain a price target.

If a downside breakout occurs, the long liquidation (open interest down) often continues. Yet even in this technically weak condition, the height measuring objective is most often reached to the downside. The ideal situation is open interest expanding after the downside breakout, but it is not a necessary condition. The propensity of the public to favor the bull side of any market is once again the major influence.

PRICE AND OPEN INTEREST INTERACTION—AN EXAMPLE

The coffee futures chart in Figure 3–10 exhibits classic price and open interest interaction:

1. The bulls were in control on the two price rallies of April and May; open interest expanded.
2. Dips in open interest preceded the price declines in late April and mid-June; this is the classic early warning signal.
3. Note the normal long liquidation that occurred as quotes moved lower after a rally.
4. A healthy bear market developed from late June onwards; open interest marched higher.
5. Open interest held flat at a relatively high level during the triangular consolidation from mid-August to late in September; this gave classical bar chartists confidence that enough fuel was present to propel prices to the traditional height measuring objective once a breakout occurred.

WHO IS RESPONSIBLE FOR THE OPEN INTEREST CHANGE?

Crowd psychology often plays an important role in the movement of futures prices. Small traders are especially susceptible to this influence. On the other side of the equation are the large commercial users of the futures markets. These hedgers, in theory, should possess the best fundamental information. The Commitments of Traders report, detailed in Chapter 10, yields insights as to the net long/short positions of the large hedger, large speculator, and small trader. In addition, the report provides the *changes* in the open positions of each category from the previous report, two weeks earlier.

In Chapter 10, the chart of crude oil in Figure 10–6 exhibits an increasing plot of total open interest. The largest open interest change emanated from in-

FIGURE 3–10

Classic Price and Open Interest Interaction

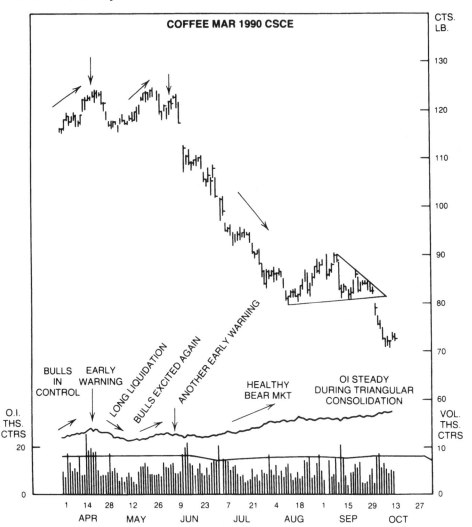

creasing participation by the large hedgers. These commercial users of crude oil were adding to existing net short positions. One month later (Figure 10–7), this market view, the view of the smart money, proved to be correct.

Particular attention should be focused on the crude oil chart (Figure 10–6). The definition of an ideal healthy bull market was operating: price up and open interest up. The knowledge that the commercial users were the large shorts did not aid in identifying the exact timing of the price top. But given the condition of the small trader heavily net long and the commercials net short, the sharp price break, when it finally came, should not have been too surprising.

Knowing *who* comprises the net long/short open positions can be immensely helpful in forecasting the tenor of the price reaction as the three main categories of traders react to adversity.

SHORT INTEREST (EQUITIES)

The concept of short interest in the U.S. stock market is completely different from open interest in futures. In any equity market that allows short sales using borrowed stock, a short interest situation might exist. Short interest is the number of shares that have not yet been purchased to cover short sales. The borrowed stock must eventually be returned to the lender.

Two schools of thought prevail as to what short interest implies: (1) either traders expecting a price decline could be initiating short sales, or (2) the shares sold short must eventually be bought back—hence a bullish condition.

Increases in takeover activity and arbitrage have further clouded the issue of how to interpret short interest statistics from an equity market.

4

GENERAL RULE FOR A HEALTHY PRICE TREND

Analyzing the strength of any given price trend can be done by combining the ideal price, volume and open interest characteristics, that is:

VOLUME AND OPEN INTEREST
SHOULD INCREASE AS PRICES MOVE IN THE DIRECTION
OF THE MAJOR PRICE MOVE

According to this rule, the most bullish condition is price moving up on increasing volume and increasing open interest; the longs are in control and the price uptrend is expected to continue. On a daily basis, this rule implies that on price-up days (when quotes close higher than the previous trading session), volume should expand and open interest should increase.

In a strong bear market when quotes close lower, volume will expand and open interest will increase. This ideal healthy price downtrend does not often occur in those markets that the public prefers to trade from the long side. These include traditional agricultural commodity futures and metals. Conversely, markets such as interest rate futures (U.S. Treasury bonds in particular) often *do* exhibit the ideal bear market characteristics of volume and open interest up on price-down days. The most bullish and most bearish technical situations are shown schematically in Figures 4–1 and 4–2.

WHICH IS MORE IMPORTANT, VOLUME OR OPEN INTEREST?

While the generalization for a healthy price trend states that volume *and* open interest should increase in the direction of the major price move, what if the two variables are in conflict? Which is more important, volume or open interest? Both

F I G U R E   4–1

Ideal Healthy Bull Market

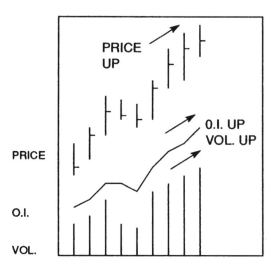

variables should be weighted equally. At times a technician will want to give slightly more emphasis to one of the readings. Three of the most obvious situations in which volume and open interest are not given equal weight are found in a short-covering rally, an upside breakout, and holiday trading.

Short Covering Rally

Extrapolating from the general rule, price up with high volume is bullish. However, if open interest drops during this same trading session, a bearish reading of that variable results. The internal condition of the market during such a trading session would be that of short covering.

A short-covering rally is a very weak technical situation. The technician can state that the decline in open interest is more bearish than the high volume is bullish. In fact, if volume is so high that it can be considered to be of blowoff proportion, the volume reading would also be bearish—signaling at least a temporary reversal of the price uptrend.

An example of a short-covering rally is found on the gold chart, Figure 4–3. The Comex gold futures generated high volume (61,746), but open interest declined (–52). Skeptics will be quick to point out that a decline of 52 contracts does not appear significant; still, there is no denying that, on balance, the 3.90$/oz. rally *was* net short covering.

An interesting technical sidelight to the volume and open interest analysis in Figure 4–3 is the series of down-sloping trendlines. They were drawn to show that simply penetrating a trendline does not automatically signal the start of a new direction in price. A three-point trendline is much greater in its technical significance than a trendline constructed tangent to only two reversals of the minor price trend. A close beyond a three-point trendline changes the prevailing price trend

FIGURE   4-2

Ideal Healthy Bear Market

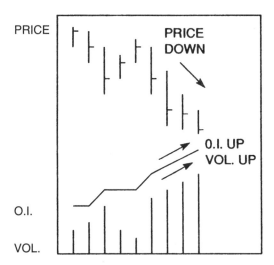

from up to sideways or down to sideways. It does not automatically change the trend direction 180 degrees.

Figure 4–4 shows that the price rally in gold did continue, rising approximately 6.50$/oz. over the next four trading sessions. But the rally was simply continued short covering and not to be trusted. Note that gold subsequently sank to below the price level where the short covering began.

Upside Breakout

Volume is especially important in validating any upside breakout on a chart. This is because of the propensity of the general trading public to look for reasons to buy to initiate longs rather than for reasons to sell to establish shorts. Since volume normally increases on upside price moves as the public buys, it must show a more-than-normal increase to assure traders that the breakout is actually valid.

There must be a fundamental factor that causes the volume to expand. Although this does not mean that the technician must ferret out that fundamental, it does mean that the volume expansion must not be due simply to technical traders activating an apparent price pattern. Some new fundamental input must have entered the market—causing the volume to expand because of increased participation by fundamental traders as well as technicians.

Thus, volume on an upside breakout is more crucial than the open interest change for that particular trading session.

Technical analysis of equity markets does not involve the use of open interest; this statistic is nonexistent in the equity market. Volume, however, has always been a determinant in technically analyzing any equity market. A noticeable increase in volume on any upside price breakout has always been a part of classical bar charting for equity technicians.

F I G U R E   4–3

Short-Covering Rally

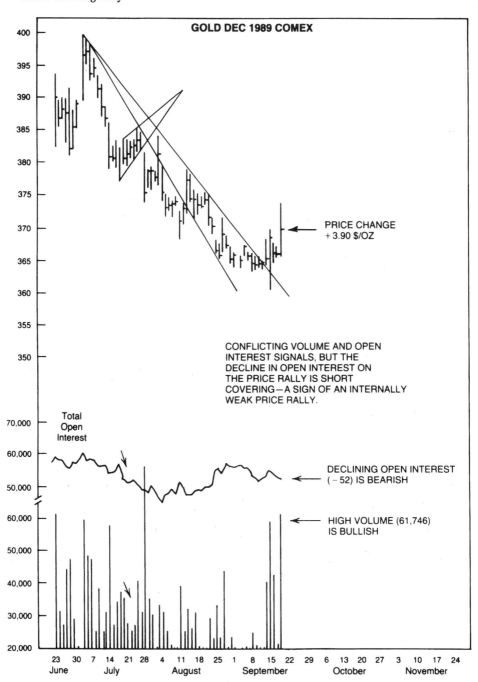

Holiday Trading

When trading is curtailed due to a holiday, volume usually contracts. In such situations, the change in open interest can be more instructive than volume.

F I G U R E   4–4

Outcome

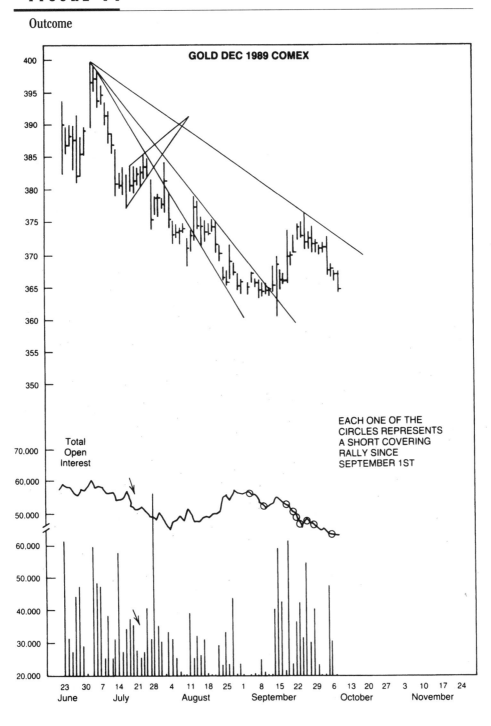

In the financial-instrument futures in particular, volume is low on business days in the United States when the Federal Reserve Bank is closed. Both the Chicago Mercantile Exchange (CME) and the Chicago Board of Trade (CBOT)

have midday (12:00 P.M.) closings on business days preceding federal holidays and three-day weekends.

Table 4–1 depicts the price and open interest changes for Monday, October 9, 1989. This day was Columbus Day in the United States, Thanksgiving Day in Canada, and Yom Kippur throughout the world. The Federal Reserve Bank was closed but the exchanges were open in the United States. With the exception of the British pound, volume was low in all eight financial instruments surveyed, and all of the markets witnessed significant (five or more minimum price tics) price changes except for the deutschemark contract, which finished unchanged.

Open interest declined in all six of the markets that could be analyzed. Even though the rule for a healthy price trend could be applied only in its most minute form (one day), the declining open interest meant that the price changes that trading session should *not* be the direction of the major price trend.

> *The premise is that open interest changes can still be used to test for the direction of the major price trend during holiday trading.*

Table 4–1 also presents the price changes the following session, Tuesday, October 10, 1989. The general rule can be tested: Did the price changes occur in what would be expected to be the direction of the *minor* price trend? Yes or No answers are noted.

The outcome of this particular experiment is inconclusive; three Yes versus three No answers resulted. This, however, does not mean the analysis was unimportant. Analysis of this type gains significance when it is extended over several trading sessions, shown in Chapter 6, "Developing a Disciplined Approach," where the analysis is expanded to five trading sessions using both volume and open interest changes.

TABLE 4–1

Price and Open Interest Changes on a U.S. Federal Reserve Bank Holiday, Columbus Day, October 9th, 1989, CBOT and CME

Markets	Price	Open Interest	Price Next Trading Session	Worked According to General Rule?
T-bonds	+	−	−	Yes
Eurodollars	+	−	−	Yes
S&Ps	+	−	−	Yes
Gold	−	−	−	No
Deutschemark	±0	+	−	No analysis possible
Swiss franc	−	−	−	No
Japanese yen	−	−	−	No
British pound (average volume)	−	−	−	No analysis possible

(Volume was "low" in all the markets.)

Eurodollar Example   Another, and more conclusive, test of the general rule during holiday trading occurred in the International Money Market (IMM) Eurodollar futures during the trading session before the Thanksgiving Day holiday in November 1989. In Figure 4–5, note the apparent upside breakout into new high

FIGURE 4–5

Volume and Open Interest in Preholiday Trading

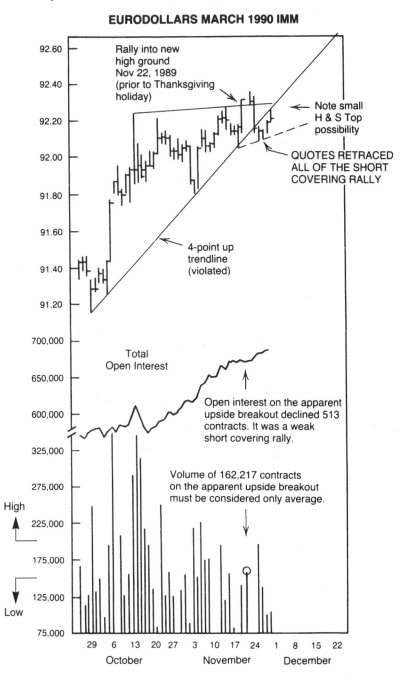

ground found on November 22. Volume needed to surpass 200,000 contracts to be considered high; this was necessary to validate the upmove and suggest purchases on the next pullback to support at 92.29. Actual volume at 162,217 was only average.[1]

Looking below the surface of this trading session reveals an even more disquieting note for the bulls: open interest declined. Here again, the skeptics may claim that the reduction was "only" 513 contracts, but the 14-basis-point rally in price *was* net short covering.

The two filters of volume and open interest change, particularly the negative open interest change, in this preholiday trade would have kept an astute technician from jumping aboard the bull bandwagon. As Figure 4–5 illustrates, subsequent price action had the result that the entire 14-tic rally was wiped out two days later.

---

1. Since it is unlikely that volume would enter the high-volume category on holiday trading, an upside breakout would rarely be validated.

CHAPTER

5

WHY TOTAL VOLUME AND OPEN INTEREST ARE USED

When constructing a chart, the technician plots total volume and total open interest for all outstanding futures contracts at the bottom of each chart. One specific contract (usually the nearest to expiration) is used to plot prices. Why, then, use *total* volume and open interest if only *one* specific contract will be traded? The answer lies in the ability to apply the guidelines for a healthy price trend (i.e., volume and open interest should increase as prices move in the direction of the major price move).

THEORETICAL BEHAVIOR

Figure 5–1 shows the hypothetical plot of the open interest of a single June XYZ futures contract. The expiration date for this contract is in June, two years hence. On the day before the exchange lists the contract for trading, the open interest in this individual contract month is zero. When the exchange states it is legal to deal in that particular expiration month, a speculator and a hedger together make a trade. Open interest slowly begins to increase, but the number of open positions in this distant month is relatively low because it is not the lead (nearby) contract.

Assuming the XYZ futures have a quarterly expiration cycle, the June future becomes the lead month with the arrival of April and May of that expiration year. Open interest in the June contract escalates dramatically. In the delivery month, open interest in the June XYZ future will drop back to zero; this is true whether the contract specifications call for physical delivery or cash settlement.

If a technician tries to measure a single-volume or open interest plot, both variables would be increasing as the contract became the lead month—no matter what prices were doing. The axiom used to determine the health of the price trend would not be applicable.

F I G U R E   5–1

Theoretical Behavior of Open Interest for an Individual Contract Month

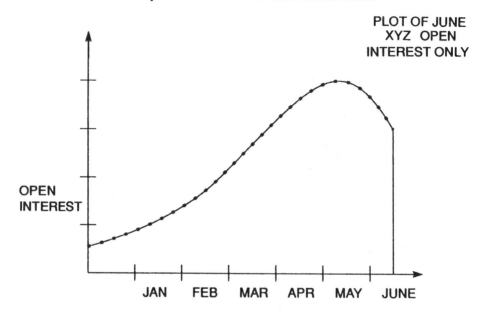

Assume the market in this example is used by sophisticated hedgers and speculators. The hedger needs to transfer risk. If exposure to risk will continue after the expiration of the June contracts, the hedger's position must be rolled into the next month. The astute speculator, desiring to maintain a market view, also would roll positions forward.

Rolling from one expiration month to the next is best accomplished by a spread order. Assume the hedger is short in futures to protect the long "cash" market inventory and the speculator is currently long in futures and desires to continue with a bullish view. Spread orders for each trader would look like the examples in Figure 5–2.

In a mature market, the level of total open interest can be expected to remain unchanged during an orderly expiration cycle. The shape of the sequential expirations would resemble that shown in Figure 5–3.

At any point in time, the summation of all the open-contract open interest (and volume) should be plotted on the chart. Applications of the principles of a healthy price trend then become feasible.

ACTUAL OBSERVATIONS

A perfect market does not exist. In reality, most plots of total open interest do record a drop as maturity of the nearby contract approaches. Specific contract specifications create unique and observable shapes to the open interest curve.

There is a distinct difference in the shape of the open interest plots in physical-delivery contracts versus cash-settled contracts. Generally, an orderly roll-

FIGURE 5-2

Typical Spread Orders to Roll Positions Forward

ABC HEDGE CO.	
BUY 50 JUNE XYZ	**SELL** 50 SEPT XYZ MKT

and

DEF SPEC CO.	
BUY 50 SEPT XYZ	**SELL** 50 JUNE XYZ MKT

over is observed in the physical-delivery contracts, while cash-settled contracts exhibit a more pronounced drop in total open interest at expiration. This is because positions in cash-settled futures can be held through expiration with no physical-delivery consequences. Figure 5–4 exhibits a series of IMM Eurodollar expirations. Note how the actual open interest curves resemble the hypothetical plot in Figure 5–3.

In Chapters 8 and 9, we will examine in detail the open interest idiosyncrasies of particular futures contracts.

ROLLOVER SURGE

Studying the life cycle of an *individual* contract can produce technical insights. These are beneficial to hedgers and speculators in timing the entry or exit of positions to coincide with periods of good volume activity. The substantial rise in volume in a single futures contract is known as the rollover surge.

The Chicago Mercantile Exchange (CME) featured the rollover surge in its August 1986 issue of *Market Perspectives*. Figure 5–5 contains charts from that issue showing volume by individual contract month of the S&P 500 and deutschemark futures. Volume has been smoothed via a 10-day moving average. This serves to highlight the rollover surge and make it more readily apparent.

FIGURE 5–3

Theoretical Shape of Sequential Expirations

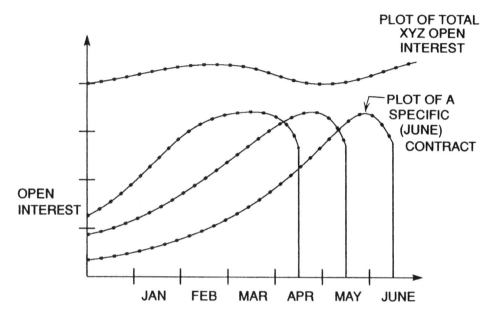

PLOT OF TOTAL XYZ OPEN INTEREST

PLOT OF A SPECIFIC (JUNE) CONTRACT

OPEN INTEREST

JAN   FEB   MAR   APR   MAY   JUNE

Not surprisingly, volume jumps dramatically in an individual contract when it becomes the lead month. Then volume often drops off prior to setting new highs again. This phenomenon can be observed in Figure 5–5. The probable explanation for the volume dip is that spread orders to roll positions forward were completed.

LIFFE's Approach

In futures contracts where volume is concentrated only in the first several expiration months, it is possible to use a different legend to represent each contract's volume. This plotting technique produces a very good graphic of the rollover process. The rollover of December 1995 to March 1996 in German bund futures on the London International Financial Futures Exchange (LIFFE) is easily seen in Figure 5–6. Also notice the dip in total open interest that occurred during the rollover; not all the December contracts were rolled forward into the March.

DISTRIBUTION OF OPEN INTEREST

Although most technical attention is focused on total open interest, a look at the distribution of open interest reveals much about the depth and sophistication of a market.

A simple look at the quantity of open contracts in the back months provides the first clue about liquidity. Agricultural futures have "crop years," a circumstance that tends to encourage old-crop versus new-crop spreads. The new-crop month often builds open interest faster than the last of the old-crop contracts.

FIGURE 5-4

Individual Contract versus Total Open Interest Plots

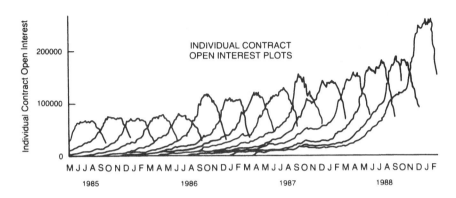

IMM Eurodollar Time Deposit Future
Open Interest 5/1/85 to 2/28/89

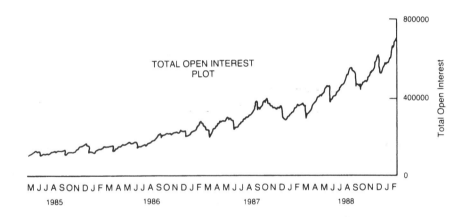

Knowledge of which month represents the first contract of the marketing season is extremely important.

To gain further insight into the amount of spread activity, the *Commitments of Traders Report* for the U.S. futures markets should be examined. In the grains, there are details on same-crop-year spreads and old-crop versus new-crop spread activity. The definition of "old crop" for any nonagricultural futures contract is defined as the current calendar year. A thorough explanation of the *Commitments of Traders Report* is found in Chapter 10.

Interest rate futures also lend themselves to a myriad of spread strategies. For example, a spread in T-bond futures creates an artificial instrument of duration equal to the time distance between the legs of spread. The resulting position is a surrogate for the term repo rate for the time period in question.

Strip trading, which involves buying or selling a series of contracts for protection against adverse interest rate fluctuations, is also popular with hedgers. Table 5–1 lists the open interest of the CBOT (Chicago Board of Trade) 30-day

Rollover Surge

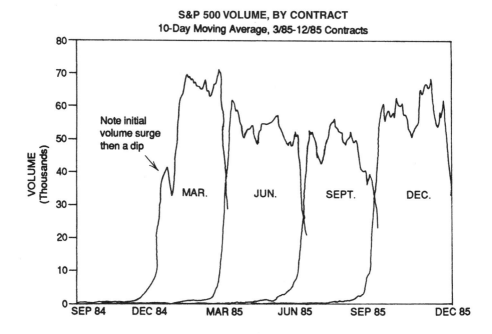

S&P 500 VOLUME, BY CONTRACT
10-Day Moving Average, 3/85-12/85 Contracts

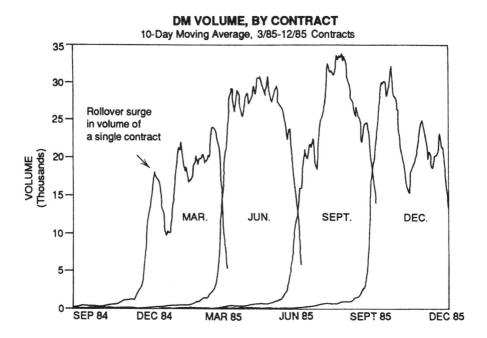

DM VOLUME, BY CONTRACT
10-Day Moving Average, 3/85-12/85 Contracts

interest rate futures. The data contains the open interest history from the contract's inception on October 3, 1988, to March 24, 1989. The distribution shows that an active back-month trade developed soon after the contract was introduced.

FIGURE 5-6

German Bund, LIFFE; Distinct Volume Scales for Each Contract Month

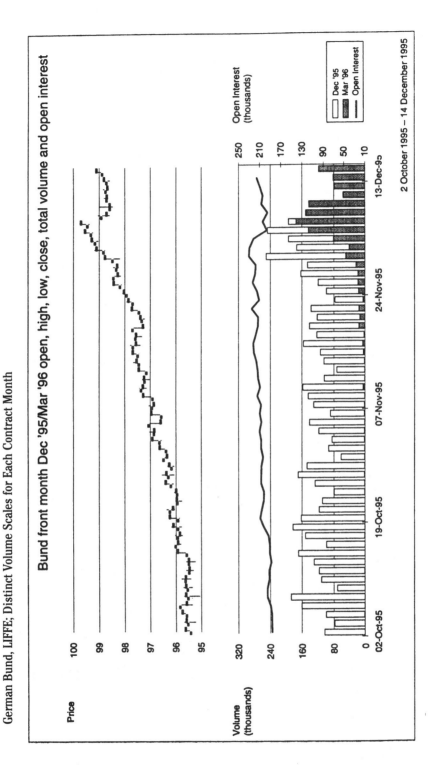

TABLE 5-1

Distribution of Open Interest in CBOT 30-Day Interest Rate Futures

							Contract Months						
	Oct	Nov	Dec	Jan	Feb	Mar	Apr	May	June	July	Aug	Sep	Total
Oct 7	220	163	153	219	143	267	0	—	2	—	—	10	1177
Oct 14	219	182	249	314	222	292	0	—	12	—	—	0	1490
Oct 21	289	236	376	410	288	312	0	—	14	—	—	0	1925
Oct 28	274	375	421	590	308	331	0	—	14	—	—	0	2313
Nov 4	—	400	560	712	316	370	22	—	36	—	—	0	2416*
Nov 11	—	344	497	677	265	234	22	—	36	—	—	0	2075
Nov 18	—	364	473	564	289	177	24	—	36	—	—	0	1927
Nov 25	—	292	604	626	407	245	24	—	36	—	—	0	2234
Dec 2	—	—	841	734	501	360	18	4	39	—	—	0	2497*
Dec 9	—	—	831	792	536	409	33	21	38	—	—	0	2660
Dec 16	—	—	1016	809	690	563	61	34	51	—	—	0	3224
Dec 23	—	—	981	810	759	820	63	37	62	—	—	0	3532
Dec 30	—	—	919	837	820	842	63	37	62	—	—	0	3580
Jan 6	—	—	—	949	774	857	83	50	73	—	—	0	2786*
Jan 13	—	—	—	976	973	723	110	67	72	—	—	0	2921
Jan 20	—	—	—	923	1089	761	152	99	68	3	—	0	3095
Jan 27	—	—	—	853	1109	802	250	190	103	4	—	0	3311
Feb 3	—	—	—	—	1186	853	196	203	117	4	—	0	2559*
Feb 10	—	—	—	—	1240	1170	248	314	230	4	—	0	3206
Feb 17	—	—	—	—	1191	1183	267	367	238	5	—	0	3251
Feb 24	—	—	—	—	1133	1266	321	311	263	25	—	0	3319
Mar 3	—	—	—	—	—	1509	484	450	358	32	—	0	2833
Mar 10	—	—	—	—	—	1447	682	512	529	47	14	30	3261
Mar 17	—	—	—	—	—	1321	762	500	560	51	29	30	3253
Mar 24	—	—	—	—	—	1339	817	526	620	63	42	44	3451

* Spot month expiration occurred.

Source: Chicago Board of Trade, *Financial Futures Professional*, 13, no. 4 (April 1989).

A look at open interest in back-month contracts, especially in short-term interest rate futures, will reveal whether commercial interests are using the contracts via strip trading. Additional insights into back-month open interest can be found in "Spread Considerations" in Chapter 8.

6

DEVELOPING A DISCIPLINED
APPROACH

Taking the theory and arriving at a market view requires discipline. Volume parameters must be derived and updated regularly. A procedure of recording open interest changes should be developed. Finally, a weighing of the evidence leading to a conclusion must occur.

SETTING VOLUME PARAMETERS

Specific parameters that define low, average, and high volume must be determined for every chart. In the computer age, it makes sense to develop a computational method of deriving the required volume parameters. A mechanical approach will be suggested, but in the end, a simplistic analysis still seems the most viable.

A statistical approach could calculate a moving average of daily volume for the last 20 trading sessions. Any volume reading beyond a .75 standard deviation on either side of the mean could be classified as low or high. But there is a major drawback to this type of approach. A purely mathematical model will not know that an important holiday or book-squaring date is artificially lowering the volume. In addition, the assumption that volume follows a normal bell-shaped distribution is suspect. Moreover, the probability of extremely low volume is less likely than the probability of extremely high volume.

Another consideration is that the volume directly relates to the level of open interest. If open interest registers a sustained increase or decrease, the volume it would support on a daily basis would be likely to increase or decrease as well.

An easier approach to creating volume parameters is to scan backward an appropriate distance on the chart. Then draw hypothetical horizontal lines representing the threshold levels of low and high volume. The appropriate distance, whether one week or two months, will depend on the specific conditions prevailing on each chart. These conditions involve holidays, dramatic open interest changes, expiration dates of options and futures, economic releases, and so on. The case studies in this book showing the derivation of reasonable volume parameters should aid in shaping a new technician's feel of what is reasonable.

In practice, the number of high and low readings observed in the period analyzed should be about equal. There also must be an adequate number of volume readings in the average category. This is to allow for situations where the market is just marking time during a consolidation. The following is a general rule of thumb:

One-third of the volume readings should fall into each category.

There is no specific determination made about blowoff volume. Any volume bar that sticks out like a sore thumb on the chart is a good candidate for blowoff volume. This, of course, would be a warning signal of a possible price trend change.

UPDATING THE PARAMETERS

Volume parameters are not static. How often must a new determination be made? A review should be made every week. Usually no revision or only a slight adjustment will have to be noted. This reevaluation is made easier once the initial parameters are set.

A worksheet requiring the analyst to make specific entries to denote volume parameters is essential. This is to make sure the technician cannot "cheat." Suppose an apparent upside breakout occurs on a price chart. Volume must then register a noticeable increase to validate the breakout. It is human nature to look at the associated volume and say, "It is high enough." But by setting a prior volume hurdle that must be surpassed, a more objective volume confirmation of the breakout will be reached.

When an apparent price reaction in opposition to the direction of the major trend occurs, the technician should write down the current best estimate of low volume. The actual turnover when it becomes available can then be compared to the predetermined figure. If the actual volume was in the low territory, the price move could correctly be labeled as only a reaction. Figure 14–4 in chapter 14 is a detailed example of how to organize price, volume, open interest, *and technical comments.*

Efforts spent in developing volume parameters will be rewarded—the process becomes easier. As you become more experienced, when you look at any new chart, the volume levels for low and high will become very apparent.

USING A WORKSHEET

The next step is to analyze a series of trading sessions with regard to the general rule for a healthy price trend. This is accomplished using a simple worksheet, such as the one in Figure 6–1. The goal of this analysis is to derive the direction

FIGURE 6–1

Volume and Open Interest Analysis—Worksheet

Contract: _____

Date: _____

High Volume: _____

Low Volume: _____

If Contract is Cash Settled: Trend
Component of Open Interest
Increase = _____

General Rule:

**Volume and Open Interest
Should Increase as Prices Move in the Direction
of the Major Price Trend**

Date	Price Δ	Volume	Open Interest Δ
_____	_____	_____	_____
_____	_____	_____	_____
_____	_____	_____	_____
_____	_____	_____	_____
_____	_____	_____	_____

SUMMARY

BULLISH   BEARISH

of the major price trend. Five trading sessions are analyzed, a full week of trading. However, any length of time period can be used if the volume parameters remain unchanged.

A CASE STUDY

The September 1989 D-Mark future in Figure 6–2 will be used as an example. The date of the analysis is Thursday morning, July 13, 1989, prior to the opening on the IMM. Wednesday's actual volume and open interest figures are available and posted on the chart. Data for the previous five trading sessions has been entered in the worksheet in Figure 6–3.

FIGURE 6–2

Overview

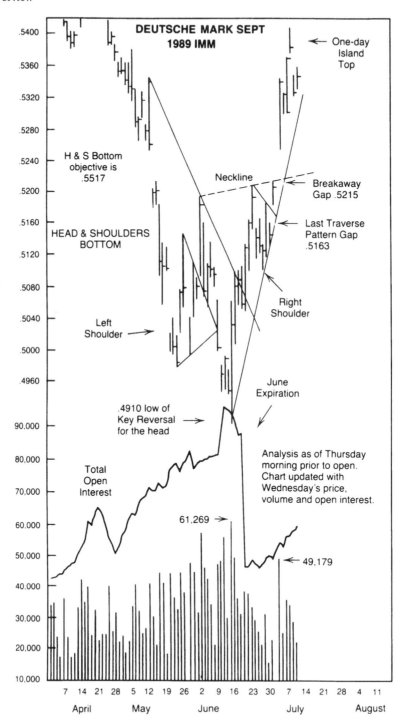

F I G U R E   6–3

Volume and Open Interest Analysis—Worksheet

Contract: Sept '89 D-Mark

Date: Thurs 7/14/89

High Volume: _____

Low Volume: _____

If Contract is Cash Settled: Trend
Component of Open Interest
Increase = _____

General Rule:

**Volume and Open Interest
Should Increase as Prices Move in the Direction
of the Major Price Trend**

Date	Price Δ	Volume	Open Interest Δ
Thurs 7/6	–16	25,232	–597
Fri 7/7	+46	36,471	+2,901
Mon 7/10	+14	34,284	+733
Tues 7/11	–58	29,750	+1,558
Wed 7/12	+22	22,658	+834

SUMMARY

BULLISH   BEARISH

The two volume parameters must now be set. The enlarged bottom portion of the chart is in Figure 6–4. The appropriate distance to scan backward on this particular chart is two weeks. The conditions were far different before the expiration of the June contract. (Note the huge drop in total open interest with the June 21 posting.) Thus, the analysis will begin with the volume posting on Friday, June 23.

Horizontal lines "guesstimating" the volume categories need to be drawn. Figure 6–5 shows this graphically. The two lines shown are at 26,000 and 32,000. These volume parameters are then entered onto the worksheet (Figure 6–6). As

FIGURE 6-4

What Comprises High, Average, and Low Volume?

The Graphic Answer Is on the Next Page

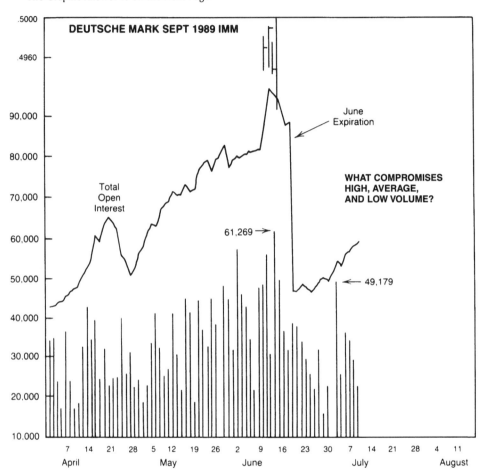

a rough check for how appropriate an estimate, note the number of high-, average-, and low-volume postings beginning Friday, June 23rd. The results are:

Four readings above 32,000.

Three readings from 26,000 to 32,000.

Six readings below 26,000.

This is close enough to meet the criteria of nearly equal readings in each category.

Open interest is building. This means that volume is likely to escalate as well. The expectation is that subsequent volume postings will increasingly enter the average- or high-volume categories. The parameters likely will be increased by the time two weeks pass.

The next step is to place each trading session's volume into one of the three

F I G U R E   6–5

Graphic Answer to What Constitutes High, Low, and Average Volume

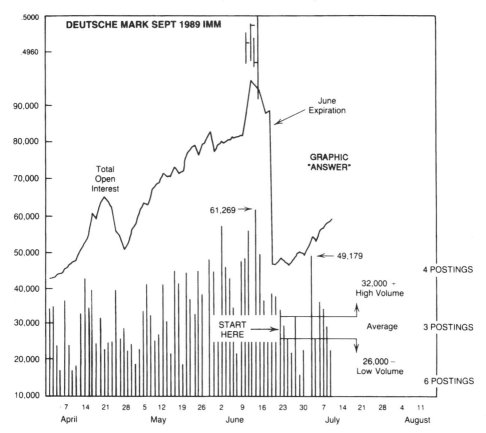

categories (or the fourth—blowoff volume—if applicable). This analysis will be detailed as each of the five trading days is examined. The result will be the completed worksheet in Figure 6–6.

In this analysis, the technician is trying to determine the direction of the major price trend by examining a series of interactions of price changes with their corresponding volume and open interest changes. The key is the general rule for a healthy price trend.

Working the general rule *backwards* determines whether the price change versus volume and/or the price change versus open interest change leads to a bullish or bearish direction for the major price trend.

Thursday

The first volume figure of 25,232 falls into the low-volume category. Prices closed down 16 tics that trading session. A low-volume sell-off is characterized as a reaction, expected in a healthy uptrending market. This price-down low-volume reading is deemed to be bullish. The words *low equals bullish* are written by the volume posting of 25,232 in Figure 6–6.

F I G U R E   6–6

Volume and Open Interest Analysis—Worksheet

With Analysis and Summary

Contract:	Sept '89 D-Mark
Date:	Thurs 7/14/89

High Volume: _____ 32,000 + _____

Low Volume: _____ 26,000 – _____

If Contract is Cash Settled: Trend
Component of Open Interest
Increase = Not applicable

General Rule:

**Volume and Open Interest
Should Increase as Prices Move in the Direction
of the Major Price Trend**

Date	Price Δ	Volume	Open Interest Δ
Thurs 7/6	–16	Low=Bullish 25,232	Bullish –597
Fri 7/7	+46	High=Bullish 36,471	Bullish +2,901
Mon 7/10	+14	High=Bullish 34,284	Bullish +733
Tues 7/11	–58	Average =? 29,750	Bearish +1,558
Wed 7/12	+22	Low=Bearish 22,658	Bullish +834

SUMMARY

BULLISH	BEARISH
7	2

Open interest declined 597 contracts in conjunction with the 16-tic price sell-off. Ideally, open interest should increase in the direction of the major price trend. Therefore:

Whatever price change occurs when open interest declines is not the direction of the major price trend.

Hence, the major trend is *not* down. This reading of price versus open interest is deemed to be bullish. The term *bullish* is noted next to the –597 open interest posting on the worksheet in Figure 6–6.

Friday
The next trading session (Friday, 7/7) saw price up (+46) on high (36,471) volume and increasing (+2,901) open interest. This is easy to read. It represents the definition of an ideal healthy price uptrend. Both interactions are bullish.

Monday
The third session analyzed (Monday, 7/10) is similar to the previous day. Increasing price, high volume, and a positive change in open interest are construed as bullish.

Tuesday
Tuesday, 7/11, is an interest trading session. Given the big price-down day (–58), did the longs panic? No. Volume did not escalate into the *high* category. At 29,750 contracts, turnover charts as average. A technician does not try to force the issue when average volume occurs. This is a neutral reading. A question mark is placed on the worksheet in Figure 6–6 to mark this as a nondirectional reading.

Open interest on Tuesday, 7/11, showed a big increase (+1,558). With a price-down day, the general rule states that this is the definition of an ideal healthy price downtrend. The word *bearish* is written on the worksheet.

Wednesday
Volume on the 22-tic price rally of Wednesday, 7/12, was a disappointment for the bulls. The longs would have preferred to see a high turnover. At only 22,658, this was a low-volume rally. Since low-volume rallies are expected in an ideal healthy down market, this is a bearish signal. The positive change in open interest on the price-up day is considered bullish. This neutralized the bearish volume reading for this trading session.

Summary
The final step is to add up the bullish and bearish readings to arrive at a "weight of the evidence" verdict about the direction of the major price trend. At seven bullish signals versus only two bearish signals, the major price trend is considered to be up.

FIGURE 6–7

Outcome

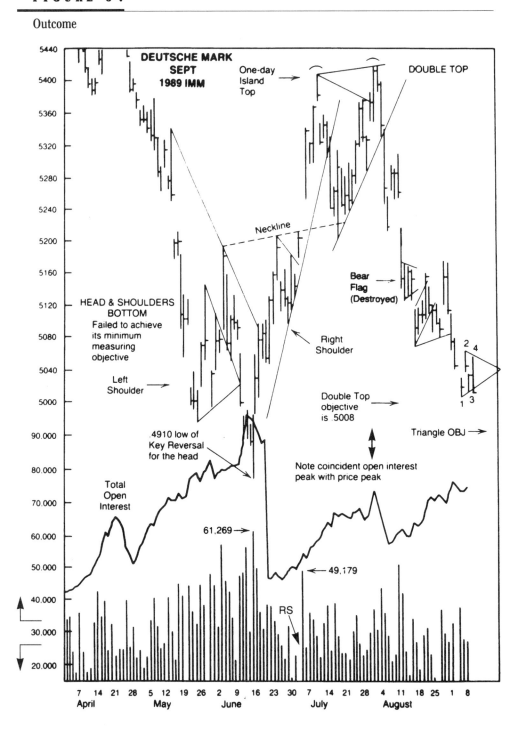

DEUTSCHE MARK
SEPT
1989 IMM

One-day Island Top

DOUBLE TOP

Neckline

HEAD & SHOULDERS BOTTOM
Failed to achieve its minimum measuring objective

Left Shoulder

Right Shoulder

Bear Flag (Destroyed)

Double Top objective is .5008

Triangle OBJ

.4910 low of Key Reversal for the head

Note coincident open interest peak with price peak

Total Open Interest

61,269

49,179

RS

Other Technical Considerations and Outcome

Two opposing price patterns were apparent to the bar chartists. These are seen in Figure 6–2. The one-day Island Top was bearish, and the Head & Shoulders Bottom (although unsymmetrical) was bullish.

The outcome of these two forces is seen in Figure 6–7. A pullback to the underlying support at the neckline occurred. Although additional bearish readings occurred in price versus volume and in open interest, the weight of the evidence still favored the bulls. This led to another price rally (to a higher high) in late July as the major trend reasserted itself.

Note the abrupt change in open interest concurrent with the price high on August 2. This exemplifies open interest acting as a coincident indicator with price.

MECHANICAL APPROACH TO ESTABLISHING VOLUME PARAMETERS

Many statistical software packages contain programs to place standard deviation bands around a mean (average). Technical analysis toolboxes often refer to this process as establishing Bollinger Bands around a price mean.

Figure 6–8 shows how Bollinger Bands can be placed at three-quarters of one standard deviation around a 20-day moving average of total *volume.*

The average 20-day volume in Figure 6–8 was 22,851 contracts. The volume levels at three-quarters of one standard deviation around this mean were 16,334 and 29,368. A purely mechanical approach to establishing volume parameters would consider these the threshold levels for high and low volume.

FIGURE 6-8

Mechanically Establishing High and Low Volume Parameters

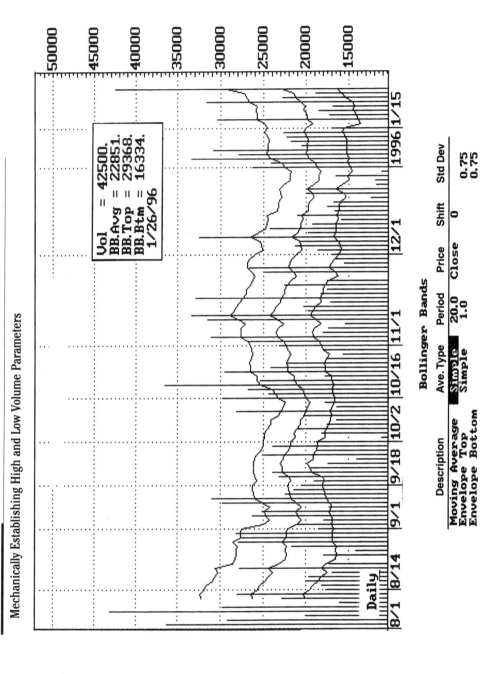

7

SPECIALIZED PROBLEMS

This chapter answers the most often asked questions regarding the interpretation of volume and open interest, which usually are associated with disturbances in the pure theory of price versus volume or price versus open interest changes.

SCALE CONSTRUCTION

Obviously a technician would like the most responsive volume and open interest scales practical. Updating a dozen daily charts by hand should present no problem for the serious trader. However, working with more than 12 charts daily would strongly suggest the need for computer software and a good printer. In any case, selection of proper scales is important. For charts constructed by hand, several observations can be noted:

> *Do not try for too much accuracy.* The actual figures are not important. Identifying the volume *category* and observing the *change* in open interest is the goal. Trying to place an open interest dot to within 1,000 contracts when the magnitude of the open interest is 300,000 is fruitless. In this situation, accuracy to within 4,000 contracts is sufficient. What is most important is that the direction of the open interest change is apparent.
>
> *The scales do not have to begin at zero.* The bottom of the chart does not need to be cluttered with black vertical lines. Identify a level of obviously "low" volume and begin the scale at that level. Should a volume figure lower than the determined level occur, simply place a dot on the scale at the minimum reading. This will serve as a "place holder" to assure the technician that the chart has been updated. This can be observed on the August 1989 Comex gold chart in Figure 7–1 on the four low-volume trading sessions during April. If a limit move artificially reduces volume to

the low category, a notation on the chart must be made. This is necessary unless the location of the tic mark on the price chart makes it clear that a locked limit situation existed.

Introduce a discontinuity between the volume and open interest scales if necessary. There is no need to have a great expanse of open space between the volume and open interest plots on the graph. Instead, drop the open interest scale so it rests only slightly above the volume scale. Should volume surpass the level of open interest (actually or due to the scale discontinuity), no problem will develop. The interaction of price, volume, and open interest will still be easily seen. This is especially true when there is no great expanse of blank chart paper between the postings of all three variables.

The Comex gold chart in Figure 7–1 shows how the open interest scale has been lowered via a discontinuity. Some mechanically reproduced charts make use of two differently denominated scales for both volume and open interest. This necessitates the use of a right-hand scale and a left-hand scale. In Figure 7–2, open interest is plotted using the scale on the left side of the chart; each small square equals 4,000 contracts. The scale on the right is used for volume and each small square is only 2,000 contracts.

This technique obviously brings the open interest scale down, eliminating white space, but it also reduces the sensitivity of open interest changes. Introducing a discontinuity in a single scale is preferable.

WHEN TO CHANGE MONTHS

Technicians should concentrate primary price analysis on the most liquid futures month. This is typically the nearby contract, closest to expiration. When does this contract begin to lose liquidity, making it necessary to change the technical emphasis to the next expiration? The answer is not standard. In many cases, it can be derived from the contract specifications.

Most futures contracts still allow the obligations to be fulfilled by actual delivery. However, the majority of market participants, including hedgers, do not want or need to participate in this process. As long as the ability to deliver forces convergence between the futures price and cash price, an honest futures quote will result. Prudent trading suggests that an open long futures position should not be held when receiving delivery is a possibility. Most futures traders are out of their element when forced to operate in the cash market.

By contrast, holding a short position in a physical-delivery contract when delivery is possible is not dangerous because the short initiates the delivery process. Even so, liquidity declines, and the spread between the bid and asked often widens appreciably.

Next we will examine some contract characteristics of the two large Chicago futures exchanges. Each trader must do the needed homework on the contracts being traded. Knowledge of the contract specs will point to the advisability of shifting to the next contract.

FIGURE 7-1

Note Discontinuity in the Scale between Volume and Open Interest

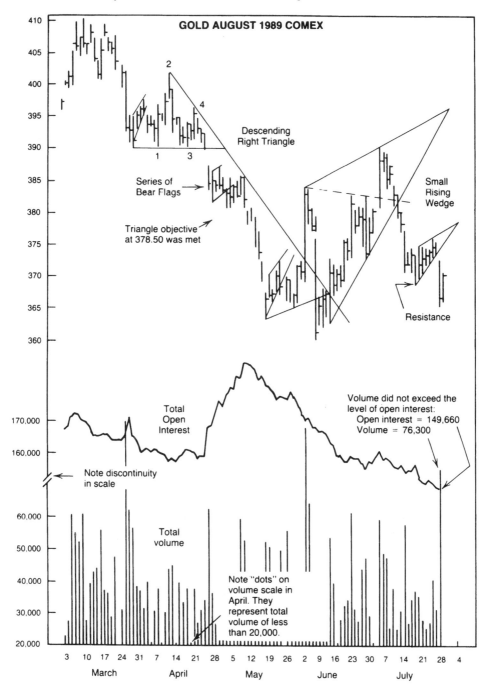

F I G U R E   7–2

Right- and Left-Hand Scales

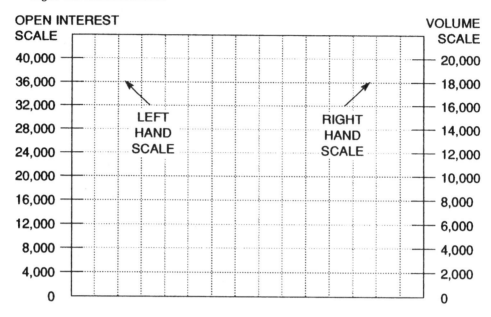

CHICAGO BOARD OF TRADE

The following sequence governs the physical delivery process on the CBOT.

First position day: Second-to-last business day preceding expiration month.

First notice day: Last business day of month preceding expiration month.

First delivery day: First business day of expiration month.

The shorts initiate the delivery process. Allocation of delivery notices begins with the oldest-dated long position. First Position Day is very important to the longs. Holding an open long contract on the close of First Position Day could result in the trader receiving a delivery notice on First Notice Day. Actual delivery would occur on First Delivery Day.

The practical ramification of this system is that all speculative longs should be closed out or rolled forward by the close of business on First Position Day.

As previously discussed, open short positions held beyond First Position Day tend to suffer from declining liquidity. A general rule for the CBOT contracts:

Be out of all short positions by the end of the first week of the delivery month.

Switching/Rollover

The Chicago Board of Trade is well aware of the desire of its customers to deal in the most liquid contracts. This necessitates "rolling" positions forward into the next month. To insure that this *physically* occurs, the most liquid month is "switched" to the "top step" of the trading pit. This top level of the trading pit has the largest area, is most easily accessible, and contains the best sight lines to the other pits and telephone desks. In actual practice on the CBOT, the individual pit brokers, scalpers, day traders, and clerks remain in the same physical location; only the month they are trading actually changes.

Typically, switching the pit occurs on First Notice Day at the CBOT. If volume and open interest in T-bonds are holding up in the lead contract, however, the T-bond pit committee might not switch the pit until a few trading sessions after First Notice Day. The smaller contracts such as the municipal bond futures (even though they have an index and do not settle via physical delivery) would switch at the same time as the more active T-bond contract.

A speculative desire to maintain long positions in a physical-delivery month sometimes arises. This stems from a very bullish market often resulting in an inverted price structure ("backwardation"). The nearby contract gains in price on the back months. An economic function is being served—a price inversion should draw existing quantities of the commodity out of storage. Playing this game can be dangerous. When sufficient deliveries occur to break the back of the squeeze, the front month often undergoes a collapse in price with respect to the back months. The London Metals Exchange is famous for its many cases of backwardation.

The conclusion to be drawn from this analysis of the CBOT's physical delivery contracts is:

> *All technical work and open long speculative positions should be concentrated on the next expiration month contract—beginning with the close two business days prior to the expiration month.*

CHICAGO MERCANTILE EXCHANGE

Physical deliveries do occur on most of the livestock futures on the Chicago Mercantile Exchange (CME). Longs can receive a delivery notice *after* the market closes on First Notice Day. Therefore:

> *All technical price work in the physical-delivery contracts should move to the next contract, beginning with the close one business day prior to the beginning of the expiration month.*

The currency and T-bill futures on the IMM present a special case in the arena of physical-delivery contracts. Delivery does not take place until *after* the last day of trading. Knowledge of the exact date (and time of day) is crucial. The last trading day in foreign-currency futures is defined as the Monday prior to the third Wednesday of the delivery month. Physical delivery then occurs two days later on Wednesday. (A detailed look at a currency expiration can be found in Chapter 8.)

> *In general, holding either long or short positions in currency futures into the first week of the delivery month presents no problems.*

The T-bill expiration is more complicated. The last trading day is defined as one business day preceding the first business day of the contract month on which a 13-week T-bill *and* a previously issued one-year T-bill has 13 weeks to maturity. The easiest method of keeping track of the last trading day is to obtain a listing from the exchange. The CME provides handy calendars listing the last trading days for both options and futures. Figure 7–3 is an example of one of these expiration cards. Note that the expiration of the T-bill options was designed to coincide with the CBOT's interest rate options. T-bill options expire in the month prior to the delivery month.

Eurodollars

Eurodollar time-deposit futures exhibit a unique open interest behavior as expiration approaches. Open interest in Euros declines rapidly in the front month *further from expiration* than any other cash-settled future. The August 1986 issue of

F I G U R E   7–3

CME T-Bill and Eurodollar Expiration Card

the CME *Market Perspectives* stated that "fifty days before expiration, less than half of total Eurodollar open interest is in the nearby compared to well over 90 percent for [other CME financial futures]."

This is due to several possible factors. Financial institutions tend to hedge using a "strip" of Eurodollar futures. There is also a desire to operate more than one month forward, so positions are rolled as the Eurodollars approach one month prior to expiration.

Table 7–1 contains an example of a rollover in Eurodollars. The March contract of the next year was rotated to the most active pit position on Monday, November 10. This was more than one month prior to the expiration of the December contract on December 18.

Technicians need to focus attention on the price charts of the most active contracts. In Eurodollars this means that a glance at the volume and open interest in the first *three* quarterly expiration months is necessary. This is because it is possible for a more distant contract to become the top-stair trading month—leaping over a nearby contract if its "customer business" is high enough. Specifically, the rule reads that whenever the five-day moving average of customer business in a deferred month exceeds that of a nearby month for two trading sessions, the more active contract is switched. In 1993, when this rule was first implemented, the lead month switched from the June contract to the December contract, skipping over the September future. In general:

Technical price work should be concentrated on the next contract month in Eurodollars, at minimum, beginning at the midmonth prior to the expiration month.

T A B L E   7–1

IMM Eurodollar Rollover

Contract	Volume	Open Interest	
		Total Outstanding	Change
Friday, November 10, 1989			
Dec '89	33,276	209,720	–3,124
Mar '90	21,876	160,995	–814
Monday, November 13 (Rollover Day)			
Dec '89	20,180	205,601	–3,101
Mar '90	31,492*	164,376	+3,381
Tuesday, November 14			
Dec '89	53,670	199,825	–5,776
Mar '90	119,248	179,892	+15,516
Expiration of December contract: December 18, 1989			

* March contract now has more volume than the nearby December contract.

Cash-settled futures, Eurodollars in particular, present another (minor) problem to students of volume and open interest. This is addressed in the "detrending open interest" case study in Chapter 8.

SIMEX

The Singapore International Monetary Exchange (SIMEX) follows the same rules and contract specifications as the CME. In this regard, the analysis of when to monitor the next trading month is similar.

One interesting sidelight (that does not contain any technical ramifications) is that the SIMEX trading pit is not switched or rotated. Most floor brokers filling orders are on salary. *Only* the "locals" physically move themselves to the area of the pit where the most action is occurring. The salaried floor brokers do not move. Thus, they become order fillers in the front month for part of the year and in the back months for another portion of the year. Since the SIMEX trading floor is much smaller than the Chicago exchanges, it is quite easy for any order filler to execute a trade in any contract month.

WEEKLY AND MONTHLY CHARTS

Volume and open interest are not usually plotted on weekly or monthly futures charts because the long-term secular growth seen in many contracts overwhelms the technician trying to discover the nuances. This is especially true on newly introduced contracts. Analysis can be undertaken, however, on "mature" futures contracts.

Weekly and monthly charts are called continuation charts. The nearby future is plotted until less than one full week or month remains until expiration. The chart is then continued by plotting the next expiration. If a large price-spread exists between the lead and back month, a gap on the chart can result when plotting the next contract. The technician must live with this. The long-term charts are used to monitor the big picture. Actual entry and exit trading decisions are usually based on a reading of the daily chart.

PERPETUAL CHARTS

Futures contracts have an inevitable expiration date. This created havoc when computer-driven technical analysis began to proliferate. This created the need for a "perpetual" futures contract chart. Many methods of constructing such a chart are possible. Common to every method is the need to specify the "roll-forward" date. For example, this could be: the 1st trading day of the expiration month, the 10th day of the expiration month, the last trading day, or a more sophisticated open interest weighted system.

Unless the transition is smoothed, a synthetic jump or drop in price will occur within the data series. Old-time futures bar chartists simply changed to a new contract month on a daily bar chart when appropriate (depending on the contract specifications) and did all the technical work on a specific chart. This remains the best alternative for analysis of volume and open interest. The price data will always be the most active future and the volume and open interest will always be total.

Even classical bar chartists have difficulty when it comes to a long-term view of the futures markets. What's needed is a methodology of switching from the nearby contract to the next appropriate contract when plotting a weekly or monthly. The criteria selected depend somewhat on the type of technical analysis being used and on the technician's particular trading style.

For calculating percentage retracements on a chart, say a 61.8 percent pull-back, it is critical to have the highest high and lowest low of the nearest-to-expire contract present on the long-term chart. On a weekly continuation chart this would entail plotting the nearest-to-expire future as long as it had at least a full week remaining until expiration. But prudent trading suggests that a trader does not have an open position in a physical-delivery future beyond the First Notice Day or First Position Day.

An excellent example is the all-time price high in U.S. Treasury bond futures. This was 122-10 on the September 1993 future. It occurred during the first week of the delivery month in September 1993. If the December 1993 contract had been used for the monthly continuation chart—it was trading at a discount to the nearby September future—there would have been a historic price high lower than 122-10.

The conclusion to this foray into longer-term analysis is that volume and open interest are seldom plotted on weekly or monthly charts. These charts are used for an overall picture of the major price-trend. The trigger for new longs or shorts is pulled based on the daily chart. Thus, plotting the nearby until less than one full week or less than one full month is left to expiration is appropriate for charts of these magnitudes. Trendlines and classical price patterns can be constructed on these longer-term charts. But trendlines and the like are *not* drawn from the expiration of one daily chart to the next. A separate daily bar chart is created and analyzed for each individual futures contract month.

SPECULATIVE VERSUS HEDGE MARKET

Examine the two graphs in Figure 7–4. Without knowing the name of what is being traded, one can comment concerning the type of market being made. Which market is dominated by speculators and which is more heavily used by hedgers?

Graph B is the speculators' market. Volume on a daily basis often exceeds the level of open interest. Day traders play a major role. They participate in price action during the trading session, but are unwilling to hold positions overnight.

Graph A is typical of a mature futures contract used by commercial interests. Hedges are placed and not grossly changed from day to day. Corn futures would be a prime example.

An interesting difference in trader attitudes is apparent in the interest rate futures in Chicago. This is seen in the two graphs of Figure 7–5. Large hedge positions in Eurodollar time-deposit futures make volume unlikely to surpass open interest levels. But at the long end of the yield curve, T-bond futures' daily volume quite often exceeds open interest. Clearly there is more speculative activity in pro-

FIGURE 7–4

Which Graph Depicts a "Hedge" Market versus a "Spec" Market?

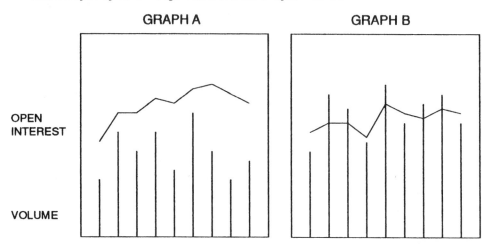

portion to the total overnight positions. Some of the T-bond turnover *is* coming from "hedgers" who are "actively managing" the position!

An important consideration is how much pure speculative activity is present. The amount of "noise" created by speculators makes placing protective stop-loss orders more difficult. For example, a 100-point move in the S&P futures (in either direction) is common every day (no matter what the major trend may be doing). Price reactions often eat into support or resistance levels by 100 points. Traders who would normally feel comfortable buying or selling an unchanged opening would wait for a 95-point dip or rally from the previous session's close before entering the S&P market. This is trying to take advantage of the normal speculative noise.

The public idiosyncrasy favoring the long side can be carried to extremes: given two charts, one the inverse of the other, the public would overwhelmingly opt to trade the market that is rising. An interbank dollar/mark chart would look like the IMM deutschemark futures chart turned upside down. But the outside speculator is trading in futures, not the interbank market. The general rule for a healthy price trend is applied in the way currencies are quoted in the futures markets.

QUIZ QUESTION

The following question has been used in Ken Shaleen's Chicago Mercantile Exchange Technical Analysis course since 1976. Students are asked to insert the word *up* or *down* to make the statement correct.

Price _____ with open interest increasing indicates the underlying _____ trend is healthy and should be expected to continue.

The answer is found in Figure 7–6. Additional questions are located in "Practical Exercises" in Chapter 16.

F I G U R E   7–5

Note Relationship of Volume to Open Interest

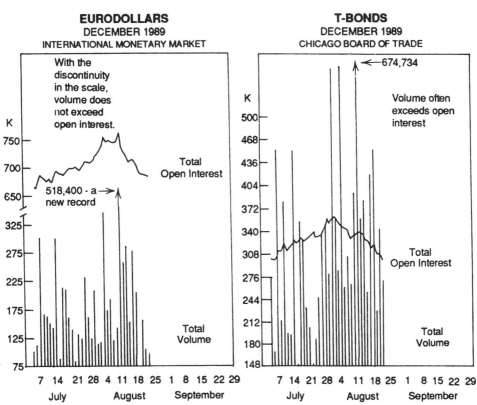

OPTIONS ON FUTURES

The *definitions* of volume and open interest on options contracts are interchange-able with the *definitions* of volume and open interest on futures. But that is where the similarity ends. Graphic analysis of an options price chart together with vol-ume and open interest interpretations are difficult, if not impossible.

Price

The time decay inherent with options created unorthodox price formations. Price pattern recognition should be applied to the underlying futures contract. An op-tions strategy can then be selected that will take advantage of the anticipated price move.

Open Interest

The options open interest analysis problem is similar to that of cash-settled fu-tures, only worse. Total-options open interest builds steadily and then collapses at expiration. Figure 7–7 of open interest in options on T-based futures illustrates the typical shape. Removal of the "trend component" of open interest increase is the

F I G U R E 7–6

Answer to the Quiz Question

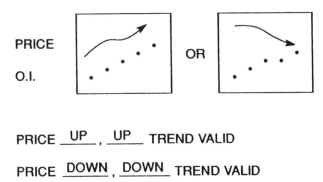

PRICE __UP__ , __UP__ TREND VALID

PRICE __DOWN__ , __DOWN__ TREND VALID

The question can be answered either with "up, up" or "down, down"! Actual test results show that an overwhelming percentage (90 percent) answer the question "up, up." Approximately 6 percent of the answers are "down, down" (true bears!). And 4 percent of the students are insightful enough to conclude that either "up, up" or "down, down" is correct.

suggested approach with cash-settled futures contracts. The concept of detrending futures open interest is found in the Eurodollar case study in Chapter 8. No attempt has been made to apply a similar detreading approach to open interest on options.

Volume

Options volume does not necessarily exhibit a regular escalation and then drop at expiration. Many options expire worthless and no offsetting action is needed. Since total options volume consists of both put and call activity, a further complication is introduced. Although it would be quite easy to plot put and call volume separately, no such attempt has been made.

Another volume factor is apparent in the graphs of total monthly deutschemark and British pound volume in Figure 7–8. In general, volume on a futures contract increases when options on the contract are listed.

Chapter 8 details the specific problem that occurs when futures open interest experiences a decline coincident with an options expiration.

EFP TRADES

Exchange For Physical (EFP) trades have the potential to cloud volume and open interest interpretation. These types of trades are conducted for a specific purpose—typically, to allow buyers and sellers to effect their cash market transactions on the basis of a negotiated price, delivery site, commodity to be delivered, and the timing of the delivery. In an EFP trade, a cash market-position is exchanged for a futures position. In its simplest form, the buyer of a physical commodity exchanges the long futures positions for the physical commodity needed.

FIGURE 7 – 7

Options on T-Bond Futures

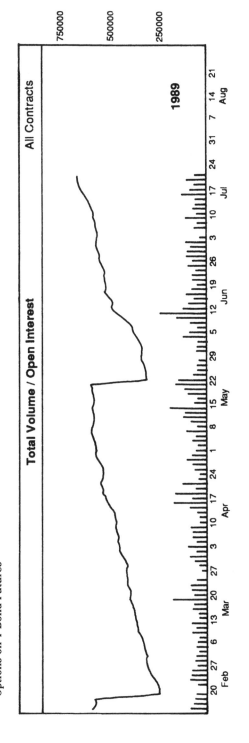

(Note severe decline in option open interest when the nearby option expires.)

Source: *Financial Update*, Chicago Board of Trade, July 21, 1989.

F I G U R E   7–8

Total Futures Volume Increases When Options Are Listed

The accompanying charts illustrate total monthly volumes for four contracts traded on the Chicago Mercantile Exchange: Deutsche mark futures and options and British pound futures and options. The graphs demonstrate the coincidence between increased volume in the underlying futures and commencement of options trading based on the currency futures contracts.

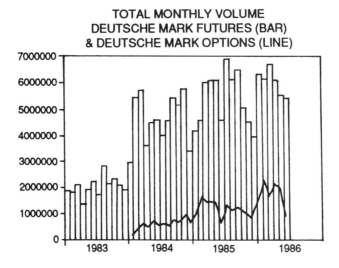

TOTAL MONTHLY VOLUME
DEUTSCHE MARK FUTURES (BAR)
& DEUTSCHE MARK OPTIONS (LINE)

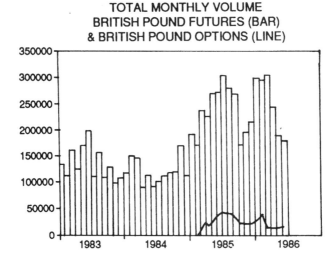

TOTAL MONTHLY VOLUME
BRITISH POUND FUTURES (BAR)
& BRITISH POUND OPTIONS (LINE)

Source: *Market Perspectives,* Chicago Mercantile Exchange, August 1986.

The seller of a physical commodity gives up the cash commodity but receives short futures positions in return.

The volume of EFP trades is kept by futures exchanges and is included in total-volume statistics. Open interest can increase, decrease, or remain unchanged due to an EFP trade. The three possible EFP situations are as follows:

1. If two parties enter into a "basis trade" and neither has a prior futures position:
   a. Party A: Sells physicals—establishes new long future.
   b. Party B: Buys physicals—establishes new short future.
   c. Result: Volume 1, open interest + 1.
2. If one side of the trade already has an open futures position (Party B is long futures):
   a. Party A: Sells physicals—receives B's long future and is now long futures.
   b. Party B: Buys physicals—passes long future to A and is even in futures.
   c. Result: Volume 1, open interest unchanged
3. If both sides have open futures positions, the transfer terminates both futures hedges:
   a. Party A: Sells physicals—receives B's long future, covering existing short, and is now even in futures.
   b. Party B: Buys physicals—receives A's short future, exiting from existing long, and is now even in futures.
   c. Result: Volume 1, open interest −1

EFP trades have been increasing as a percentage of total volume in the financial-instrument futures. For example, EFPs in T-bond futures amounted to 0.3 percent in 1986; by the start of 1990 the percentage was estimated at 4.0 percent. EFPs in grain and oilseed trading in Chicago averaged 5.5 percent in 1986. This is a representative figure and EFP trading remains fairly static at this percentage level.

Currency futures EFPs on the IMM averaged 8–9 percent in the liquid contracts for 1989. With the advent of GLOBEX electronic trading, it could have been argued that there would be far less need for EFP trades. But the percentage increased to 13 percent in 1995, even with electronic trading available to offset an open currency futures position. A substantial amount of the EFP business took place in the one-half-hour suspension between GLOBEX and regular trading hours. When truly seamless futures trading (no suspensions) becomes a reality, the percentage of EFP trades should decline.

S&P 500 EFPs amounted to 1.2 percent of total volume in 1989. In 1995 this percentage dropped to 0.5 percent (see Table 11–3 for a one-day reading of S&P EFPs in early 1996). EFPs were only 0.25 percent of livestock futures in 1989; by 1995 the percentage was negligible. EFPs in the interest rate products at the CME was a very small 0.10 percent of total volume in 1995.

EFP trades in the more cash-oriented exchanges constitute a higher percentage of volume. Wheat EFPs amount to 15 percent of volume on the Kansas City Board of Trade. The percentage reached 25 percent on the Minneapolis Grain Exchange in the mid-1980s. The flexibility afforded by negotiating an EFP trade is also increasing its use in the oil industry via the New York Mercantile Exchange's petroleum futures.

Examples of how the exchanges disseminate the number of EFP trades can be found on the samples of the various Daily Information Bulletins in Appendix H. EFP trades are similar to any other futures transaction in the way volume or open interest is recorded. To summarize:

EFP trades have not proved to be a problem for the technical trader analyzing total-volume and open interest statistics.

MUTUAL OFFSET SYSTEMS

The most successful mechanism for transferring open futures positions to another exchange exists between the IMM and SIMEX. This interexchange link allows designated contracts that are bought/sold on one exchange to be sold/bought on the other and offset. The system is especially useful to active international money market dealers. In 1989, it was estimated that 30 percent of SIMEX Eurodollars contracts were transferred to the IMM, mostly for the purpose of liquidation. This percentage climbed to nearly 50 percent of SIMEX Eurodollar volume in 1995.

Since any trade is placed with a profit motive, it won't disturb the premise that volume and open interest figures can be used to monitor traders' viewpoints.

VOLATILITY TRADES

The same logic is applied to "volatility trades." A volatility trade occurs when an options trader effects both the options and futures trade in the options pit. The trader is viewing whether the market is over- or understating volatility in the options price. The two transactions are counted individually for volume and open interest purposes. These trades, of course, boost volume and open interest figures but do not distort technical analysis of either market.

BASIS TRADES

The difference between the cash or spot market price and the nearest to expire future is referred to as the basis. Arbitrage between the cash market and the nearest to expire future is what keeps the futures or any forward market in line. As with spread trading (future versus future, discussed in Chapter 8), basis trading is thought to approximate a fairly low but stable percentage of trades every day. In this regard, basis trading is not expected to distort the analysis of volume or open interest.

Some exchanges, notably the LIFFE, makes it very easy to establish basis trades via its Basis Trading Facility (BTF). For a look at how much volume this type of trading generated, a technician can consult LIFFE's *Daily Information Bulletin* (sample in Appendix H). At mid-1996, for example, basis trading in the German bund futures amounted to 0.85 percent of total bund volume.

LINKAGES

In an attempt to see if open-outcry trading would attract more business than electronic dealing, LIFFE and the CBOT proposed to enter into an agreement to trade selected products of the other exchange. The volume would belong to the exchange where the trade was consummated and the open interest would belong to the home exchange where the transaction is cleared.

Technicians will simply treat this evolution as another trading session in the international 24-hour trading day, summing the volume for all the sessions and posting the open interest under the price bar containing the tic mark for the close corresponding to the open interest report. This phenomenon will be discussed in detail in Chapter 14, "24-Hour Trading."

CHAPTER

8

IDIOSYNCRASIES RELATIVE TO THE <u>GENERAL RULE</u>

Technical use of volume and open interest has evolved since the inception of traditional agricultural futures, which began in the United States in 1877 with the inception of wheat trading in Chicago. As new contracts continue to be introduced, technicians should apply the criteria for a healthy price trend, appreciating the specific traits of each contract type. The detailed nuances of contracts introduced since 1972 are found in Appendix B, "Historical Overview."

This chapter contains macro observations of how open interest acts in a transition from a bull market to a bear market, and it also includes a micro look at contract specifications.

MARKETS IN TRANSITION

Since open interest is expected to increase in the direction of the major price trend, what happens to open interest as a market reverses trend? If open interest exhibited perfect hypothetical characteristics, it would have to rise continually. But this does not happen.

Open interest normally declines in the initial stages of a new bear market.

This is especially true in markets that the public likes to trade from the long side, such as the traditional agricultural commodities and metals. Open interest declining is a result of both longs and shorts exiting from their positions. But the driving force emanates from the selling pressure of liquidation by participants with current long positions. Confused shorts are also closing out positions; they do not realize the trend has finally turned down—in their favor.

Open interest often declines to roughly the "steady state" condition that prevailed before the start of the previous uptrend. After liquidation has brought the open interest down to this low level, then open interest may begin to exhibit the ideal situation by moving up. At this stage the price downtrend becomes more readily apparent and the shorts may begin to show their strength by pressing their winning positions. Would-be longs begin bottom picking and open interest begins to increase. The result is a healthy bear market.

AN ANOMALY?

Chapter 6 suggested using the general rule for a healthy price trend to identify bullish or bearish price versus open interest changes on a daily basis. Seeing open interest dip along with prices was deemed a bullish reading. It now appears that open interest will decline at the initial stages of any bear market. Obviously, a conceptual difficulty arises. To clarify this problem:

> *Price down, open interest down is not an automatic signal to initiate new long positions.*

A better label to affix to this technical occurrence would be *not bearish*.

Confusion may still exist about the difference in meaning between *bullish* and *not bearish*. When open interest declines, the direction of the price change that trading session is not the direction of the major price trend. Thus, price down, open interest down does not reflect the ideal healthy bear market. To twist this reflection around to mean that the market must therefore be bullish is to assume too much.

In summary, when prices decline and open interest declines, no automatic buy signal occurs. This is because the price dip might be the start of a major sell-off and not simply a correction. At this stage, the ability to locate underlying support becomes crucial. Until the price sell-off violates classical support levels, the sell-off remains only a correction.

The initial discussion may have appeared to suggest that new positions should be taken based upon open interest changes only. Entry into a new position entails a price move that is confirmed by proper volume and open interest changes. A violation of a trendline or support/resistance level on the price chart will stop-out a trade.

The gold chart (Figure 8–1) is a typical example of how open interest reacts during an important market turn. This phenomenon is observed in a transition from a bull market to a bear market.

PHYSICAL-DELIVERY CHARACTERISTICS

When physical delivery settles a futures contract, total open interest is reduced by the number of deliveries against the expiring contract. At this time, some decline in the plot of total open interest is usually observable. Specific contracts experience far greater open interest drawdowns. This is due to the contract specifications, the nature of what is being traded, and who is trading it.

F I G U R E   8–1

Market in Transition

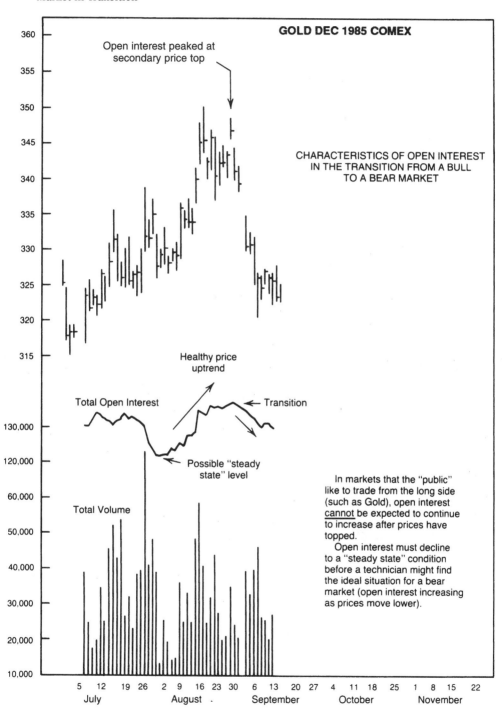

GOLD DEC 1985 COMEX

Open interest peaked at
secondary price top

CHARACTERISTICS OF OPEN INTEREST
IN THE TRANSITION FROM A BULL
TO A BEAR MARKET

Healthy price
uptrend

Total Open Interest   Transition

Possible "steady
state" level

Total Volume

In markets that the "public"
like to trade from the long side
(such as Gold), open interest
cannot be expected to continue
to increase after prices have
topped.
Open interest must decline
to a "steady state" condition
before a technician might find
the ideal situation for a bear
market (open interest increasing
as prices move lower).

DELIVERY WHILE NEARBY IS STILL TRADING

Chicago Board of Trade deliveries (T-bonds, grains, etc.) can take place anytime during the delivery month. Deliveries can occur both before and after the last trading day. On the CBOT, the last day of trading, typically, is eight full business days before the end of the contract month.

In grain and oilseed futures, the general consensus over the years has been that roughly 2 percent of all open positions are settled via the delivery process. In 1995, the average deliveries as percentage of average open interest ranged from 3 percent in corn to 11 percent in wheat. This does not take into account how many bushels were re-delivered. Thus, the generally accepted 2 percent historical figure is probably still a good guesstimate.

The decline observed in open interest as these physical-delivery futures move toward expiration is orderly and fairly predictable. The T-bond case study in Chapter 9 will examine the expected changes in open interest on approaching important days (such as First Delivery Day). In 1995, the average deliveries in T-bond futures as a percentage of average open interest was 3.64 percent. This is an accurate figure because most of the deliveries occurred in the last few days of the contract month, due to the "positive carry" that was being earned on actual cash bonds.

Any contracts open in the lead month after the last trading day on the Chicago Board of Trade must be fulfilled via delivery. Thus, the technician has a good idea of the magnitude of the total open interest decline that must be posted after trading in the lead contract ends.

DELIVERY AFTER TRADING IN NEARBY CEASES

The graphic change in the open interest plot of the IMM foreign exchange futures is very dramatic due to the settlement process occurring on a single day. This is the third Wednesday of the contract month. Trading in the expiring contract stops two business days *preceding* the delivery day. This last trading day, typically, is Monday of the third week of the contract month. Thus, the magnitude of the open interest drop due to the deliveries is known when the open interest statistics for Monday's trade are released.

The average deliveries as a percentage of average total open interest ranged from 36 percent in the Japanese yen to 63 percent in the British pound in 1995. These large deliveries stem from the fact that dealer arbitrage traders utilize the physical-delivery mechanism.

Currency Futures Example

When total open interest declines substantially because of heavy deliveries into the expiring contract, a technician must temporarily look further into the open interest changes to gain an understanding of what traders are thinking. A prime example is the IMM foreign-currency expirations in September 1989. The delivery day was Wednesday, September 20, 1989. The changes in open interest for that trading session are found in Table 8–1.

TABLE 8–1

Open Interest at the Conclusion of Delivery Day
Wednesday, September 20, 1989
IMM Foreign Currency Futures

	D-Mark	Swiss Franc	Japanese Yen	British Pound
Sept '89	−30,904	−14,429	−30,115	−9,555
Dec '89	−758	−89	−2,190	−784
Mar '90	+111	−14	+80	+67
June '90	+92	0	0	0
Total	−31,459	−14,532	−32,225	−10,272

Trading in the September contracts ceased on Monday, September 18. The magnitude of the open interest drop in the expiring September contracts was known on Tuesday morning, September 19, after the release of volume and open interest statistics for Monday.

The large drops in open interest in the expired September contract masked what was really taking place. What is important to the technician is that open interest declined in the most active December contracts. The price changes on Wednesday, September 20, were as follows:

	D-Mark	Swiss Franc	Japanese Yen	British Pound
Dec '89 contract	+34	+34	+31	+118

The analytical conclusion was that the price rally was a net short covering, a signal of a weak rally. In addition, small price gaps were posted on three of the four high-low-close bar charts.

The gaps on the IMM charts were properly classified as "pattern gaps." This meant that gaps were found *within* a trading range or congestion area and would quickly be filled (gaps are discussed in further detail in chapter 14). Declining open interest added credibility to this technical interpretation. In fact, successful day-trade short sales could have been initiated on the openings Thursday morning. Closing the gaps was the objective. Open interest changes were available at 2:45 A.M. Chicago time on Thursday morning September 21. This means that spot forex dealers in Europe had ample time to position themselves with long dollar views before the resumption of dealing in North America.

When futures trading began on Thursday morning in the United States quotes were lower. The lower openings on the IMM were a reflection that the previous day's rallies were suspect. Nimble day traders in the U.S. futures markets did have room to initiate shorts even on the lower openings. The gaps, even lower than the openings, were the targets. This information is illustrated in Table 8–2.

The graphic portrayal of the Wednesday and Thursday price activity is shown in Figures 8–2 through 8–9.

FIGURE 8–2

Before

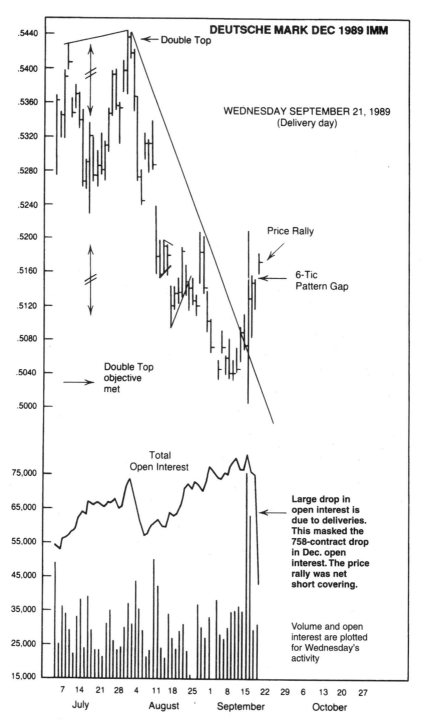

DEUTSCHE MARK DEC 1989 IMM

← Double Top

WEDNESDAY SEPTEMBER 21, 1989
(Delivery day)

Price Rally

6-Tic
Pattern Gap

Double Top
objective
met

Total
Open Interest

**Large drop in
open interest is
due to deliveries.
This masked the
758-contract drop
in Dec. open
interest. The price
rally was net
short covering.**

Volume and open
interest are plotted
for Wednesday's
activity

7   14   21   28   4   11   18   25   1   8   15   22   29   6   13   20   27

July   August   September   October

F I G U R E   8–3

After

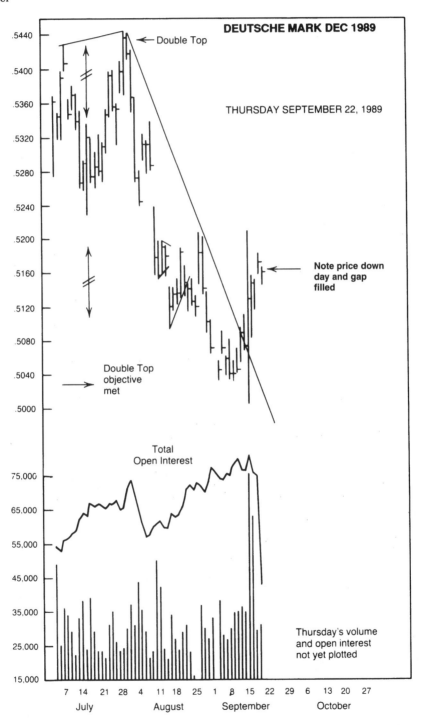

DEUTSCHE MARK DEC 1989

Double Top

THURSDAY SEPTEMBER 22, 1989

Note price down
day and gap
filled

Double Top
objective
met

Total
Open Interest

Thursday's volume
and open interest
not yet plotted

July   August   September   October

FIGURE 8–4

Before

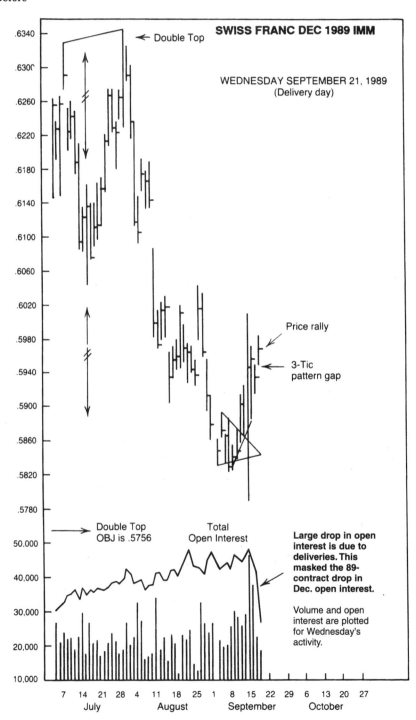

FIGURE 8–5

After

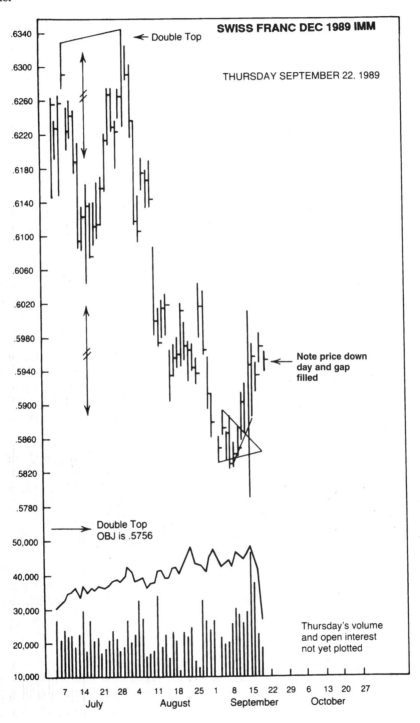

SWISS FRANC DEC 1989 IMM

THURSDAY SEPTEMBER 22. 1989

← Double Top

→ Note price down day and gap filled

→ Double Top OBJ is .5756

Thursday's volume and open interest not yet plotted

FIGURE 8-6

Before

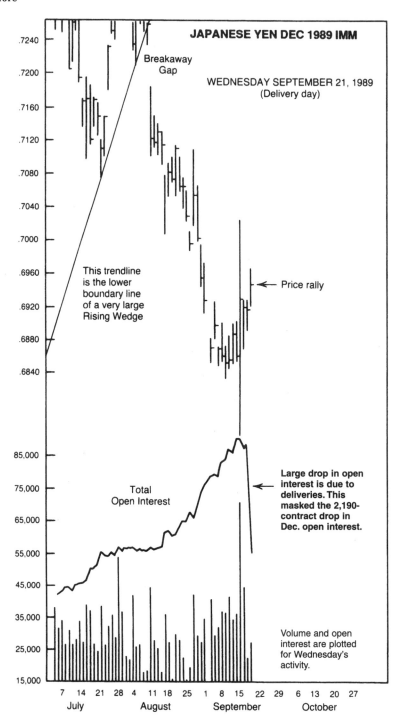

FIGURE 8–7

After

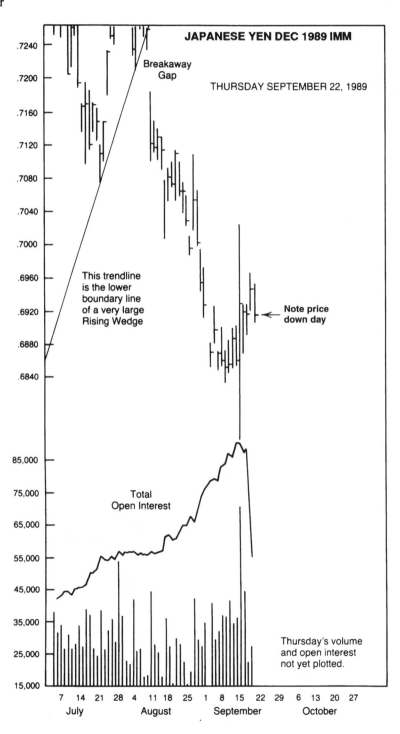

JAPANESE YEN DEC 1989 IMM

Breakaway Gap

THURSDAY SEPTEMBER 22, 1989

This trendline is the lower boundary line of a very large Rising Wedge

Note price down day

Total Open Interest

Thursday's volume and open interest not yet plotted.

.7240
.7200
.7160
.7120
.7080
.7040
.7000
.6960
.6920
.6880
.6840

85,000
75,000
65,000
55,000
45,000
35,000
25,000
15,000

7 14 21 28   4   11 18 25   1   8   15 22 29   6   13 20 27
July   August   September   October

FIGURE 8–8

Before

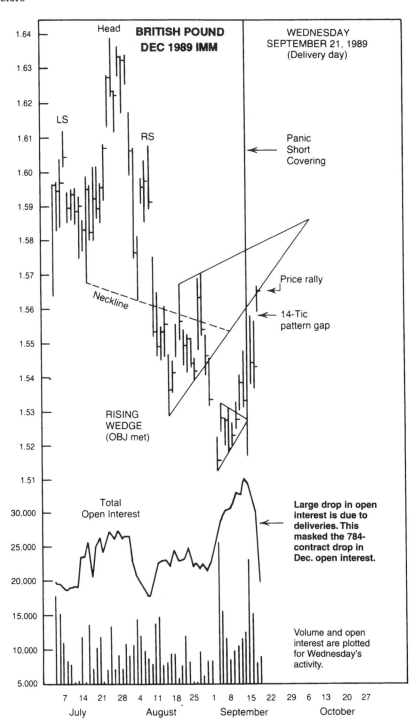

F I G U R E   8–9

After

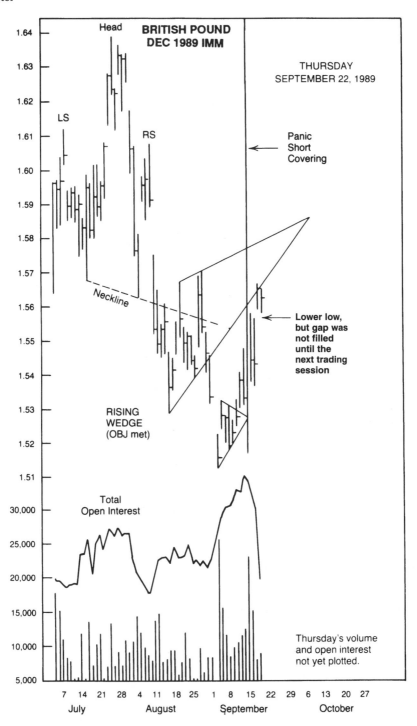

T A B L E   8–2

Price Changes Thursday, September 21, 1989—IMM Foreign Currency Futures

	D-Mark	Swiss Franc	Japanese Yen	British Pound
Open	−16	−11	−5	−28
Gap	−20	−20	No Gap	−86
Low	−25	−28	−42	−64
Close	−13	−15	−32	−24
Comment	Gap Filled	Gap Filled	No trade based on a gap; but OI did indicate a selloff was likely	Gap not filled; it was closed the next trading session.

Note: This table summarizes the outcomes noted in Figures 8–3, 8–5, 8–7, and 8–9.

CASH SETTLEMENT

The Chicago Mercantile Exchange introduced the first futures contract settled in cash rather than by physical delivery. This occurred when the Eurodollar time deposit future began trading on December 9, 1981. The first stock index future soon followed with the Value Line contract on February 24, 1982, on the Kansas City Board of Trade.

In a cash settlement future, there is no threat of delivery for the longs. Therefore, no urgent need exists to roll positions forward as expiration approaches. Obviously, there is no delivery mechanism for the shorts either.

Both sides can hold their open positions until and into the last day of trading. The exchange then simply marks the price of the expiring futures contract to the underlying cash market and all positions are offset. This forces the convergence of the futures with the cash market. If both sides were to roll forward in equal numbers, the plot of total open interest would be unaffected. In actual practice, without the inducement to roll, open interest in the lead contract plunges to zero, and the total open interest curve undergoes a severe drop. This creates a problem for the technician who is trying to analyze open interest changes.

General Configuration of Open Interest in a Cash-Settled Future

The total open interest plot of all cash settled futures reflects the same general configuration. Total open interest increases rather steadily and then drops precipitously as the lead month expires. The Euromark chart in Figure 8–10 exhibits this pronounced shape.

Although this tendency occurs to some extent on all futures charts, it is much more pronounced on a cash-settled contract. Therefore, an additional level of analysis is required for this type of contract. Ken Shaleen first used the technique of "detrending" Eurodollar open interest in his technical analysis course at the Chicago Mercantile Exchange in the mid-1980s.

DETRENDING OPEN INTEREST

A technician must try to isolate the normal trend component of the open interest increase. This does not require the use of high-powered regression analysis. A simple eyeball approach examining the last few expiration cycles, is sufficient. No more than four should be necessary. A trendline of best-fit is then placed through the open interest line. This is done in Figure 8–10. Note that this is not a trendline in the classical bar charting sense. The line is not constructed tangent to lows but rather represents the general slope or gradient of the open interest line.

A simple procedure is to move sideways 10 trading sessions. Then count up to the line of best fit, obtaining the number of contracts increased during the 10-session period. Dividing the results by 10 yields the normal trend component of open interest for each trading session.

Eurodollar Example

The IMM Eurodollar future is one of the most straightforward contracts to analyze. Four quarterly expirations are examined. These are seen in Figure 8–11. The eyeballed slope of the open interest trendlines for the four quarters of 1988 is summarized in Table 8–3.

TABLE 8–3

Eurodollars: Slopes of Open Interest Trendlines
(from Figure 8–11)

1st quarter 1988	1,800	per trading session
2nd quarter 1988	2,800	per trading session
3rd quarter 1988	3,400	per trading session
4th quarter 1988	2,800	per trading session
	10,800/4 = 2,700 contracts*	

*See Appendix D for a mathematical determination.

Note that no consideration is given to trend prices (up, down, or sideways). The period under analysis (the year 1988) did, however, exhibit all three price trend conditions.

The result of this example, on average, is total open interest increased by 2,700 per trading session in the IMM Eurodollar futures, no matter what prices did! Armed with this statistic, a technician has a benchmark with which to analyze open interest changes in later time frames.

An increase in total IMM Eurodollar open interest of 1,000 contracts would actually represent a sub-trend increase! For determining the health and direction of the major price trend, the opening interest change would be considered a decline of 1,700 contracts. The direction of the price change in that particular trading session would not be considered the direction of the major price trend.

For more thorough analysts, Appendix D—Mathematically Detrending Open Interest—provides a "check" of the eye-balled line of best-fit for the first

FIGURE 8–10

General Configuration of Open Interest in a Cash-Settled Future

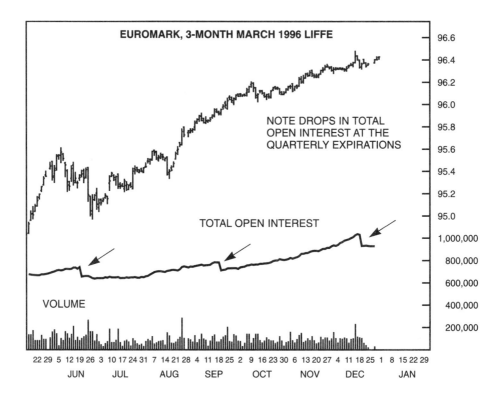

quarter of 1988. The slope of the line as calculated mathematically was 2,015 contracts per trading session. This is close to the 1,800 contract figure derived by simply looking at the plot of total Eurodollar open interest.

APPLICATION TO A CURRENT CONTRACT

March 1989 Eurodollars

Prices on the March 1989 IMM Eurodollar chart were in a healthy price downtrend, see Figure 8–12. A relatively rare Head & Shoulders Continuation Top forecasted a downside move to 90.14. That forecast objective was achieved.

A disciplined trading strategy dictated removing ¼ to ½ of all existing shorts. Any head & shoulders measuring objective is only a minimum. Prices can continue to decline much further than the minimum target. The obvious question is: When should a trader cover the remaining shorts? One answer is contained in the analysis of open interest changes. The smart money had been the shorts. When the shorts determined that the March Eurodollar had dropped enough, they began taking profits. This is reflected in a subtrend increase (or actual decrease) in total open interest.

FIGURE 8-11

Detrending Open Interest in a Cash-Settled Future

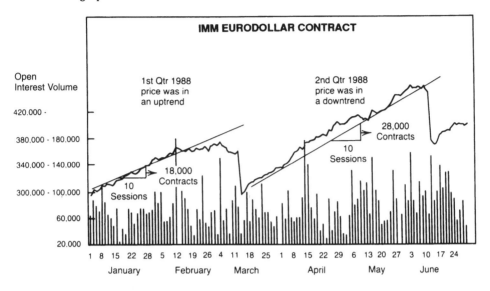

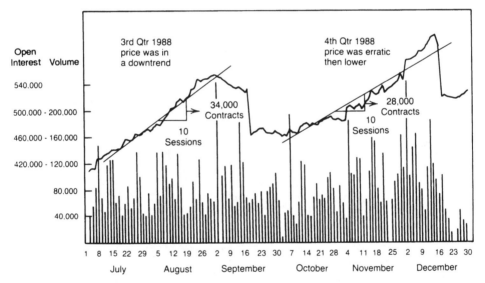

On the price-down day, Friday, February 17, 1989, open interest declined 558 contracts. This was not only a subtrend increase, but also an actual decline. This statistic was released by the CME clearinghouse and available to technicians at 1:46 A.M. Saturday, February 18. The information was ready for use by interest rate traders on SIMEX or LIFFE before the resumption of trading in the United States.

Open interest declined the next trading session as well. By then, price and open interest showed that a healthy bear market was resuming. Figure 8–13 shows how Eurodollar quotes continued to fall and the increase in open interest resumed.

F I G U R E   8–12

Comparing Actual Open Interest to the Trend Component

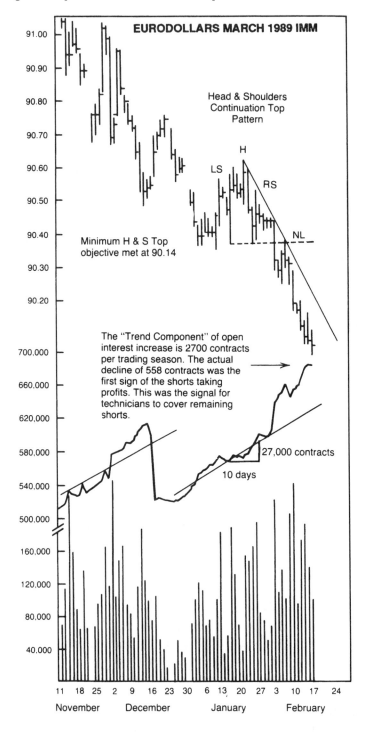

FIGURE 8–13

Outcome

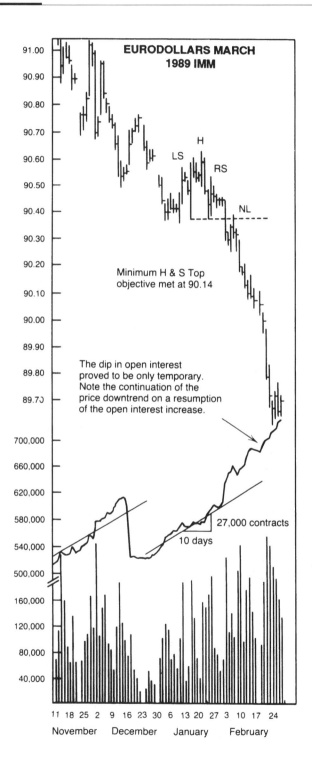

EURODOLLARS MARCH 1989 IMM

Minimum H & S Top objective met at 90.14

The dip in open interest proved to be only temporary. Note the continuation of the price downtrend on a resumption of the open interest increase.

27,000 contracts

10 days

In this example, an analyst would have received a premature signal to cover shorts. But the discipline of following this approach, using open interest changes as a guide, does pay off in the long run.

An aggressive trader wanting to reinstate positions would see that the resumption of the price downtrend generated healthy, positive open interest changes. Because the rollover of positions from the March contract into June was beginning, new shorts would have been placed in the June Eurodollars.

A note concerning reestablishing a position is in order. Many nondisciplined traders find it difficult to open new shorts at a price level lower than where previous shorts were covered. The same is true about not wanting to chase a bull market. If the technical signs point to a continuation of the major price trend, new positions must be initiated even if prior positions proved to have been closed out prematurely.

OPTIONS EXPIRATION

Typically, futures open interest will experience a drop in the nearby contract when the option on it expires. Often, this decline in open interest is enough to cause the total open interest line to drop.

Extreme caution should be used to avoid reading too much into the interaction of the price change versus the total open interest change of that trading session. It is wise to look below the surface of total open interest and examine the changes in the back months. This is the same technique as the one suggested for analyzing the situation when the nearby futures expire.

Table 8–4 contains the changes in open interest, both total and lead month, for the December 1989 expiration of the popular options contracts that trade in the large Chicago markets.

To gauge the possible decline of the futures open interest, it may be instructive to see how many in-the-money options were exercised. The hedge ratio (delta) could be large enough to affect the futures open interest appreciably if delta-neutral options strategies were being used. Futures positions created from options exercises would be offset versus existing open futures positions; futures open interest would decline.

Table 8–4 shows that open interest in the December 1989 futures declined at the expiration of its options series in all but the D-mark contract. The D-mark situation was abnormal. At this time, D-mark open interest was surging to new-record levels. This was strong enough to suppress the normal tendency of the lead futures open interest to decline at options expiration.

An open interest decline in the lead contract is often of sufficient magnitude to pull down the *total* open interest as well. In the December 1989 T-bond options, 61,875 in-the-money options were exercised on November 18, 1989. The total T-bond futures open interest declined 12,757 contracts. Contrast this to the December 1989 corn futures. Big increases in the back-month open interest during the same option expiration were large enough to cause total open interest to remain unchanged.

Total futures open interest increased in live cattle and live hog futures when

TABLE 8–4

Analysis of Futures Open Interest Changes at the December 1989 Options Expiration

	In-the-money Options at Expiration	Dec Futures Open Interest Change	Total Open Interest and Change
T-bonds	41,261 calls 20,614 puts	−17,699	361,294 −12,757
Wheat	2,831 calls 622 puts	−332	52,119 0
Corn	7,767 calls 8,520 puts	−1,857	199,189 +127
Soybean meal	1,171 calls 178 puts	−788	64,356 −151
Live cattle	4,559 calls 0 puts	−145	80,636 +4,506
Live hogs	922 calls 0 puts	−470	37,645 +362
D-marks	24,714 calls 379 puts	+483	116,219 +4,730
J-yen	2,151 calls 14,734 puts	−1,609	61,363 −173
British pound	4,183 calls 530 puts	−529	27,514 +649

the December 1989 options expired on November 24. It is unusual that no in-the-money puts were exercised. This stems from the dynamic bull market in both cattle and hogs. New "life of contract" price highs were posted during trading on the day the December options expired. CME rules state that "no new strike prices shall be listed if less than 10 calendar days remain to maturity." There were no in-the-money put options trading!

No specific relationship concerning the magnitude of the in-the-money options versus futures open interest declines at options expiration is being proposed. The bottom line is this:

A technician must be aware of the options expiration dates. Be prepared to look at open interest changes in more detail on these dates.

SEASONALITY

Does the analysis of volume and open interest need to be modified due to seasonal influences? For volume, the answer is no. Day-to-day volume comparisons are more important than any seasonal factor. Assessing open interest changes, especially in the agricultural futures, may require a seasonal adjustment.

The Commodity Research Bureau, now owned by Knight-Ridder, periodically updates a study of the seasonal-volume and open interest variations of the more active U.S. futures. Figure 8–14 exhibits the seasonal variations in corn. The

FIGURE 8–14

Corn: Seasonal Trend of Open Interest and Volume

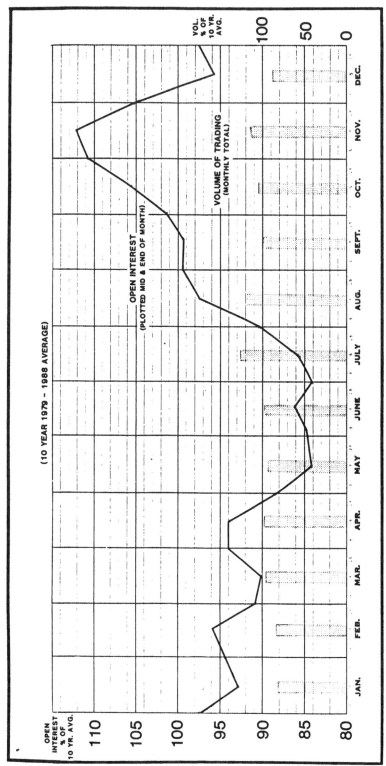

Source: Commodity Research Bureau, 75 Wall Street, 22nd Floor, New York, NY 10005.

graph is constructed with a percentage scale. The absolute level of open interest is most often different from year to year, but the percentage changes during any year do exhibit a regular pattern. In fact, comparison of this study for the 10 years ending in 1988 produces a high correlation to the same type of study for the 10 years 1955–1964. The only difference is the two relative lows in open interest now expected in mid-May and late June as opposed to a single low at the end of July back in 1955–1964. With the emergence of bigger crops and earlier grain and oilseed harvests in South America, the slight movement of the expected seasonal open interest low can be explained. Additional studies are located in Appendix G.

Knight-Ridder's CRB *Futures Perspective* chart service makes the seasonal analysis task easier by including a graphic history of average open interest for the previous six years. The historic open interest plot is displayed on the chart of the nearby future together with the current open interest.

Refer to the pork belly chart in Figure 8–15. Note the price uptrend into mid-August. Is this a healthy price uptrend and is it expected to continue? The standard answer would be no because open interest is declining. What does the open inter-

F I G U R E   8–15

Weak Price Uptrend: Downside Reaction Likely

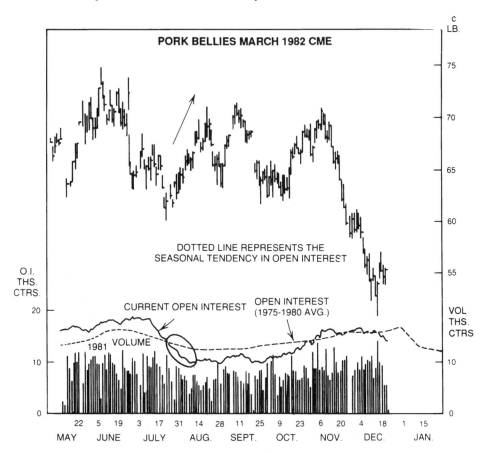

est in this particular commodity normally do at this time of the year? The dotted line represents the average open interest for the years 1975–1980. Open interest normally declines between mid-July and mid-August. How does this seasonal influence change the analysis? Since the current decline in open interest is at a much steeper rate than would normally be expected seasonally, the same conclusion is reached. The price uptrend is unhealthy and it would be expected to reverse soon.

Financial-instrument futures (currencies, interest rates, stock index futures) do not exhibit enough seasonality to alter the analysis. There are times of the year when cash market trading or interbank dealing will slow. Mid-December to the end of the calendar year is a good example. But these times of book-squaring are very evident. A detailed analysis of historic open interest curves is unnecessary.

The method used by the Commodity Research Bureau to construct the seasonal open interest line is simple: the total open interest figures at the beginning and middle of each month of the previous six years are added and the result divided by six. The plotted results tend to smooth out the open interest drops that occur when the lead contract expires. The circled areas of the graphs in Figures 8–16 and 8–17 do not contain seasonal influences; this is a smoothed expiration effect. The shallow declines in the historic open interest curve are the effect of the nearby contract's expiration.

OPEN INTEREST AS A COINCIDENT INDICATOR

In bull markets, open interest often acts as an indicator with price. Open interest peaks coincide with price peaks. Price becomes the driving influence. When longs

FIGURE 8–16

Smoothed Historical Open Interest: Wheat Example

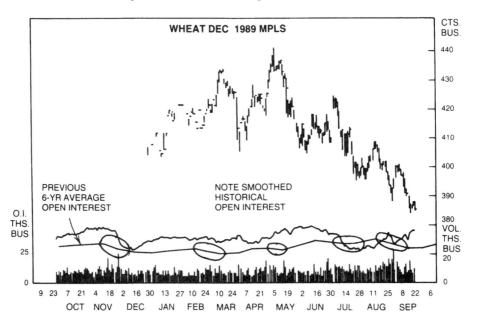

FIGURE 8–17

Smoothed Historical Open Interest: S&P 500 Example

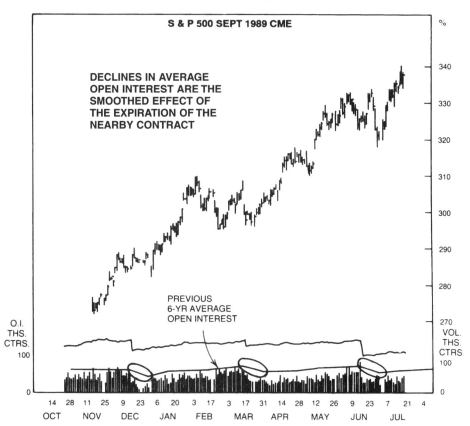

are getting stopped-out on a sell-off, the financial press often mislabels the price decline as "profit taking."

Figures 8–18 through 8–20 contain examples of open interest as a coincident indicator in livestock, currency, and grain markets. The tendency of open interest to coincide with turns in the foreign-exchange markets will be explored in more detail in Chapter 9, "Specific Market Behavior."

SPREAD CONSIDERATIONS

Spread trading is a popular strategy in the futures markets. Much of the spreading in agricultural and livestock futures is based on the life cycle of the commodity. Financial-instrument spreads rely on the economic judgment about the relationship of the two contracts. Does heavy spread trading hamper the usefulness of volume and open interest statistics? No. The analytical process of examining open interest changes of individual contract months determines if spreading is indeed taking place.

F I G U R E   8–18

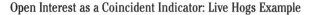

Open Interest as a Coincident Indicator: Live Hogs Example

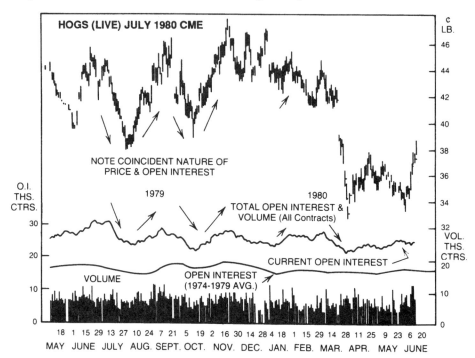

The spreading does not distort the volume and open interest statistics. A spread trade is initiated because the trader believes that a profit can be made. The trader has a difference of opinion with the current pricing of the two variables. A difference of opinion is what creates a market and price change. The technician tries to monitor this willingness to place open positions. Even if one of the legs of the spread resides in the cash, spot, or forward market, the motivation remains to make a profit. This means that normal arbitrage activities do not mask the price determination function of futures markets.

The more popular spreads are transacted on a single-order ticket. Execution takes place as a single transaction. The important point is that a single number—the price differential—is what is being traded. Thus, the hopes, fears, and moods that influence a trader are reflected in a single number—the spread. Technical analysis of the spread itself thus becomes possible.

Although a spread can be transacted in a single operation and the spread quote may actually appear on the "tape," exchanges do not publish spread volume or open interest. This statement is not absolutely true now that considerable electronic futures trading is occurring. The Chicago Mercantile Exchange's Volume Analysis (see Table 11–3) includes the volume of spread trades that are transacted on GLOBEX.

But, in general, spread volume and definitely spread open interest statistics are not available for close examination. A look at changes in the individual con-

FIGURE 8–19

Open Interest as a Coincident Indicator: Japanese Yen Example

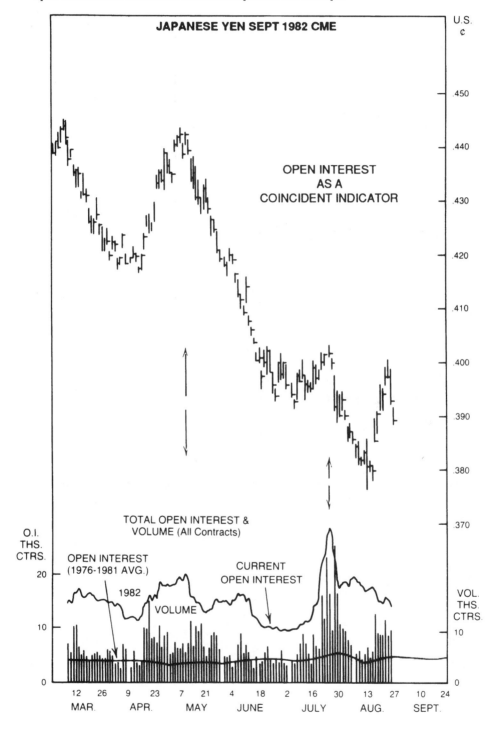

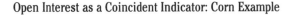

FIGURE 8–20

Open Interest as a Coincident Indicator: Corn Example

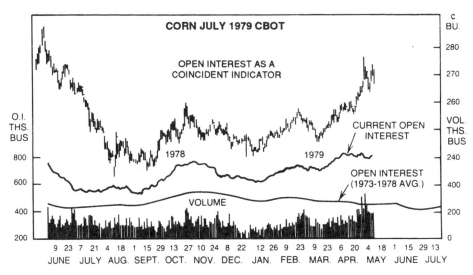

tract months often reveals that a spread transaction was highly likely. The Commitments of Traders Report (Chapter 10) is also an excellent source for uncovering how much spread activity has occurred. Old-time grain traders have often remarked that the first hint that market conditions were changing was in the movement of spread relationships.

STORABLE VERSUS PERISHABLE COMMODITIES

The simple definition of a storable futures contract is one in which a delivery resulting from a long futures position can be held for an extended period of time (i.e., three months) and then be redelivered via a short position in a more distant contract. Spreads using storable commodities lend themselves to carrying charge calculations. The "full carry," can be computed. Full carry is the maximum differential that a more distant future should trade above a nearby future.

Spreads involving storable commodities tend to be more stable than spreads involving perishable commodities. Live hog futures on the CME are a typical example used to describe a perishable commodity contract. Live hogs received via a long position in July will not meet the contract specifications for a delivery into a short August live hog future a month later. In this regard, U.S. Treasury bond futures would be considered storable, whereas U.S. T-bill futures would be considered perishable.[1]

---

1. A tiny window exists where a delivery resulting in T-bonds with less than 15 years and three months to First Call Date would not be eligible for delivery three months hence.

CASH & CARRY TRANSACTIONS

Storable commodity futures lend themselves to a "cash & carry" analysis. Holding cash market inventory that is easily deliverable into an existing short position allows an implied interest rate return to be calculated. Comparing this return to other short-term interest rates, such as Eurodollar yields, may reveal more favorable returns. If true, the open interest in this futures market would be swelled by this factor. This problem would arise only in a storable commodity such as gold that was trading very close to full carry. In grain futures, even in times of surplus, the spreads rarely move beyond 80 percent of full carry.

TAX SPREADS

Prior to 1982 technicians had to be aware that some spread trading occurred solely to obtain preferential tax treatment. These spreads were executed mainly in storable commodities, particularly metals. The logic was that metals should tend to trade near full carry. Many would-be tax spreaders received an unwelcome education in the effects of increasing prices, increasing interest rates, a yield curve inversion, and increasing physical demand in the silver bull market of 1979!

The important point to realize is that historical analysis of any storable futures contract before 1982 must be conducted with the knowledge that tax spreading may have been a factor. Beginning in 1982, futures spreads were marked-to-market, meaning that all realized and unrealized gains and losses are taken into account for U.S. tax purposes.

The following two observations should aid in the historic analysis of any storable commodity futures charts of the late 1970s and early 1980s:

> The month of June in the United States represented a critical month with respect to tax planning. Positions placed in any futures contract that expired the following calendar year would have more than six months to run in the present calendar year. A holding period of 6+ months qualified a long position for preferential tax treatment. June was the last chance for traders to place positions that had the possibility of "long term" (6+ months on long positions) capital gains (taxed at a lower rate) in the current calendar year.
>
> January was another important calendar month. This is when the bulk of the tax spreads were unwound. When tax spreading was prevalent, total open interest often experienced a drastic decline in the first few days of the new calendar year.

The gold charts of 1980 in Figures 8–21 and 8–22 exhibit the distinct fall and rise in open interest due to tax spreading.

Looking Below the Surface

When trying to investigate spread activity, the technician should examine individual contract month open interest. The actual CBOT volume and open interest sheet in Table 8–5 shows the spreads (probably butterfly spreads for non-U.S.-based tax purposes) that were removed on January 3, 1984. Tax spreads using T-bond futures were very popular in the early 1980s.

FIGURE 8–21

Tax Spreads Being Removed

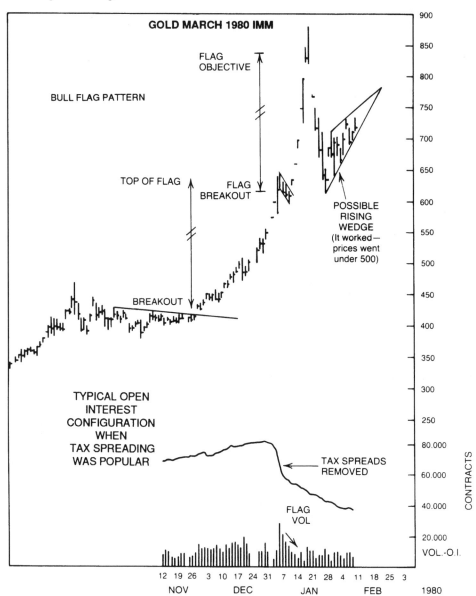

F I G U R E   8–22

Tax Spreads Being Placed

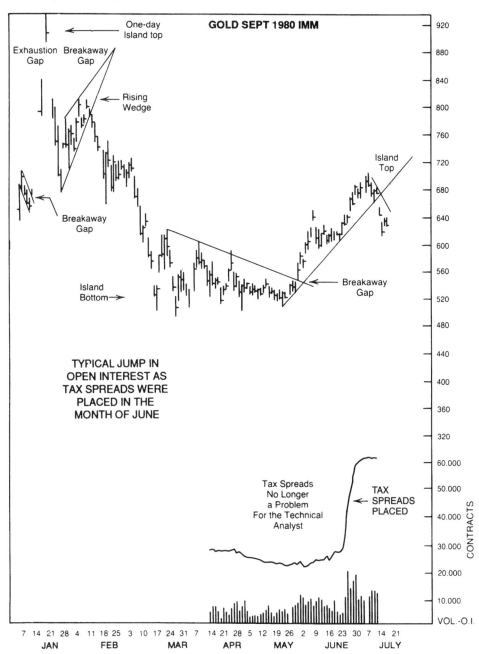

GOLD SEPT 1980 IMM

One-day Island top

Exhaustion Gap

Breakaway Gap

Rising Wedge

Breakaway Gap

Island Bottom→

Island Top

Breakaway Gap

TYPICAL JUMP IN
OPEN INTEREST AS
TAX SPREADS WERE
PLACED IN THE
MONTH OF JUNE

Tax Spreads
No Longer
a Problem
For the Technical
Analyst

TAX
SPREADS
PLACED

CONTRACTS

920
880
840
800
760
720
680
640
600
560
520
480
440
400
360
320

60.000
50.000
40.000
30.000
20.000
10.000
VOL.-O.I.

7 14 21 28   4 11 18 25   3 10 17 24 31   7 14 21 28   5 12 19 26   2 9 16 23 30   7 14 21
JAN   FEB   MAR   APR   MAY   JUNE   JULY

TABLE 8–5

Spreads Being Removed

141 West Jackson Blvd.
Chicago, Illinois 60604
Futures Trading and Open Interest in Commodities Traded on The Chicago Board of Trade,
Tuesday, January 3, 1984
#001 Daily Volume of Trading –Sales– Including Exchanges of Futures for Cash, The Close of
Business. Cash Exchanges Are Included in Trading Volume. Subject to Further Correction.

Commodity	Mth	Yr	Trading Volume	Cash Exchange	Transfers	Open Interest At Close	Open Interest Change	Delivery Notices
T-bonds	Mch	84	50,543	228	461	111,022	2,056+	
	Jun	84	3,332		5	29,510	765–	
	Sep	84	4,821			12,173	3,198–	
	Dec	84	6,893			7,943	4,028–	} NOTE
	Mch	85	6,385		1	5,887	2,814–	
	Jun	85	2,398			3,410	800–	
	Sep	85	21			1,314	5+	
	Dec	85	27			561		
	Jun	86				1,084		
	Sep	86	1			26		
Total			74,421	228	467	174,120	9,544–	

Note the reductions in Sep 84, Dec 84 and Mar 85 open interest. It certainly looks like a 2000 × 4000 × 2000 butterfly spread was re-moved.

9

SPECIFIC MARKET BEHAVIOR

Each category of futures markets possesses unique volume and open interest characteristics. These idiosyncrasies are due to both individual contract specifications as well as what is being traded. This chapter will isolate some of the distinctive traits of the U.S. Treasury bond and currency futures in particular. The matrix in Table 9–1 at the end of this chapter summarizes the findings and provides a general framework for beginning an open interest analysis on any futures contract.

CONTRACT SPECIFICATIONS

Open interest in the *nearest to expire* futures contract would normally be expected to decline:

1. When options on the futures expire.
2. When receiving delivery is first possible.
3. On the last day of trading.
4. On the last delivery day.

In various futures contracts, some or all of the above conditions may occur on the same day. For example, options on the IMM Eurodollar futures expire on the last day of trading of the futures contract. An analysis of open interest changes on any futures contract must include a consideration of the four important benchmark dates listed above. The CBOT's Treasury bond contract will be examined in detail to demonstrate the theoretically expected open interest behavior; then a comparison will be made to what actually occurred.

TREASURY BONDS

The important dates unique to T-bond futures are:

1. Options expiration: Noon of the Friday preceding First Notice Day by at least five business days.
2. First Position Day: Two business days preceding delivery month (Longs could receive notice of delivery prior to the opening on First Notice Day).
3. First Notice Day: Last business day of month preceding delivery month.
4. First Delivery Day: First business day of delivery month.
5. Last Trading Day: Eighth full business day prior to end of delivery month.
6. Last Delivery Day: Last business day of month.

Under the hypothesis that open interest would be expected to decline on these dates, a theoretical shape of a total open interest curve has been constructed in Figure 9–1. This hypothetical open interest curve was created without regard to the price changes that may have occurred. The theory being tested is that *the influence due to the contract specifications will overwhelm the open interest changes due to market conditions.*

F I G U R E   9–1

Theoretical Total Open Interest Curve for CBOT Treasury Bond

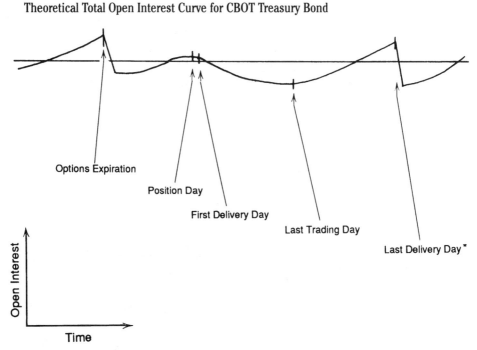

*Assuming positive carry, that is, overnight repo rate is less than bond yield.

The next step is to examine actual open interest curves to determine if reality conforms to the hypothetical curve postulated in Figure 9–1. Twenty-four consecutive T-bond expirations between 1984 and 1989 were examined. The last two years in the study are shown in Figure 9–2. Five of the important dates are indicated by arrows. First Notice Day was not analyzed.

An actual total open interest curve has been created by observation of the 24 actual curves. This plot is shown in Figure 9–3. Note the similarities and difference when the actual is compared to the hypothetical:

1. Open interest in T-bonds does decline at options expiration. In only 3 of 24 expirations did total open interest fail to decline on the Friday of options expiration or on the Monday immediately following.

2. Open interest declined two-thirds of the time on First Position Day. This shows that futures market participants are well aware of the ramifications of First Position Day. Open contracts in the nearby contract were liquidated so actual delivery would not occur.

3. Open interest increased on First Delivery Day in 17 of 24 expirations. This was due to the fact that new positions were being placed in the next-to-expire or later futures contract.

4. There is a definite tendency for total T-bond open interest to drop on the last day of trading in the nearby contact. This occurred 18 of 24 times.

5. On only 2 of 24 expirations did open interest fail to decline on either of the last two delivery days. This means that the shorts were waiting until the last possible moment to deliver physical T-bonds. The positive carrying charges (short-term interest rates lower than long-term rates) prevailing during the time frame analyzed was the fundamental factor creating this idiosyncrasy.

Bear Market Considerations

There is a definite tendency for open interest in T-bond futures to increase as prices move lower. This means that it is common to find the definition of an ideal healthy price downtrend with respect to the interaction of price and open interest changes. This is because:

Treasury bond futures are driven by the perception of the potential short hedgers.

Fund managers have a natural long position in cash T-bonds. When they become nervous about increasing rates, they have only two choices: liquidate cash market holdings and move to a shorter maturity on the yield curve, or place a short hedge in bond futures. When these potential short hedgers become actual short hedgers, their selling pressure forces futures even lower, and open interest most often rises.

The opposite side of the coin is that price rallies in T-bond futures often occur on declining open interest. This phenomenon does not neatly fit the defini-

FIGURE 9-2

T-Bond Open Interest Curves with Important Dates Indicated

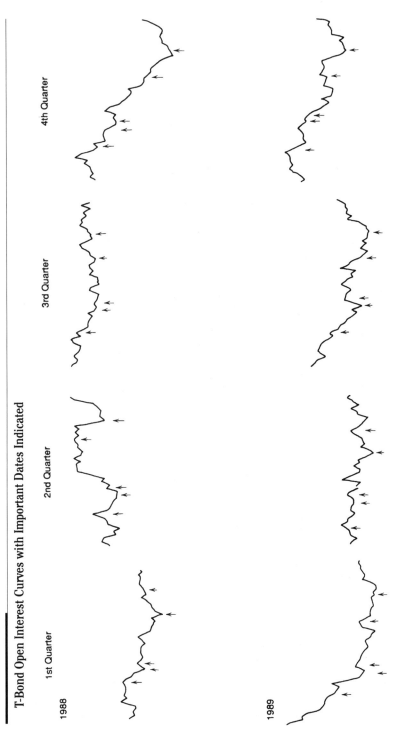

FIGURE 9-3

Actual Total Open Interest Curve for CBOT Treasury Bond Futures

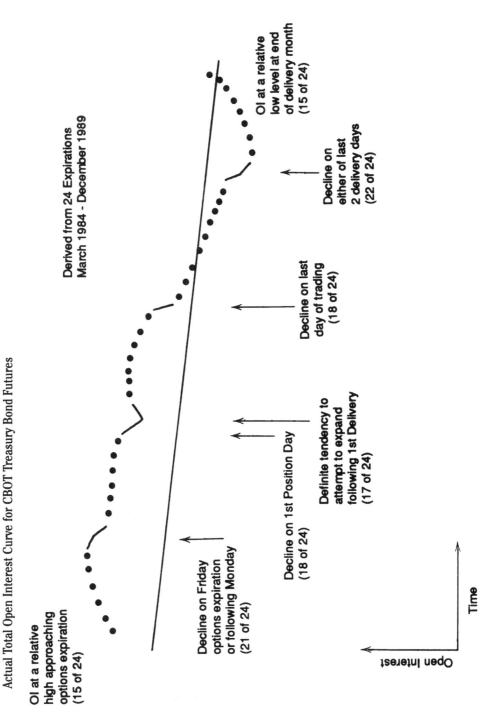

OI at a relative
high approaching
options expiration
(15 of 24)

Derived from 24 Expirations
March 1984 - December 1989

OI at a relative
low level at end
of delivery month
(15 of 24)

Decline on
either of last
2 delivery days
(22 of 24)

Decline on last
day of trading
(18 of 24)

Definite tendency to
attempt to expand
following 1st Delivery
(17 of 24)

Decline on 1st Position Day
(18 of 24)

Decline on Friday
options expiration
or following Monday
(21 of 24)

Time

Open Interest

tion of a healthy bull market. But where did the general rule for a healthy price trend (developed in Chapter 4) come from? Answer: From almost 150 years of *wheat* futures trading on the Chicago Board of Trade.

The trading of interest rate futures, denominated and invoiced in terms of *price* has only been in existence since late 1975. The first glaring example of a major T-bond futures price rally on declining open interest occurred after the successful Fed tightening and ultimate subduing of the U.S. inflation rate by the Paul Volcker-era U.S. Federal Reserve System in mid-1985 to mid-1986.

This is when astute T-Bond technicians first learned that substantial price rallies could occur on sustained "short covering," In actuality, the holders of cash market fixed instruments were simply returning to their natural position—long.

Another notable short covering rally in T-bond futures of significant proportion (76-00 to 96-00) began with the "flight to quality" that took place during and after the U.S. equity market crash of 1987.

A textbook example of T-bond open interest acting in both ideal bullish and bearish fashion is found on the March 1996 T-bond chart in Figure 9–4. Of note on this chart as well is the decline in total open interest as bond prices swung back and forth, creating a complex head & shoulders top on the daily chart.

Other Interest Rate Futures

When U.S. Treasury bond futures were first listed by LIFFE, in London, the contract actually acted according to the general rule for a healthy price trend—in both directions. However, as the contract achieved its critical mass and became a viable hedge vehicle, it began to show the characteristics of being driven by the propensity of the short hedgers. Might not this phenomenon be present in other interest rate futures?

The U.S. bond futures seem to be the most susceptible by far to the influx of new short hedgers. But as other interest rate futures mature and are more fully utilized by hedgers, open interest may tend to show a propensity to increase during major price declines and to dwindle during sustained price rallies. The three-month British pound interest rate futures contract, short sterling, that trades on LIFFE exhibited this characteristic during the bear market of 1994 and the bull market of 1995 (see Figure 9–5).

Year-End Phenomenon

Another clearly observable trait in T-bond futures is the normal calendar year-end decline in total open interest. Nine years, from 1981 to 1989, were surveyed. Total open interest declined to a relative low on the last business day in December in eight of the nine years. Only December 1982 did not reflect this end-of-year open interest decline. This means that an analysis of any T-bond futures chart from late November to the end of December must take the seasonal downward pull on open interest into consideration. The particular price chart being analyzed would more than likely be the March contract of the next calendar year.

FIGURE 9-4

Ideal Open Interest Trends in Both a Bull and Bear Market

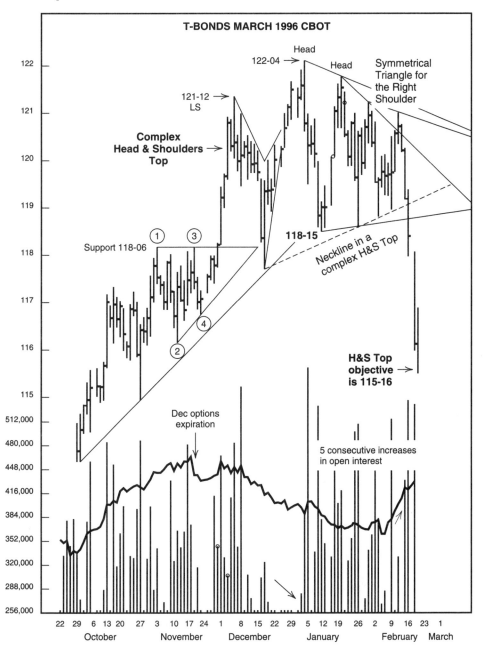

An extrapolation of the year-end phenomenon is the bounce back in open interest that occurs as a new calendar year begins. The entire seasonal tendency in T-bond open interest can be seen in the decline and subsequent increase in the average open interest line in the March contract in Figure 9–6.

FIGURE 9-5

Definite Propensity of Open Interest to Increase During a Bear (price) Market

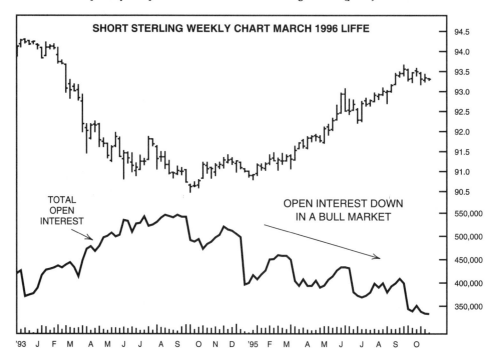

CURRENCIES

An idiosyncrasy of the IMM foreign exchange futures has been apparent for many years:

There is a definite tendency for open interest in the currency futures to peak coincident with price reversals.

This statement is generally true for all important price reversals on the currency charts and particular prevalent with price tops on the IMM futures charts. Although this phenomenon may be visible only 50 percent of the time, it can be a very useful filter for decision making—especially to foreign-exchange dealers operating in non-U.S. time zones. This is because the actual open interest changes from the Chicago Mercantile Exchange clearinghouse become available in late-afternoon dealing in Asia and in prime European dealing hours. Chapter 12 details the use of the important internal futures statistics by foreign-exchange dealers. Figure 9–7 shows an amazing coincident interaction between price *and* open interest. In fact, there was a head & shoulders top on both the price and open interest plots of the D-mark future. But note: classical bar charting (e.g., price pattern analysis) is not being suggested on either volume or open interest plots.

A plausible explanation for this phenomenon of coincidence of price changes and open interest peaks is that U.S. futures players will trade a bullish foreign-currency market, but retreat to their natural "long dollar" positions when

FIGURE 9-6

Year-End Open Interest Phenomenon in T-Bond Futures

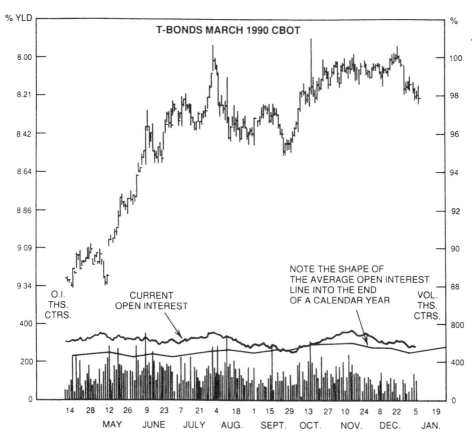

the non-U.S. currencies are falling in price. Remember that the IMM currency futures are quoted in American terms, the reciprocal of the European (interbank) terms. The tendency for the small trader to favor the long side of the IMM currency futures can easily be documented by examining the seasonal normal open interest graphs in Appendix E.

The remaining figures in this chapter (Figures 9–8 through 9–10) exhibit the coincident nature of price and open interest in the other three most active IMM foreign exchange futures. An additional example can be found on the September 1989 D-mark chart in Chapter 6, Figure 6–7. This phenomenon was observable in 1980 and is still operating in 1996. The "controlled devaluation" of the yen versus the U.S. dollar in 1995 and into 1996 was another example (not shown) of coincident interaction with open interest and price in the bear market on the various yen futures charts.

This idiosyncrasy allows open interest to be used as a corroborative tool in conjunction with other forms of technical analysis such as chart interpretation. Thus, open interest changes can highlight the fact that perceptions of foreign-exchange dealers are changing.

F I G U R E   9–7

Open Interest as a Coincident Indicator

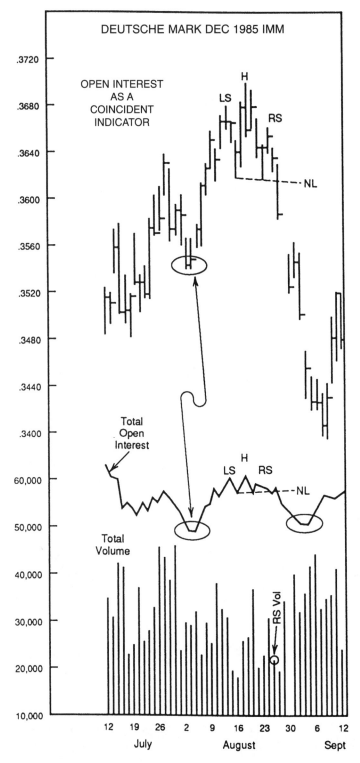

FIGURE 9-8

Open Interest as a Coincident Indicator

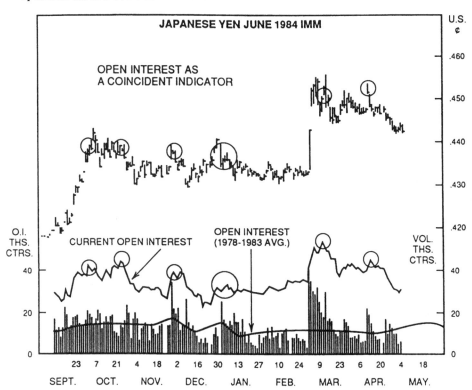

SUMMARY

All traders/dealers must think about what they are trading and ask a basic question: What are the idiosyncrasies of the futures contract they are trying to analyze? The answer lies in the contract specifications and who is trading that particular future. Table 9–1 summarizes some of the expected idiosyncrasies in open interest from several of the major futures groups. As exchanges set up more electronic trading, linkages with other exchanges, and more exotic products, the list is sure to grow.

F I G U R E   9–9

Open Interest as a Coincident Indicator

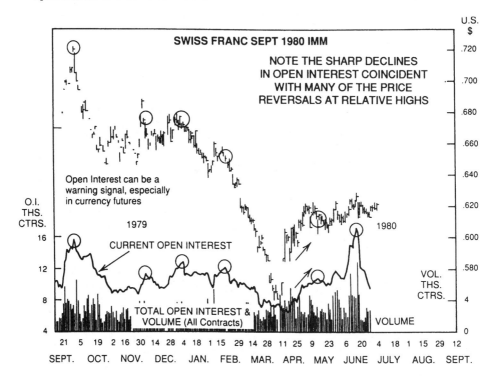

FIGURE 9–10

Open Interest as a Coincident Indicator

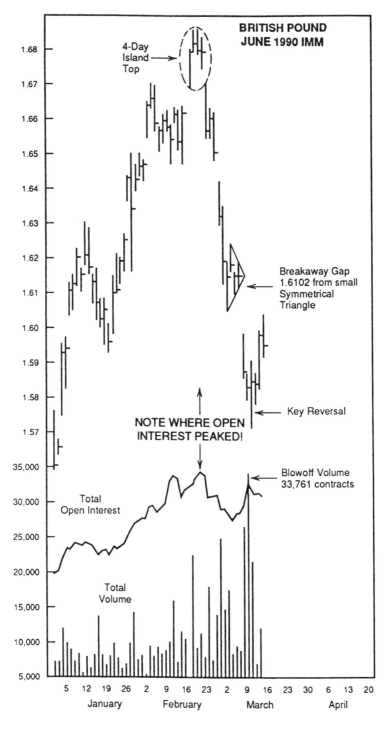

T A B L E   9–1

Summary Matrix of Open Interest Idiosyncrasies

	Option Characteristic	Delivery Type	Other Considerations
T-bonds	Options expire in month prior to futures expiration (OI ⤳)	Physical delivery; first Position Day is two business days prior to expiration month (Watch for OI ⤳)	1. On Last Delivery Day (OI ↓ if positive carry) 2. OI likely to increase in a bear market. 3. At year end (OI ⤵)
Eurodollars	Options expire on last trading day for futures (OI ↓)	Cash settled, but rollovers begin at mid-month *prior* to expiration month (Watch volume & OI in nearby versus deferred to know when to start charting deferred)	Severe ↓ in OI at futures/options expiration—must "detrend" OI curve
Currencies	Options expire second Friday prior to third Wednesday of contract month (OI ⤳)	Physical delivery; third Wednesday (OI ↓ arbitrage unwound)	OI reversal often found at price reversals
Grain/livestock & any agricultural commodity	Options expire in month prior to futures expiration (OI ⤳)	Physical delivery (OI ⤳)	Seasonal OI factor must be considered
Stock index	Options expire on same day as futures (OI ↓)	Cash settled (OI ↓)	Can chart prices until last trading day (OI ↓)
Metals	Options expire in month prior to futures expiration (OI ⤳)	Physical delivery (OI ⤳)	Unusual to find OI increasing in a bear market

10

COMMITMENTS OF TRADERS REPORT

The first part of this chapter is an examination of the Commitments of Traders Report as it existed at the end of 1990. The latter part of this chapter will update this type of analysis for the report as it existed at the end of 1995.

In the U.S. futures markets, the Commitments of Traders Report yields important insights as to the internal makeup of the markets each month. Every trader has thought: "Wouldn't it be amazing to view a market where the positions of all the participants were known?" This would give the trader the perspective of looking into a goldfish bowl; the movements of each player would be readily observable. This, of course, does not exist. However, this chapter will explain what the report is and how it can be used and will examine some practical applications.

Exchange clearing members, futures commissions merchants, and foreign brokers are required to file daily reports with the Commodity Futures Trading Commission (CFTC) listing any trader's positions on their books that exceed the minimum reporting level. The reporting limit for the IMM Eurodollar futures, for example, was 400 or more contracts in 1990. This has since been expanded to 850 contracts in 1996. Other reporting levels are listed in Appendix E.

Positions of the reportable traders are classified as to whether they are commercial or noncommercial. The term commercial is applied to any reportable position used for hedging. For analysis purposes, this reporting commercial category will be referred to as Large Hedgers. The other large trader category (the noncommercials) will be labeled the Large Speculators.

The nonreporting category is derived by subtracting the reported positions from the total level of open interest. These Small Traders consist of both hedgers and speculators. The exact number of nonreporting traders is unknown.

Prior to May of 1995, the CFTC released the report on approximately the 11th day of each month. The data is from the previous month. Sample pages from

September 29, 1989, are shown in Tables 10–1 and 10–2. The pertinent facts are published in tabular format as a regular feature of the *CRB Futures Perspective* chart service, published by Knight-Ridder Financial. The information covering the September 29, 1989 commitments report is shown in Table 10–3.

Pioneering work in the application of the commitments report has been chronicled by William L. Jiler in the CRB yearbooks. Graphs of the normal long or short positions, by category of trader, were updated in the 1990 and 1996 CRB yearbooks. The most recently updated graphs are located in Appendix E. Ten years of information were used to construct the graphs.

UPDATING THE REPORT

Did the Commitments Report lose its usefulness because it was two weeks old when released? No. With some analysis, the report can be brought up-to-date. An educated guess can be made as to which way the three major categories of traders are facing. Exact figures are not possible.

Each category has distinct traits:

1. The *Large Speculators* are professionals. They will not let prices move too far against them. In the face of an adverse price movement, the Large Speculators will adjust their positions.
2. The *Large Hedgers,* by definition, have an equal and offsetting cash market position. One should not feel sorry for the Large Hedgers if futures prices move against them. Hedgers are not likely to panic in the face of apparent adversity.
3. The *Small Traders,* on the other hand, may lack the capital and discipline to be successful traders. This does not mean that this category will be incorrect in their market judgment, but they often panic, causing a sharp short-covering rally or a massive long liquidation. This is especially true when all the Small Traders want out of a losing position at the same time.

At the end of the reporting period, the technician starts with the known status (either net long or net short) of each category. Begin by covering the ensuing price activity. Move to the right on the chart, day by day, seeing who was helped or hurt by the price movement. Note the daily change in total open interest to see how much shifting of positions was likely. Understanding each of the three main categories of traders, a technician can make a guess as to what each group's likely reaction would be. This process yields a good estimate of the present positioning.

APPLICATION

Note the distinct differences in direction that open interest moved on the December 1989 live cattle and live hog charts in Figures 10–1 and 10–2. Live cattle futures registered a net *decline* of 14,555 contracts in the two-month period ending September 2, 1989. During the same time, live hogs were undergoing a net *increase* of 6,909 contracts.

TABLE 10-1

Commitments of Traders Report—Live Cattle

Live Cattle—Chicago Mercantile Exchange
Commitments of Traders in All Futures Combined and Indicated Futures. September 29, 1989

Reportable Positions

Futures	Total Open Interest	Noncommercial — Long or Short Only Long	Noncommercial — Long or Short Only Short	Long and Short (Spreading) Long	Long and Short (Spreading) Short	Commercial Long	Commercial Short	Total Long	Total Short	Nonreportable Positions Long	Nonreportable Positions Short
Contracts of 40,000 Pounds											
All	66,848	13,801	7,115	3,471	3,471	13,396	25m863	30,668	36,449	36,180	30,399
Old	35,716	9,406	5,111	0	0	6,006	14,052	15,412	19,163	20,304	16,553
Other	31,132	6,875	4,484	991	991	7,390	11,811	15,256	17,286	15,876	13,846
Changes in Commitments from August 31, 1989											
All	−11,186	3,963	−5,662	−2,817	−2,817	−8,025	1,129	−6,879	−7,350	−4,307	−3,836
Percent of Open Interest Represented by Each Category of Traders											
All	100.0%	20.6	10.6	5.2	5.2	20.0	38.7	45.9	54.5	54.1	45.5
Old	100.0%	26.3	14.3	0.0	0.0	16.8	39.3	43.2	53.7	56.8	46.3
Other	100.0%	22.1	14.4	3.2	3.2	23.7	37.9	49.0	55.5	51.0	44.5
Number of Traders in Each Category											
All	122	49	22	14	14	31	32	85	66		
Old	91	35	18	0	0	18	25	53	43		
Other	83	32	17	6	6	21	18	53	41		

Concentration Ratios
Percent of Open Interest Held by the Indicated Number of Largest Traders

	By Gross Position				By Net Position			
	4 or Less Traders		8 or Less Traders		4 or Less Traders		8 or Less Traders	
	Long	Short	Long	Short	Long	Short	Long	Short
All	9.4	22.5	15.3	29.5	8.5	21.1	13.9	27.1
Old	12.3	23.0	19.2	32.9	12.3	20.7	17.6	30.6
Other	14.2	26.3	22.4	34.5	14.2	26.0	21.6	34.1

TABLE 10-2

Commitments of Traders Report—Live Hogs

Live Hogs—Chicago Mercantile Exchange
Commitments of Traders in All Futures Combined and Indicated Futures, September 29, 1989

Reportable Positions

Futures	Total Open Interest	Noncommercial Long or Short Only — Long	Noncommercial Long or Short Only — Short	Noncommercial Long and Short (Spreading) — Long	Noncommercial Long and Short (Spreading) — Short	Commercial — Long	Commercial — Short	Total — Long	Total — Short	Nonreportable Positions — Long	Nonreportable Positions — Short
Contracts of 30,000 Pounds											
All	30,875	10,386	2,910	2,521	2,521	4,045	6,347	16,952	11,778	13,923	19,097
Old	5,393	2,251	922	0	0	610	930	2,861	1,852	2,532	3,541
Other	25,482	9,601	3,454	1,055	1,055	3,435	5,417	14,091	9,926	11,391	15,556
Changes in Commitments from August 31, 1989											
All	4,930	3,590	−325	1,133	1,133	172	517	4,895	1,325	35	3,605
Percent of Open Interest Represented by Each Category of Traders											
All	100.0%	33.6	9.4	8.2	8.2	13.1	20.6	54.9	38.1	45.1	61.9
Old	100.0%	41.7	17.1	0.0	0.0	11.3	17.2	53.1	34.3	46.9	65.7
Other	100.0%	37.7	13.6	4.1	4.1	13.5	21.3	55.3	39.0	44.7	61.0
Number of Traders in Each Category											
All		99	21	19	19	11	18	74	48		
Old		33	7	0	0	4	6	21	13		
Other		92	21	8	8	10	17	63	41		

Concentration Ratios

Percent of Open Interest Held by the Indicated Number of Largest Traders

	By Gross Position — 4 or Less Traders — Long	By Gross Position — 4 or Less Traders — Short	By Gross Position — 8 or Less Traders — Long	By Gross Position — 8 or Less Traders — Short	By Net Position — 4 or Less Traders — Long	By Net Position — 4 or Less Traders — Short	By Net Position — 8 or Less Traders — Long	By Net Position — 8 or Less Traders — Short
All	11.3	15.7	19.7	21.8	9.8	14.1	17.0	18.9
Old	18.0	20.1	31.3	29.1	18.0	20.1	30.9	29.1
Other	13.0	16.7	21.4	23.3	11.3	14.5	18.2	19.7

TABLE 10-3

CRB Summary of the Commitments of Traders Report

Commitments of Traders—Large Hedgers, Speculators, and Small Traders
Open Interest Positions Shown in Percent (Rounded) as of September 29, 1989

	Large Hedgers				Large Speculators				Small Traders			
	Long	Short	Net	△	Long	Short	Net	△	Long	Short	Net	△
Cattle (LV)	20	39	(−19)	−16	21	11	(10)	14	54	46	(8)	0
Cattle (FE)	16	18	−2	−8	21	8	13	12	56	68	−12	−5
Cocoa	63	71	−8	0	12	14	−2	−2	24	14	10	3
Coffee	51	80	−29	−1	15	6	9	−8	32	12	20	9
Copper	41	43	−2	23	10	9	1	−15	47	46	1	−9
Corn	47	39	8	0	14	8	6	0	34	48	−14	0
Cotton	59	61	−2	19	9	11	−2	−13	27	22	5	−4
Crude Oil (NY)	55	62	−7	−7	7	6	1	4	33	27	6	3
Gold (Comex)	66	56	10	−19	4	11	−7	9	21	24	3	10
Heating Oil #2	40	73	−33	−9	24	1	23	9	36	26	10	0
Hogs	13	21	(−8)	0	34	9	(25)	12	45	62	(−17)	−11
Unleaded Gas	49	71	−22	−23	19	*	18	17	27	23	4	5
Lumber	42	44	−2	−8	21	7	14	9	30	42	−12	−2
Orange Juice	59	45	14	−4	6	24	−18	−1	31	26	5	6
Platinum	39	60	−21	−25	19	15	4	18	38	21	17	7
Pork Bellies	5	16	−11	0	39	31	8	15	47	45	2	−16
Silver (Comex)	23	69	−46	−17	20	9	11	11	52	17	35	5
Soybeans	38	33	5	−2	9	14	−5	−5	43	43	0	7
Soybean Meal	56	50	6	1	5	8	−3	2	34	36	−2	−2
Soybean Oil	47	50	−3	−7	6	6	0	0	40	37	3	7
Sugar "11"	35	4	−59	−20	33	*	32	13	32	6	26	7
Wheat (CHI)	41	27	14	−8	14	16	−2	3	36	48	−12	6
Wheat (K.C.)	44	61	−17	−6	10	8	2	1	44	29	15	5
Eurodollar	62	61	1	1	3	2	1	−1	33	35	−2	1
Muni Bonds	48	71	−23	4	28	17	11	−7	22	11	11	2
T–Bills (90 Day)	29	60	−31	−6	43	16	27	19	27	23	4	−13
T–Bonds	47	50	−3	0	14	9	5	0	36	38	−2	−1
T–Notes	75	70	5	6	6	6	0	−6	19	24	−5	−2
NYSE Composite	18	13	5	14	34	42	−8	−4	35	32	3	−11
MMI–Maxi	57	38	19	14	22	27	−5	3	22	35	−13	−15
S&P 500	70	60	10	6	8	17	−9	−1	22	23	−1	−4
British Pound	39	62	−23	−76	22	7	15	32	39	31	8	44
Deutsch Mark	26	76	−50	−71	34	5	29	44	39	19	20	26
Japanese Yen	49	48	1	−42	12	15	−3	20	35	33	2	23
Swiss Franc	27	38	−11	-32	22	22	0	9	49	38	11	23

Note: Applies only to C.O.T. Table.

△ equals change in percent net from previous month (PLUS—increased long or decreased short; MINUS—increased short or decreased long).

Note: Positions do not equal 100% because intermarket statistics are not included.

*Less than .05%

Source: Commodity Research Bureau Circulation Dept. P.O. Box 92144, Chicago, IL 60675-2144. Fax (312) 454-0239.

F I G U R E   10–1

Greater Decline in Open Interest than Would Be Seasonally Expected

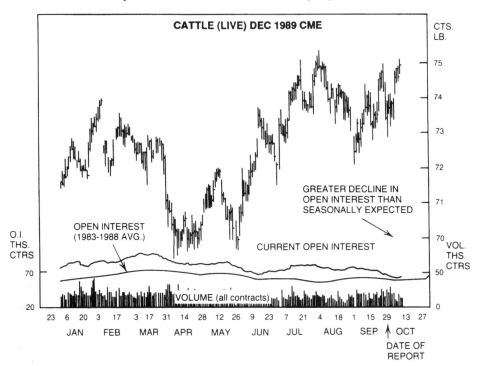

Figures 10–1 and 10–2 also contain the smoothed line of average interest in the previous six years. Open interest in live cattle would normally be declining slightly during this time frame. But the current decline is much more severe than what would be seasonally expected. The live hog situation is even more curious. The current open interest increase is markedly different from the normal expected decline.

The September commitments report can be used to determine which category of trader was increasing or reducing holdings during September, and their bullish or bearish orientation. The next step in the analysis is to compare the current situation to the historic net long or short position of each group at the end of September. This is done using the graphs in Figures 10–3 and 10–4. These graphs are the historic *percentage* split of open interest for each group.

The more the current postings deviate from the historic norm, the more strongly this category of trader feels about the direction of prices.

Prior testing by the Commodity Research Bureau (CRB) has determined that the "Large Hedgers and Large Speculators had the best forecasting records, and the Small Traders, the worst by far." In addition, "the Large Hedgers were consistently superior to the Large Speculators." Armed with this knowledge, a trader can compare his views with that of the "smart money."

F I G U R E   10–2

Greater Increase in Open Interest than Would Be Seasonally Expected

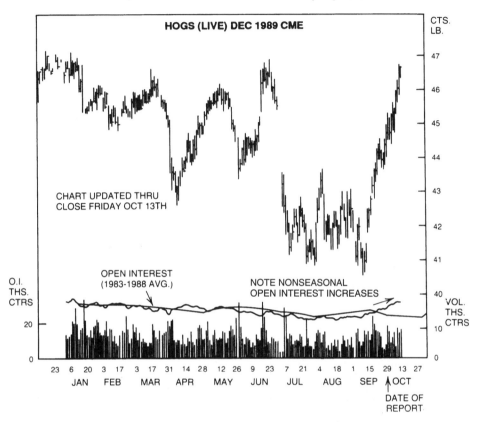

Live Cattle

From the commitments report in Table 10–1, the noncommercial reporting traders (Large Speculators) were long 13,801 contracts of the 66,848 contracts open at the end of September. This represented 20.6 percent of the total open long positions. The percentage for each category (long and short) is found on the "all" line in the middle of the commitments report. Also notice that the Large Speculators had short positions that amounted to 10.6 percent of the total open contracts on the short side of live cattle futures.

The CRB version of the commitments report in Table 10–3 also lists the (rounded) percentage long and short by category. The spread category is excluded. The CRB then goes one step farther. The "net" column is derived by subtracting the percent short from the percent long. The Large Speculators were 21% − 11% = +10% = 10% net long live cattle futures on September 29. The Large Hedgers were 20% − 39% = −19% = 19% net short. The Small Traders stood at 54% − 46% = +8% = 8% net long.

The change in positions from the previous month is shown in both reports. The change in the *number of contracts* is seen in Table 10–1. The CRB (Table

F I G U R E   10–3

Seasonally Normal Positions

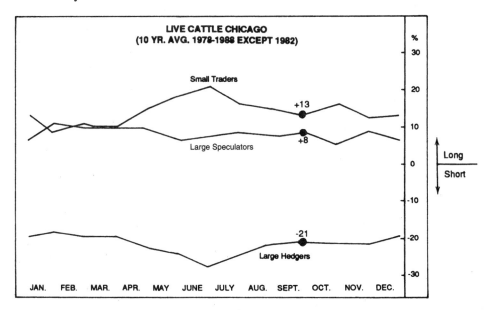

10–3) details the *percentage* shift in the "delta" column. For example, the Large Speculators were adding to longs (+3,963 contracts) and decreasing shorts (–5,662 contracts) during September. This shift is reflected in the +14 percent figure in the delta column for the Large Speculators in Table 10–3. This means the Large Speculators increased their net long positions by 14 percent (from –4 percent to +10 percent).

INTERMEDIATE ANALYSIS

Using the net positions and the changes in open interest from the previous month yields these observations:

1. *Large Speculators:* Have made a complete shift from net short to net long.
2. *Large Hedgers:* Adding to shorts; reducing longs; still net short.
3. *Small Traders:* Decreasing both longs and shorts (confused); still net long.

Next, using the seasonally normal live cattle graph in Figure 10–3, the month-end normal percentage long or short position for each category is obtained. The results are summarized in Table 10–4.

Now answer the question: Do any of the current situations represent a material deviation from the norm? If so, this reflects that group's bullish or bearish bias.

F I G U R E   10–4

Seasonally Normal Positions

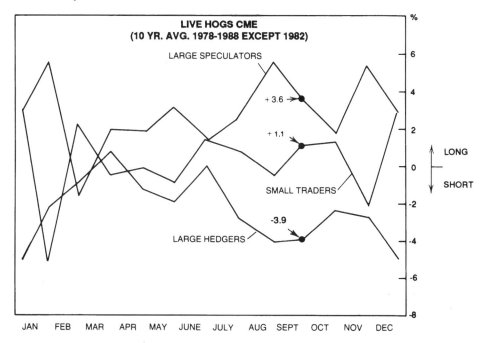

Past work by the *Commodity Research Bureau* has determined that deviations of less than 5 percent from normal should be disregarded. Also, deviations of greater than 40 percent from normal reflect an unusual situation. This is a caution flag and traders should be "wary."

The conclusions to be drawn from the cattle worksheet in Table 10–4 are:

1. The Large Speculators are slightly more bullish than normal: 10 percent now versus 8 percent usually.
2. The Large Hedgers are slightly less bearish (short hedged) than normal: –19 percent now versus –21 percent usually.
3. The Small Traders are definitely not as bullish: 8 percent now versus 13 percent usually.

Only the Small Trader category represents a deviation of 5 percent or more from normal, the difference between +13 percent and +8 percent. By using the track records of the three categories of trades, a long position would be favored. The desired position is one that sides with the Large Hedgers and Speculators, in this particular case, against the Small Traders. The price of the December 1989 live cattle future on October 12 was 74.62; this was the price when the commitments report was available. Quotes continued higher, setting a life of contract high of 76.25 on November 24 and continued even higher in the expiration month, reaching 77.42 on December 14.

T A B L E   10–4

Live Cattle—September 29, 1989: Worksheet

Current Situation	Trader Category	Historic Normal
+10%	Large Speculators	+ 8%
−19%	Large Hedgers	−21%
+ 8%	Small Traders	+13%

Live Hogs

Analysis of live hogs begins by stating the situation at the end of September. From the commitments report table (10–2) it can be ascertained that the Large Speculators (net long) correctly determined that hog futures were in a price uptrend. The Small Traders (net short) were fighting the price trend.

Prices continued higher into the end of the second week of October when the commitments report was released. Because open interest continued to climb, the assumption is made that all categories of traders are continuing to operate with the momentum in force at the end of September. Given the changes in open interest during September, these observations result:

1. *Large Speculators:* Adding to longs, reducing shorts; now more heavily net long than previous month.
2. *Large Hedgers:* Adding slightly to both longs and shorts; still net short.
3. *Small Traders:* Adding heavily to shorts; still net short.

The current situation shows an extreme imbalance from normal. This is portrayed in Table 10–5. The Small Traders are heavily net short when the expectation for this category would be net long. The Large Speculator position is also far from average—being much more bullish than normal (i.e., +25 percent versus ordinarily only +3.6 percent). The Large Hedger is more bearish (short hedged) than usual. But the deviation from normal (the difference between −3.9 percent and −8 percent) is less than 5 percent. Thus the Large Hedgers are not overly bearish.

This analysis strongly suggests that a long position in hog futures was the desired side of the market. The price of the December 1989 live hog future on October 12, 1989, when the report was available, was 46.57. Quotes moved higher, setting a life-of-contract high at 51.90 on November 27 and continued even higher into the expiration month reaching 52.85 on December 14.

AN UPDATED LOOK AT THE COMMITMENTS REPORT

The CFTC increased the frequency of the commitments report from once a month to biweekly in 1990 and introduced a new report which adds options, as futures-equivalent positions. This Futures + Options Commitments Report "delta adjusts"

T A B L E   10–5

Live Hogs—September 29, 1989: Worksheet

Current Situation	Trader Category	Historic Normal
+25%	Large Speculators	+3.6%
− 8%	Large Hedgers	−3.9%
−17%	Small Traders	+1.1%

the options positions of the reportable traders. It should yield a more accurate overall picture of the market make up. Because this report began in May of 1995, the 20 charts of the 10-year-average seasonally normal graphs in Appendix E are for futures only, not combined futures + options. A general observation of the most obvious idiosyncrasy has been added to each of the graphs.

The traditional approach to analyzing the commitments report, as detailed in the beginning of this chapter, has not changed. This is summarized in Table 10–6.

A Slightly Different Approach

A slightly different approach to analyzing the commitments report will be investigated. Instead of beginning with an actual futures price chart, we will first analyze each of the historic 10-year-average commitments graphs. We will determine what constitutes the most obvious feature of the seasonally normal commitments chart at that specific date. Then we will note the makeup of the three categories from the comparable current commitments report. If the two are materially different, the implication is that there is a strong directional belief on the part of the participants.

January 1996 Example

The first look at the strategic positions of the three categories in 1996 was available with the January 2 commitments report, released Monday January 8. The expected (normal) situation on 20 historic-average charts at the beginning of each calendar year was compared to the actual makeup on January 2, 1996. Particular attention was focused on the current position of the Large Hedger versus their normal stance. Four of the 20 futures markets examined had pronounced differences with respect to both sign (long or short) and magnitude (greater than 5% deviation). These were T-bonds, crude oil, cotton, and coffee. An example of the commitments report for crude oil is shown in Table 10–7. The seasonally normal commitments graph for crude oil is in Figure 10–5.

T A B L E   10–6

Traditional Approach to Analyzing the Commitments of Traders Report

1. Examine a futures price chart for:
   a. Any unusual changes in total open interest, especially upward,
   b. Ascertain the direction of the price trend using conventional trendline analysis.
2. Refer to the current commitments report to delineate the positions of the three categories of traders. This answers the questions of who has been correct in their market judgement. It also reveals who has been wrong—and has provided fuel for the price move.
3. Compare the current positions to the seasonally normal positions of each category at that date.
   a. If any of the current positions differ more than 5% from the historic norm—a definite directional bias exists.
   b. Deviations of less than 5% should be disregarded.
   c. Deviations of greater than 40% from normal indicate an unusual situation. This is a caution flag and traders should be "wary."
4. Make the assumptions that:
   a. The Large Hedgers are the smartest money.
   b. The Small Traders have the worst track record.
   c. The Large Speculators used to be smarter; now this category is becoming dominated by trend following funds.
5. The most distinct conclusions:
   a. **Bullish:** Large Hedgers are more heavily net long than usual,
      Large Speculators are clearly net long, and the
      Small Trader is net short more than normal.
   b. **Bearish:** Large Hedgers are more heavily net short than usual,
      Large Speculators are clearly net short, and the
      Small Trader is net long more than normal.

The situation of the four commodities under investigation:

1. *Treasury Bonds:*

Expectation = Large Hedgers would be net long 2.3%

Actual situation = this contingent was net short 9.1%

Forecast = *Bearish*

2. *Crude oil:*

Expectation = Large Hedgers would be net long 3.3%

Actual situation = this contingent was net short 14.0%

Forecast = *Bearish*

3. *Cotton:*

Expectation = Large Hedgers would be net short 15.0%

Actual situation = this contingent was net long 14.1%

Forecast = *Bullish*

4. *Coffee:*

Expectation = Large Hedgers would be net short 20.3%

Actual situation = this contingent was net long 8.8%

Forecast = *Bullish*

TABLE 10-7

Crude Oil Commitments Report (Futures Only)

CRUDE OIL, LIGHT 'SWEET' – NEW YORK MERCANTILE EXCHANGE

COMMITMENTS OF TRADERS IN ALL FUTURES COMBINED AND INDICATED FUTURES, JANUARY 2, 1996

(CONTRACTS OF 1,000 BARRELS)

	TOTAL OPEN INTEREST	REPORTABLE POSITIONS								NONREPORTABLE POSITIONS	
		NON-COMMERCIAL				COMMERCIAL		TOTAL			
		LONG OR SHORT ONLY		LONG AND SHORT (SPREADING)							
		LONG	SHORT	LONG	SHORT	LONG	SHORT	LONG	SHORT	LONG	SHORT
ALL	358,747	49,036	11,222	15,850	15,850	210,425	260,819	275,311	287,891	83,436	70,856
OLD	297,575	49,209	10,520	10,411	10,411	166,989	218,124	226,609	239,055	70,966	58,520
OTHER	61,172	37	912	5,229	5,229	43,436	42,695	48,702	48,836	12,470	12,336

CHANGES IN COMMITMENTS FROM DECEMBER 26, 1995

	TOTAL	LONG	SHORT	LONG	SHORT	LONG	SHORT	LONG	SHORT	LONG	SHORT
ALL	15,405	466	-700	1,200	1,200	11,087	11,937	12,753	12,437	2,652	2,968

PERCENT OF OPEN INTEREST REPRESENTED BY EACH CATEGORY OF TRADERS:

	TOTAL	LONG	SHORT	LONG	SHORT	LONG	SHORT	LONG	SHORT	LONG	SHORT
ALL	100.0%	13.7	3.1	4.4	4.4	58.7	72.7	76.7	80.2	23.3	19.8
OLD	100.0%	16.5	3.5	3.5	3.5	56.1	73.3	76.2	80.3	23.8	19.7
OTHER	100.0%	0.1	1.5	8.5	8.5	71.0	69.8	79.6	79.8	20.4	20.2

NUMBER OF TRADERS IN EACH CATEGORY

	NUMBER OF TRADERS	LONG	SHORT	LONG	SHORT	LONG	SHORT	LONG	SHORT
ALL	134	39	16	13	13	57	59	104	82
OLD	133	39	16	12	12	55	58	102	80
OTHER	26	2	2	4	4	16	16	20	20

CONCENTRATION RATIOS

PERCENT OF OPEN INTEREST HELD BY THE INDICATED NUMBER OF LARGEST TRADERS

	BY GROSS POSITION				BY NET POSITION			
	4 OR LESS TRADERS		8 OR LESS TRADERS		4 OR LESS TRADERS		8 OR LESS TRADERS	
	LONG	SHORT	LONG	SHORT	LONG	SHORT	LONG	SHORT
ALL	22.4	25.6	34	36.7	11.9	14.0	18.9	21.4
OLD	20.8	25.2	30.9	37.0	12.1	16.2	19.9	23.7
OTHER	43.9	43.0	59.0	57.9	35.4	32.8	46.0	44.4

141

FIGURE 10-5

Crude Oil: Seasonally Normal Commitments

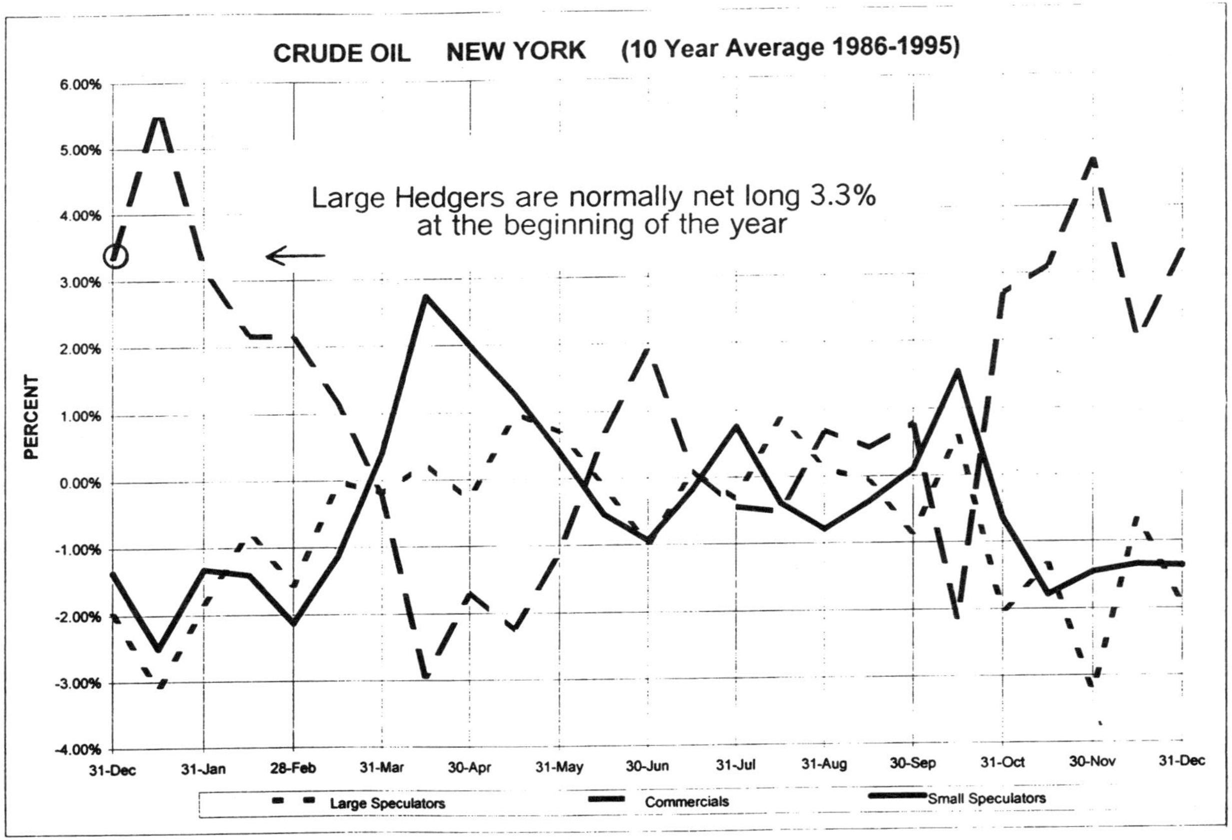

CRUDE OIL   NEW YORK   (10 Year Average 1986-1995)

Large Hedgers are normally net long 3.3% at the beginning of the year

In the four situations isolated, the Large Hedgers in T-bond and crude oil were definitely inclined to hold net short futures positions on January 2, 1996. The cotton and coffee Large Hedgers were holding net long futures. *In the previous 10 years, on average, these four Large Hedgers were facing exactly the opposite direction*—and by considerably more than a 5 percent swing, but less than 40 percent.

The remaining 16 historically normal charts versus actual situations examined did not show a difference in sign from what was expected of the Large Hedgers. The grain and oilseed commitments did show a more bullish (than the normal bullish) bias on the part of both speculative categories.

The Large Hedgers are not always immediately correct in their market view. But if prices do start moving in their direction, the other side—the Small Trader—will begin to panic. The Large Speculator will receive a trend change signal and attempt to move to the sidelines. This environment creates the potential for an "air-pocket" in futures price movement against the positions of the Small Trader.

Adding Options

With the advent of the Combined Commitments of Traders Report in May of 1995, an analyst will want to make sure that the addition of futures-equivalent options positions does not alter the bias of each category enough to negate the forecasting implications. This combined commitments report is released the day after the futures-only report. In the January 2, 1996, case study, the addition of options did not change the long/short classification of any category of any of the four situations under study, with one minor exception, T-bonds. A detailed observation of the T-bond reports is shown in Table 10–8. A positive sign equals net long; a negative sign equals net short.

The comparison of the futures-only positions to futures + options shows that the Small Trader is now net long 5 percent. These traders are taking a bullish view via positive-delta options positions. These could be short T-bond put options. But a much more likely scenario is that the small trader is long T-bond calls. This bullish bias on the part of the Small Trader increases the *bearish* forecast of the Commitments Report.

T A B L E   10–8

Comparison of the Two Commitments Reports for January 2, 1996

U.S. Treasury Bonds			
Trader Catetory	Futures-Only Report	Futures + Options Report	Conclusion
Large Hedger	–9.1%	–7.8%	Still net short
Large Speculator	+9.5%	+2.8%	Still net long
Small Trader	–0.5%	+5.0%	Now net long

Technical Analysis

Technically orientated traders might now want to apply their favorite technical tool to the price charts of the bonds, crude oil, cotton, and coffee. The first step is to identify the direction of the current price trend and then look for any technical signs of a reversal. A classical bar chartist would see a very different look to the four price charts. A technical comment on each of the four charts could be summarized as follows:

> *T-bonds:* A price sell-off in the last few trading sessions (early January) violated underlying support at the former price high of 121-12. This is the first major criteria necessary for a head & shoulders top price-pattern to form.
>
> *Crude oil:* A strong price uptrend is underway with no classical price signs of a top. This chart is shown in Figure 10–6.

FIGURE 10–6

Crude Oil Chart When January 2 Commitments Report Was Available

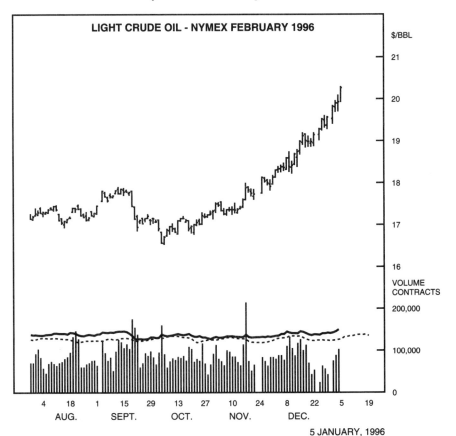

Cotton: Quotes have been moving net sideways within a large 7 cent/lb. trading range between 80.00 and 87.00.

Coffee: A definite price downtrend is in progress, with quotes below the 100.00 cent/lb. overhead resistance on the March 1996 future.

The Outcome

By the beginning of the next month, February 2, 1996, the following observations could be made:

T-bonds: Still within a large trading range between 118 and 122. Result of forecast: Result not in.

Crude oil: Refer to Figure 10–7 to see the sharp price break of more than 2.50 $/bbl. Result of forecast: Large profit.

Cotton: A rally of 3.45 c/lb. occurred. Result of forecast: Large profit.

Coffee: A rally of 13.30 occurred. Result of forecast: Large profit.

F I G U R E   10–7

How It Came Out

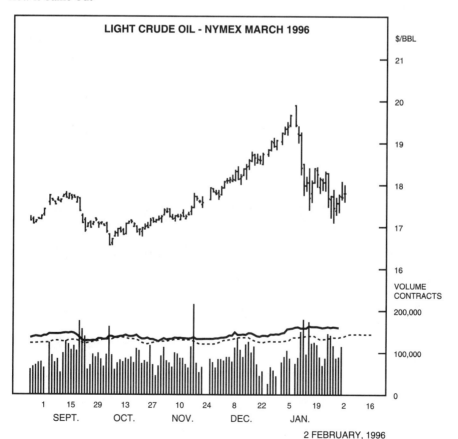

SUMMARY

The crude oil chart in Figure 10–7 is representative of the profitable outcomes in three of the four situations investigated. The directional forecasts based on the commitments report were impressive. Only the T-bonds failed to produce a clear-cut price move. However, any (small) trader with long T-bond call options would have been holding wasting assets.

WHERE TO OBTAIN THE DATA

The easiest method of accessing the Commitments of Traders Report is directly from the CFTC's Internet site at http://www.cftc.gov/cftc/. The Chicago Board of Trade was also making the reports available on its web site at http://www.cbot.com/. Knight-Ridder's *CRB Futures Perspective* weekly chart service summarizes the report in percentage format.

SPREAD ANALYSIS

Reportable positions of the large noncommercial spreaders are also contained in the Commitments of Traders Report. A glance at the magnitude of this category, in relation to the total open interest, provides some measure of the size of the spread trading factor.

Note the net positions of the three major categories in the "old" versus "other" lines of the report. Old refers to the "old-crop," and "other" to "new-crop." These terms originated when the CFTC began the report. At that time only agricultural futures were traded. The newer "commodities," without a defined marketing season, use calendar years in place of crop years. In this case, any future expiring in the current calendar year is considered "old-crop." An idea of the traders' bias can be ascertained by looking at the participation of traders in the old versus other categories.

PRIMARY DEALER POSITIONS REPORT

For interest rate futures traders, the Market Reports Division of the Federal Reserve Bank of New York produces a report somewhat similar to the CFTC's commitments report. The Primary Dealer Positions Report contains the net immediate and futures positions of primary dealers in U.S. government securities, agency securities, and other money market instruments. An example of the report is found in Table 10–9. The report is released with one month's delay. Comparison of the primary dealers report and the commitments report shows a distinct correlation of the dealers' positions to the Large Hedger net long or short positions.

T A B L E   10-9

Primary Dealers Positions Report

For Week Ended December 6, 1989
(Daily Average Figures: Par Value; in Millions of Dollars)

Type of Security	Net Immediate Position	Change from Previous Week	Net Futures Position	Change from Previous Week	Net Forward Position	Change from Previous Week
U.S. government securities:						
Treasury bills	19,716	1,574	-11,781	-1,355	979	-610
Coupon securities:						
Due in 1 year or less	-2,891	517	0	0	1,346	0
Due after 1 year but within 5 years	11,048	2,394	-703	-237	-750	341
Due after 5 years but within 10 years	-6,640	2,711	-2,384	153	-117	-63
Due after 10 years	-5,868	-25	-7,177	592	-810	-328
Total	15,365	7,171	-22,045	-848	648	-662
Federal agency securities:						
Agency securities:						
Due in 1 year or less	3,821	998	0	0	-1	-8
Due after 1 year but within 5 years	1,329	-156	0	0	-28	-9
Due after 5 years	3,124	55	0	0	-120	-353
Mortgage-backed securities						
GNMA	6,360	1,208	0	0	-8,901	-1,171
Other	17,744	-798	0	0	-6,942	251
Total	32,377	1,307	0	0	-15,993	-1,290
Other money market instruments:						
Certificates of deposit:						
Domestic	3,535	128	0	0	-27	3
Foreign	3,586	413	21,872	-5,086	2	18
Bankers' acceptances	2,258	428	0	0	0	0
Commercial paper	8,875	1,292	0	0	-2	-2
Total	18,254	2,261	21,872	-5,086	-28	18

CHAPTER

11

SUPPORT AND RESISTANCE

The subset of technical analysis encompassing "support and resistance" is particularly fraught with misconceptions and just plain bad interpretation. This chapter will explore the best definition of the terms and look deeper into a single trading day in an attempt to reduce the size of the support or resistance area.

SUPPORT

The classic chart definition of underlying support is a "former top," shown in Figure 11–1. The daily price high of the former top begins the support level. Sell-offs often eat into the support. But if the damage is kept to a minimum, the price uptrend on the chart remains intact.

A market should encounter support as quotes sell off to the area of a former price top because traders remember this price level. This is subconscious. Traders are not specifically looking at a chart. If traders are "on the market," they remember trading at the former price level and are motivated to deal in this price area again. The would-be bulls buy to establish new longs. The shorts buy to cut their losses.

Perhaps only one lot traded at the daily high. This implies that quotes would have to sink further before finding price levels at which a substantial number of contracts changed hands. The Market Profile and the CBOT's Liquidity Data Bank or CME's Volume Analysis aid in determining where support (or resistance) should be the strongest. This will be examined later in this chapter.

RESISTANCE

The classic definition of resistance is a "former bottom." This is shown in Figure 11–2. Resistance is always overhead. A price rally will encounter selling pressure (resistance) as it approaches the former bottom price. Traders with existing long

FIGURE 11-1

Definition of Support

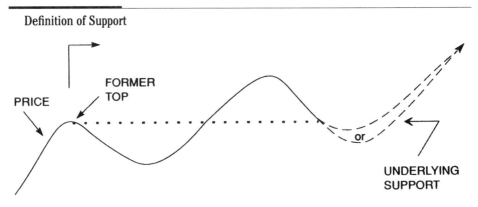

positions realizing they are "long and wrong" will be trying to sell out to mitigate their losses. Traders on the sidelines, with the knowledge that the direction of the major price trend is downward, will be selling to establish new shorts. This selling pressure builds as a price rally approaches the former price bottom on a chart.

MISCONCEPTIONS

If 100 percent of all the traders in the world were shown the two schematic charts in Figure 11–3, the great majority would refer to the price high on the chart as resistance and the price low on the other chart as support. This is incorrect. Resistance or support is supposed to stop a price move and reverse its direction. If it was true that a price high was always resistance and a price low was always support, then a trending market would never exist. And double tops and double bottoms as reversal patterns would be numerous. But, this is not the case. Markets tend to trend most of the time, rather than reverse. And the "double" formation is not a common reversal pattern.

Traders should not have a preconceived notion that a price rally has to stop at a level that it (temporarily) stopped at before—or that a price sell-off has to bounce off of a price level that stopped a sell-off previously. These price extremes are more properly referred to as benchmarks. A technician is very interested in what will happen as quotes test the benchmark high or low. But it should not be automatically assumed that these benchmark prices will stop the subsequent price movement. Relating this concept to volume:

The lower the volume on the sell-off to test support, the more likely the support will hold.

The lower the volume on the rally to test resistance, the more likely the resistance will hold.

The strength (ability to halt the price move) of the support or resistance, in theory, should be directly proportional to the amount of dealing previously done

FIGURE 11–2

Definition of Resistance

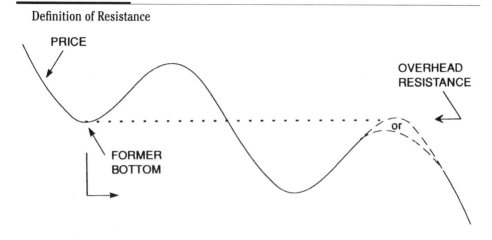

at that particular price level. Quotes may have to eat into support or resistance until a sufficient amount of prior trading is encountered to finally produce the friction necessary to stop the price move. Looking at the distribution of price versus volume *within a trading session* should be instructive in determining where the strongest support or resistance may be encountered.

MARKET PROFILE

In the early 1980s, the Chicago Board of Trade began collecting price information by half-hour time brackets to produce a better audit trail. The breakdown of a trading session by price and predetermined time periods, creates a diagram. The CBOT referred to this diagram as the Market Profile.

A revised bracketing system was introduced in January 1990, shortening the time bracket to 15 minutes, and a newer system was implemented with the requirement to identify trades in 5-minute segments within each bracket. An example of the half-hour profile for the September 15, 1989, regular trading session of the U.S. Treasury bond futures is found in Table 11–1. The "Z" time bracket represents the first 10 minutes of trading from 7:20 to 7:30 A.M. local time.

The daily T-bond chart in Figure 11–4 shows why the profile of September 15 was of interest to technicians. Underlying support on any price sell-off would be expected at 97-28 on the December T-bonds. This was the daily high on September 15.

A look at the profile in Table 11–1 shows that "single prints" occurred in the "H" time bracket from the daily high at 97-28 through 97-23. Looking at the price profile only, one can infer that not much volume occurred until the fat part of the distribution (between 97-20 and 97-05). Volume interpretation is enhanced with the information contained in the Liquidity Data Bank.

F I G U R E   11–3

Benchmark Prices

NOT RESISTANCE

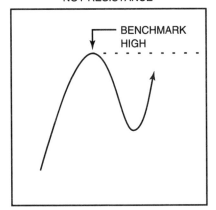

NOT SUPPORT

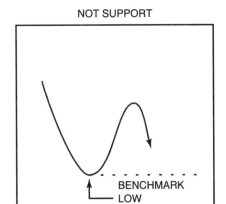

LIQUIDITY DATA BANK

The CBOT provides a record of volume (by contract month) at each price during a trading session. This is the Liquidity Data Bank (LDB). Initially, the LDB identified the percent of volume traded by local floor traders (category CTI1) and commercial clearing firms (category CTI2). This has since been expanded to shown additional categories of traders. The study of the Market Profile and Liquidity Data Bank has developed into its own subset of technical analysis.

The LDB for September 15, 1989, is shown in Table 11–2. It shows that 70 percent of the volume on September 15 was in the "value" area (between 97-05 and 97-20). Classic underlying support should start at the former price daily price high of 97-28. The profile and LDB show that much stronger support should be present at the beginning of "value" at 97-20.

The outcome of the subsequent price pullback to the support area is shown in Figure 11–5. The low of the sell-off was 97-18 (slightly into the value area). Observe that this successful test of support on Friday, October 13 concluded with a strong close at 98-17, up 11 tics for the day.

The LDB provides a detailed look at *where* the volume occurred within a trading session. The location of heavy volume is expected to provide support or resistance. The Chicago Board of Trade Clearing Corporation actually updates the LDB hourly between 8:30 A.M. and 4:30 P.M. local Chicago time. The final report for the day is released at 7:30 P.M.

T A B L E   11–1

Market Profile: December 1989 T-Bonds, September 15, 1989

LIQUIDITY DATA BANK   VOLUME DETAIL REPORT FOR DAY SESSION   89/09/18
Copyright Chicago Board of Trade 1984.   ALL RIGHTS RESERVED.   09:45:02
FOR 89/09/15 US BONDS   DEC 89   UPDATED 89/09/15 22:45:23

NOTE Volume figures shown are actual number of contracts multiplied by 2.

TRADE PRICE	TOTAL VOL.	%	LOCAL	COMMERCIALS	HALF HOUR BRACKET TIMES
96 23/32	3200	0.3	41.4	27.5	E
96 24/32	9354	0.9	57.2	7.0	E
96 25/32	6938	0.7	59.9	12.2	E
96 26/32	8960	0.8	62.4	13.2	E
96 27/32	7418	0.7	53.1	20.4	E
96 28/32	9938	0.9	59.9	12.8	EFK
96 29/32	19274	1.8	59.6	14.3	EFK
96 30/32	15628	1.5	54.6	13.1	AEFK
96 31/32	15026	1.4	54.1	11.5	AEFK
97	26256	2.5	53.7	12.9	AEFK
97 1/32	20778	2.0	55.4	16.8	AEFK
97 2/32	31256	3.0	56.8	13.7	AEFK
97 3/32	30008	2.8	54.6	17.3	ABEFGK
97 4/32	18410	1.7	54.5	14.2	ABEFGK
97 5/32	24632	2.3	52.6	14.1	ABCDEFGK
97 6/32	38048	3.6	54.7	13.1	$ABCDEFGKL
97 7/32	53008	5.0	55.1	14.9	$ABCDGKL
97 8/32	56910	5.4	58.7	11.6	Z$ABCDGKL
97 9/32	57584	5.4	59.8	12.2	Z$ABCDGHKL
97 10/32	62150	5.9	54.2	13.3	Z$ABCDGHKL
97 11/32	35980	3.4	59.9	12.7	Z$ACGHKL
97 12/32	33926	3.2	57.1	12.1	$AGHKL
97 13/32	31404	3.0	60.2	11.7	$AGHIJKL
97 14/32	45838	4.3	55.6	14.0	$AGHIJKL
97 15/32	73142	6.9	55.1	11.5	$AGHIJKLM
97 16/32	71450	6.7	55.1	13.1	$AGHIJKLM
97 17/32	46780	4.4	55.3	12.4	$AGHIJKL
97 18/32	44666	4.2	53.2	18.6	$AHIJK
97 19/32	40818	3.9	54.6	12.6	$HIJK
97 20/32	43408	4.1	48.6	15.1	$HIJK
97 21/32	15240	1.4	56.0	12.1	$HIJK
97 22/32	19454	1.8	54.5	8.0	$H
97 23/32	12506	1.2	51.2	13.9	H
97 24/32	10664	1.0	55.7	5.1	H
97 25/32	4920	0.5	58.3	9.1	H
97 26/32	9016	0.9	48.5	18.6	H
97 27/32	4868	0.5	39.6	20.4	H
97 28/32	62	0.0	53.2	0.0	H

Note: The CBOT's method of organizing the data is such that the daily *low* is located at the top of the page. This convention takes some time getting used to.

FIGURE 11–4

Locating Underlying Support at a Former Price High

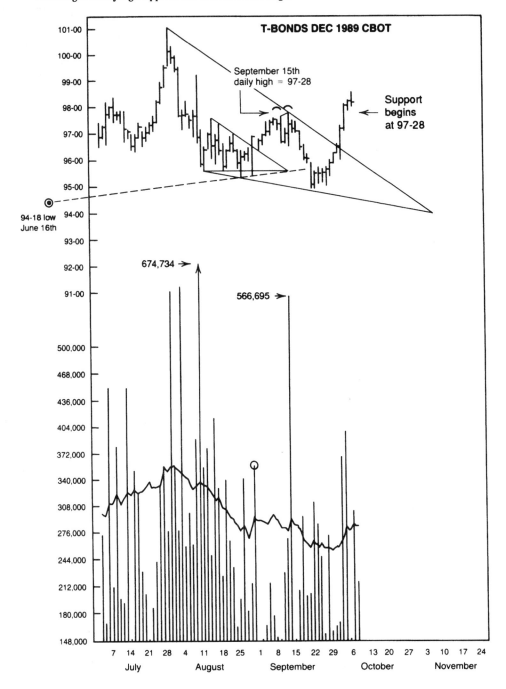

F I G U R E 11–5

Support Was Successfully Tested

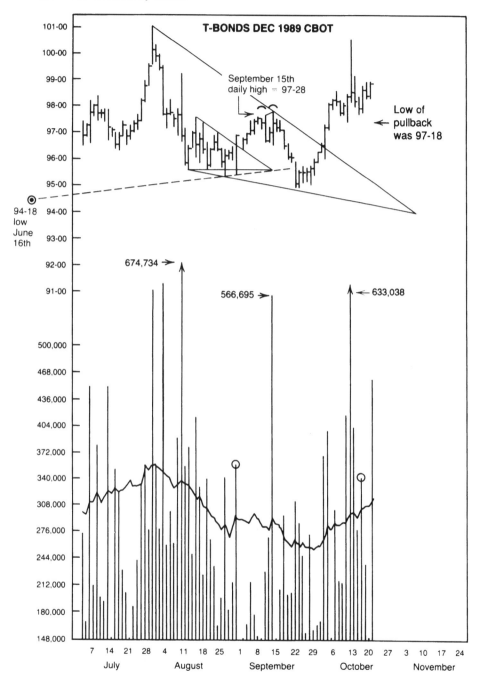

T A B L E   11–2

Liquidity Data Bank Volume Summary
December 1989 T-Bonds, September 15, 1989

LIQUIDITY DATA BANK		VOLUME SUMMARY FOR DAY SESSION					89/09/18
Copyright Chicago Board of Trade 1984. ALL RIGHTS RESERVED.							09:44:25
FOR 89/09/15 US BONDS DEC 89						UPDATED 89/09/15 22:45:23	

NOTE Volume figures shown are actual number of contracts multiplied by 2.

CATEGORY	PRICE	TOT	VOL	%	CITI%	CTI2%	BRACKETS
OPEN	97	8/32	176644	16.7	57.5	12.4	Z$ABCDGZHKL
TO	97	10/32					
CLOSE	97	15/32	144592	13.7	55.1	12.3	$AGHIJKLM
TO	97	16/32					
HIGH	97	28/32	62	0.0	53.2	0.0	H
QUADRANT	97	28/32	205622	19.4	52.4	14.0	$AHIJK
1 TO	97	18/32					
QUADRANT	97	17/32	458254	43.3	56.5	12.6	Z$ABCDGHIJKLM
2 TO	97	9/32					
QUADRANT	97	8/32	299306	28.3	55.5	14.0	Z$ABCDEFGKL
3 TO	97						
QUADRANT	96	31/32	95736	9.0	56.9	13.5	AEFK
4 TO	96	23/32					
LOW	96	23/32	3200	0.3	41.4	27.5	E
70% OF	96	20/32					
TOT VOL	97	5/32	759744	71.7	55.6	13.2	Z$ABCDEFGHIJKLM

TOT VOLUME US BONDS	DEC 89 = 1058918	TOT VOLUME US BONDS = 1083150

CME: VOLUME ANALYSIS

The two large Chicago futures exchanges are always engaged in competition. The CBOT has its LDB. The CME has its Volume Analysis. In essence, they are both the graphic and/or data representations of price versus time. Table 11–3 contains the Volume Analysis for S&P 500 stock index futures in early 1996. Technicians will note that Table 11–3 details the amount of reported spread and EFP trading for that trading session.

T A B L E   11–3

CME Volume Analysis: S&P 500 January 29, 1996

```
        CME VOLUME ANALYSIS - CONTRACT INQUIRY FOR  01/29/96

                        S & P 500                    OPEN INT:       -88344

        TRADE     TOTAL      TOTAL   CTI-1  CTI-2  CTI-3  CTI-4
        PRICE       %        SALES     %      %      %      %    HALF HOURS **
```

TRADE PRICE	TOTAL %	TOTAL SALES	CTI-1 %	CTI-2 %	CTI-3 %	CTI-4 %	HALF HOURS **
62625	1.0	1052	36.2	5.1	3.0	55.6	%GI8
62620	2.9	3190	36.1	4.0	3.0	56.9	%#GI8
62615	1.1	1210	52.6	4.3	5.2	37.9	%GI8
62610	3.2	3441	52.2	5.6	2.3	39.9	%#GI68
62605	1.0	1058	53.3	5.4	9.5	31.9	GI68
62600	2.8	3029	48.3	7.3	2.5	41.9	GI68
62595	.6	606	46.9	5.8	3.1	44.2	GI68
62590	1.3	1438	51.7	5.2	6.1	37.1	GI68
62585	.7	756	51.3	3.2	1.1	44.4	GIK68
62490	2.7	2916	46.1	6.7	5.1	42.1	GKMQSVWY246
62485	1.3	1432	53.1	4.1	3.4	39.5	GKMQSVWY246
62480	2.7	2960	50.3	7.7	3.1	38.9	GKMQSVWY246
62475	1.4	1578	50.3	4.4	6.3	39.1	GKMQSVWY246
62470	2.3	2558	51.7	7.0	4.5	36.7	GKMQSVWY246
62465	1.4	1580	52.2	5.2	7.0	35.6	GKMQSVWY246
62460	3.6	3942	50.6	7.1	4.7	37.6	GKMQSVWY246
62455	1.4	1474	55.5	3.3	6.3	34.9	GMQSVWY24
62450	3.0	3276	47.7	8.9	2.8	40.6	$GKMQSVWY24
62355	.4	412	44.7	3.9	3.2	48.3	MO
62350	.3	284	46.8	3.5	1.4	48.2	O
62345	.1	64	37.5			62.5	O
62340	.1	56	30.4			69.6	O
EFP'S	.1	110				100.0	
SPRDS	1.2	1350	34.4	17.1	15.5	33.0	
TOTAL	100.0	109148	49.0	6.0	4.0	41.0	

```
                          ** HALF HOURS IDENTIFIED BY 1ST BRACKET

                                     Inquiry Data System Screen
```

12

ASIAN AND EUROPEAN FOREIGN-EXCHANGE DEALERS' USE OF FUTURES VOLUME AND OPEN INTEREST TO OBTAIN A MARKET VIEW

This question should be posed in discussing technical analysis with foreign-exchange (forex) dealers: What was the turnover in spot dollar-mark dealing yesterday? Because interbank dealing is an over-the-counter market, an exact answer is not available. But turnover (volume) figures are important inputs to a technical approach. There are additional questions. Were new positions being opened? Was it simply long liquidation on a price sell-off? On a price rally, was it net short covering? These types of questions also cannot be answered sufficiently.

A viable futures market, one that has achieved a critical mass, produces exact high-low-close price figures as well as volume and open interest statistics. But futures trading represents only a small percentage of world currency trading.

This chapter will explain the theoretical interpretation of the data and will illustrate, via an actual example, how a market view is technically established. The premise:

A currency futures pit is a microcosm, diminutive but analogous to the larger interbank system.

Thus, clearinghouse statistics can be used as a surrogate in the absence of interbank data. This is for analytical purposes. The forex dealer will continue to operate in the interbank forex market. The dollar-mark trader will simply be utilizing the additional statistics available from the D-mark futures.

THE ASIAN AND EUROPEAN ADVANTAGE

Asian and European forex dealers have an advantage with respect to the release of currency futures data from the International Monetary Market (IMM) in Chicago. During 1988, the average time availability of volume and open interest figures for the previous trading session was 2:50 A.M. Chicago time. This meant that technical interpretation of the previous day's activity could begin four and one-half hours before the resumption of U.S. currency futures trading at the normal 7:20 A.M. Chicago open.

In late 1988, currency futures positions could be initiated on either the Singapore International Monetary Exchange (SIMEX) or the London International Financial Futures Exchange (LIFFE). Forex futures have been delisted on LIFFE, but since June of 1992 currency futures trades were possible on GLOBEX electronic dealing. Obviously, forex dealers will analyze the data and take a market view in their own medium, the interbank market. These dealers face an additional conceptual step. A bullish looking chart of spot D-mark–dollar (European terms) will obviously be the reciprocal of the bearishly construed $/DM (U.S. terms) futures chart.

OBTAINING THE DATA

The Chicago Mercantile Exchange has both a recorded message telephone tape system and a World Wide Web (WWW) page on the Internet. The telephone system is referred to as the MercLine. Relevant numbers and addresses can be found in Chapter 15, "The Data." Callers to the telephone update enter specific three-digit message codes to obtain volume and open interest statistics and a wide variety of additional information. Selected message codes can be found in Chapter 15. For the case study in this chapter, the code used for the IMM currency statistics was 131.

All MercLine information must be accessed from a Touch-Tone telephone and not a rotary dial telephone. In 1996, futures statistics were available on the MercLine system as early as 3:00 A.M. (Chicago time) and as late as 6:00 A.M., one hour and 20 minutes before the open. The average release time was 4:30 A.M.

After the advent of electronic dealing (GLOBEX), the 7:20 A.M. beginning of regular open outcry trading is referred to as a resumption rather than an opening. In 1996, the statistics via the telephone were available earlier than on the WWW page, which because of special reports generated for the CME Daily Bulletins, had a 6:00 A.M. release deadline.

ANATOMY OF A REVERSAL

The following example will show how forex dealers could have obtained an important insight into the changing internal conditions of the dollar–mark. Figure 12–1 represents trading in D-mark futures for Wednesday, November 23, 1988. The actual volume and open interest are posted on the chart. Reference will be made to both local Chicago time and Greenwich mean time (GMT).

Wednesday 23 November—19:58 GMT
The spot D-mark was quoted at 1.7180 in U.S. interbank dealing at 19:58 GMT on Wednesday, November 23, 1988. The March 1989 IMM D-mark future was in the process of closing at .5894. This was two points (.0002) higher than the pre-

F I G U R E   12–1

November 24, 7:45 GMT—When Volume and Open Interest were First Available

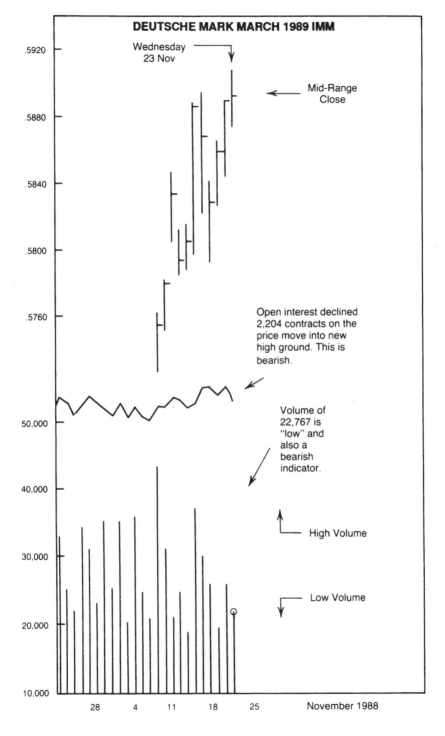

vious day's settlement price. In addition, the futures settlement price would be as close to the middle of the session's trading range as possible. This is referred to as a midrange close and is shown in Figure 12–1.

Technicians often regard a midrange close as a minor trend change indicator. In this case, the direction of the minor price trend going into Wednesday's IMM trade was up (weaker dollar). Therefore, it would not be unusual to expect a slight price sell-off in the D-mark future on the IMM the next trading session, based on price action alone.

Wednesday, 23 November—22:04 GMT

Australian forex dealers did little to move the dollar-mark relationship. Spot DM was quoted at 1.7165. This was to be expected as no new technical or fundamental input was available. The midrange close in the United States, however, should have alerted technicians to a possible change in the minor price trend of the dollar-mark.

Thursday 24 November—7:45 GMT

Although Thursday, November 24, was the Thanksgiving holiday in the United States (exchanges closed), the Chicago Mercantile Exchange released the volume and open interest statistics as usual. The CME statistics department had the information on the automated telephone system at 1:45 Chicago time (7:45 GMT). Thus, the vital data was available at 2:45 P.M. local Singapore time.

VOLUME ANALYSIS

A reasonable definition of total D-mark futures volume parameters at the time was: high volume = above 34,000; low volume = below 24,000. Forex dealers could obtain the D-mark futures volume and then:

1. Volume of less than 24,000 would be considered low.
   a. And would imply that the previous trading session's price rally was unhealthy.
   b. And is bearish for D-mark futures.
   c. Therefore, *buy dollars.*

Or

2. Volume between 24,000 and 34,000 would be considered average.
   a. And is a neutral indicator.
   b. Therefore, no interbank action is suggested.

Or

3. Volume above 34,000 would be considered high.
   a. And the price rally in the D-mark futures would be considered healthy.
   b. And is bullish for D-mark futures.
   c. Therefore, maintain a bearish view on the dollar.

Outcome

Actual D-mark futures volume for Wednesday, November 23, totaled 22,767. This was a technical signal to buy dollars.

OPEN INTEREST ANALYSIS

Similarly, forex dealers could obtain the IMM D-mark open interest change and then:

1. A decline in open interest would:
    a. Be short covering on the price push into new high ground on the chart.
    b. Be bearish for D-mark futures.
    c. Therefore, *buy dollars.*

Or

2. An increase in open interest would:
    a. Be a sign of a healthy price trend.
    b. Be bullish for D-mark futures.
    c. Therefore, maintain a bearish view on the Dollar.

Outcome

The actual total open interest change was a decrease of 2,204 contracts. This was a technical sign to buy dollars.

Of note was the fact that open interest on the IMM Swiss franc, Japanese yen and British pound futures also declined. This was in conjunction with price upmoves on the IMM futures. Thus, the previous dollar bears, in general, were undergoing a change of attitude and were unwilling to hold short dollar positions.

Most U.S.-based futures traders assumed they had no choice but to wait for the resumption of trading in the United States on Friday before shorting the D-mark futures. SIMEX was open and trading the D-mark futures at the time the Chicago volume and open interest data was released. As an update to this case study, readers should refer to the discussion in Chapter 14 ("24-Hour Trading") concerning electronic futures dealing during U.S. holidays.

A major question addressed in this case study is: Did Asian or European forex dealers respond to the blatant warning signals of a price change in dollar-marks?

DEALER RESPONSE

Thursday 24 Nov—16:57 GMT   There was very little reaction in the Asian time zone. In Europe, the dollar declined slightly to 1.7140 D-marks in Zurich at 16:57 GMT Thursday. This presented an excellent opportunity for astute technicians to accumulate long dollar positions. By the time of the normal close of currency futures trading in Chicago (had the exchange been open on Thursday), the dollar was quoted at 1.7130 in Sydney (21:23 GMT). The dollar was weaker still in Hong Kong at 1.7100 D-marks (3:09 GMT Friday 25 Nov).

INTERVENTION

Sometime prior to the opening of the futures market in Chicago on Friday, November 25, the Bank of Japan bought dollars. At 13:12 GMT (eight minutes prior to the IMM's opening), the dollar was quoted at 1.7210 in Copenhagen.

IMM TRADING

Friday 25 Nov 1988—13:20 GMT   The March D-mark futures opened at .5881. This was a drop of 13 tics (.0013) from Wednesday's close. In the first 10 minutes of trade, the dollar strengthened to 1.7248 in Frankfurt. Then a real battle developed. D-mark futures rallied up to the daily high of .5907 in the next 30 minutes of trading. When the dust finally settled, the March future had gained six tics (.0006) but was *unable* to post a new life-of-contract high. In spot dealing, the dollar-mark was back down to 1.7165 in New York (20:20 GMT).

ADDITIONAL ANALYSIS

What did volume and open interest have to say about the D-mark's *attempt* to make new price highs on the IMM? Friday's total D-mark volume was only 14,064 contracts, definitely low. This was a bearish signal for a price rally in the D-mark futures. Open interest increased 647 contracts and was bullishly construed. This neutralized the bearish volume consideration. Often volume and open interest do conflict, but an overall consensus usually emerges. In this case, the dominant technical influence remained Wednesday's low volume and declining open interest in conjunction with a price rally into the new high ground. (Note that volume and open interest statistics for Friday were available when the Asian forex markets began dealing on Monday, November 28.)

FOLLOW-UP

Sunday 24 Nov—23:31 GMT   A violent move took place in the dollar. From 1.7133 in Tokyo (23:31 GMT), the U.S. currency strengthened to 1.7290 in Singapore (2:17 GMT Monday). It is interesting to note that at the same time, the T-bond futures were rallying in price (Sunday evening trading) at the Chicago Board of Trade.

By 13:14 GMT Monday, November 28 (six minutes prior to the IMM's opening), the dollar was quoted at 1.7322 in London. This caused a gap opening to the downside in the D-mark futures in Chicago. The March contract closed 60 points (.0060) lower. Volume did expand to 24,445, but was considered only average. Open interest increased 2,365 contracts. This was a classic sign of a healthy bear market.

A price rally in D-mark futures later in the week closed the gap on the chart, but quotes did *not* make new contract highs. In fact, a classical head & shoulders top formation was the resulting pattern on the IMM D-mark chart. Figure 12–2 graphically summarizes the outcome.

CONCLUSION

This insight into the use of volume and open interest statistics should provide the Asian and European forex dealers incentive to use their time zone advantage in shaping a technical market view. As in any approach to trading, discipline is a key ingredient. It takes discipline to monitor the statistics on a daily basis, but it pays off!

F I G U R E   12–2

Outcome

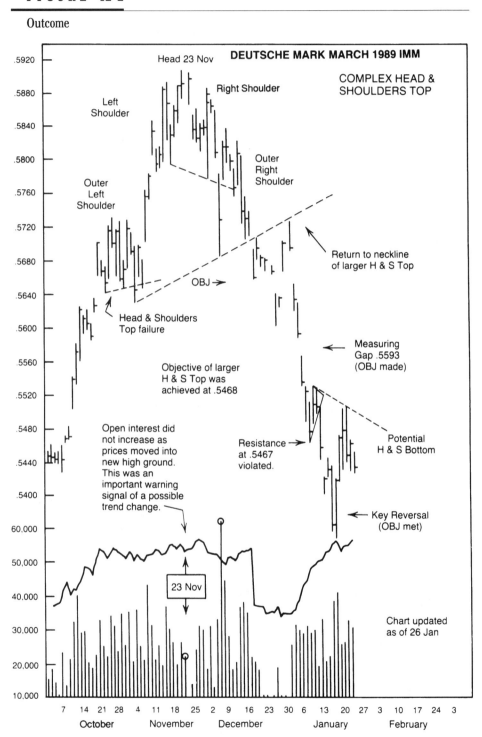

13

CASE STUDIES

This chapter will investigate specific technical situations in which there is particular utility to doing volume analysis and/or open interest analysis.

ANALYZING EQUITY MARKET PRICE MOVES

Since open interest is nonexistent in the equity market, stock index futures can be used to judge the quality of a price move in the overall market. Note the headlines from *The Wall Street Journal* in Figure 13–1. U.S. stock prices moved into new high ground, as did the stock index futures. On the surface, the price up move looked strong. But the change in open interest in the S&P 500 futures told a different story for that trading session.

Figure 13–2 shows that total S&P futures open interest declined 3,962 contracts on the 10-point price rally. "Investors anxious not to miss another rally" (the opening sentence of the newspaper article in Figure 13–2) were far from evident. The rally in the S&P futures was actually net short covering.

Volume on the S&P futures of 42,914 could only be categorized as average. The combination of declining open interest and lackluster volume would make technicians very nervous about following the rally.

S&P 500 Follow-Up

The S&P 500 futures opened 60 points lower the next trading session. A run at the previous day's life-of-contract high resulted in a new high by the minimum allowable price fluctuation (a .05 increase). The close, however, was not lower, so a key reversal day was not created. A key reversal is a new life-of-contract high with a lower close. It is a minor trend change indicator for technical traders.

Figure 13–3 shows that the continued move into new high ground over the

F I G U R E   13–1

Typical Newspaper Headline

THE WALL STREET JOURNAL THURSDAY, OCTOBER 5, 1989

Stocks Set New Record At 2771.09

Bonds Flat as Dealers Await New Figures; Dollar Trades Mixed

WEDNESDAY'S MARKETS

By Douglas R. Sease
Staff Reporter of THE WALL STREET JOURNAL

Investors anxious not to miss another rally boosted stock prices to a new high.

The Dow Jones Industrial Average climbed 16.53, to 2771.09, in moderately active trading, setting a second-consecutive record. Currency traders bid the dollar higher against the yen, but the U.S. currency was off against the mark. Long-term bond prices barely budged as traders awaited key economic data scheduled for release tomorrow.

Stock-market analysts said the surprise rally that sent stock prices to new highs Tuesday jolted money managers into action. Fearful they may be left behind if a big new rally is getting under way, portfolio managers jumped into the market, sending the industrial average up more than 22 points by early afternoon. Most of those gains evaporated in a brief mid-afternoon sell-off, but a late rally involving computer-assisted buy programs restored much of the lost ground in the closing half hour of trading.

Traders took a mixed view of yesterday's action. Trading volume, while continuing at better levels than prevailed through much of September, still doesn't signal a bull market. More disturbing, only 831 issues on the New York Stock Exchange posted gains, while 656 issues fell. Analysts look for more than 1,000 advancing issues to indicate broad support for a rally.

But on the bright side, technology stocks, which have been lagging the overall market, perked up. **International Business Machines**, dogged in recent days by expectations of poor third-quarter results, gained 2¼, to 108¼.

next several trading sessions was, on volume even lower than 42,914! A technician could not be bullish.

A small key reversal finally occurred on Tuesday, October 10, 1989. Quotes retraced all the ground gained since the push into the new high territory. Figure 13–4 shows the "crash of 1989."

F I G U R E   13–2

Bullish Price Move?

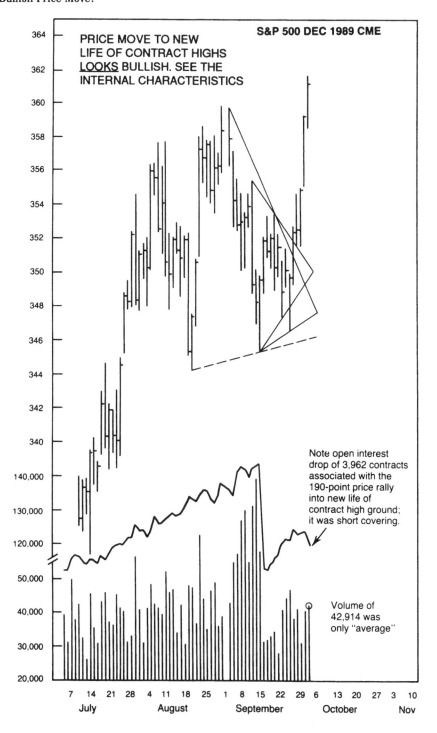

S&P 500 DEC 1989 CME

PRICE MOVE TO NEW
LIFE OF CONTRACT HIGHS
LOOKS BULLISH. SEE THE
INTERNAL CHARACTERISTICS

Note open interest
drop of 3,962 contracts
associated with the
190-point price rally
into new life of
contract high ground;
it was short covering.

Volume of
42,914 was
only "average"

FIGURE 13–3

Price Rally into New High Ground on Declining Volume

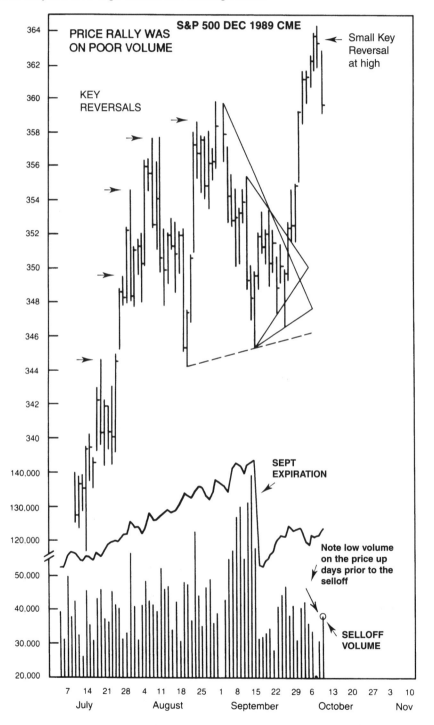

FIGURE 13–4

"Crash of 1989"

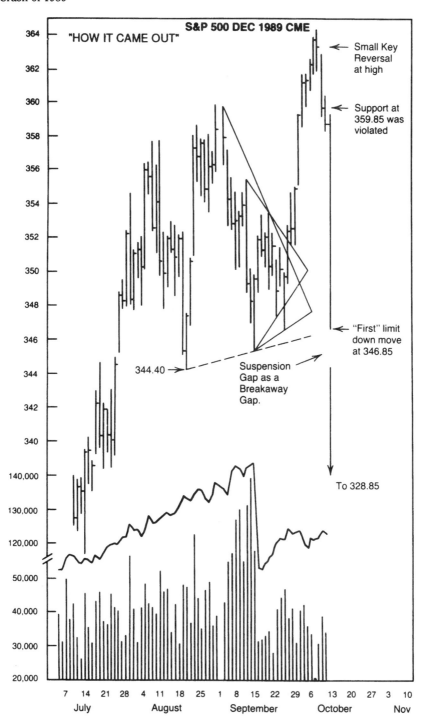

KEY REVERSAL DAY

With online, real-time quotations and analytical tool boxes filled with software, technicians are becoming more myopic in their time horizons. Rather than waiting for a classical bar charting price pattern to develop, they are asking: What will happen tomorrow? Tomorrow often refers not only to the next day but the next major time zone as well. Asian traders post their U.S. futures charts in the morning to obtain a view for dealing in their market that day.

The key reversal day is one of the most widely known yet least understood minor trend change indicators. A high percentage of traders jump to the erroneous conclusion that a key reversal marks the end of a major price move. It might, but this is too simplistic. Regarding the key reversal as a *minor* trend change indicator constructs a much safer trading plan. The key reversal is only helpful in gauging what might happen in the next trading session.

Key Reversal at a Price High

The definition of a key reversal (K-R) high is a new life-of-contract high and a lower close. It forecasts a lower price low (than the K-R price low), the next trading session. If prices have not set a new life-of-contract high (only a new high for the current price rally), a lower close on such a day would be called a reversal day; it is not a key reversal day. The price action on a key reversal high and the theoretical next trading session is depicted schematically in Figure 13–5A.

Key Reversal at a Price Low

A key reversal low is a new life-of-contract low and a higher close. A higher price high (than the K-R price high) is expected, usually the following trading session. The price action on a key reversal low is shown schematically in Figure 13–5B. Note that no close is shown on the day after either of the key reversal examples

FIGURE 13–5

Key Reversal Days

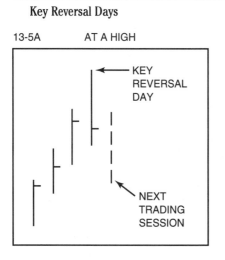

13-5A   AT A HIGH

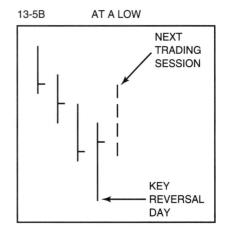

13-5B   AT A LOW

in Figure 13–5. The location of that close is not part of the definition of whether the key reversal worked as expected.

Expanding the Definition of Whether a Key Reversal Day Worked

What is expected following a key reversal low trading session? Quotes should make a higher price high than the key reversal day *before making a lower low.* This more rigorous definition allows for a higher high and then a collapse to new life-of-contract lows the next trading session. Thus, the key reversal calls for quick action by the technical trader.

Important to the understanding of the key reversal phenomenon are several additional criteria. If you presume that a key reversal day is forming, "leading off" by taking a position early in the day can be extremely hazardous. Seldom does a key reversal make itself evident early in the trading session. More often, the price move to a higher or lower close occurs in the last 20 minutes of trading. Evidence of a key reversal early in the day is more likely to result in the price's making a violent move to a new contract low or high before the late price move in the opposite direction.

Price gyrations, often expanding the range for the day several times in both directions, will generate high volume. Thus, a key reversal that occurs on average or low volume should not be trusted. Access to knowledgeable sources on the trading floor or in the dealing room for an estimate of volume activity *during* the day's trading is ideal.

24-Hour Markets

What about key reversal price postings on charts of financial instruments that are truly international in scope, with viable dealing in Asia, Europe, and North America? The foreign-exchange markets in the major currencies have always been in this category. And now the futures markets are at or approaching 24-hour trading days. The premise developed in Chapter 14, "24-Hour Trading," is that a 24-hour chart *is* the chart that should be used for technical analysis in these markets. After traders in each major time zone in the world (starting with New Zealand, Australia, Tokyo, and so on, thru Asia, the Middle East, Europe, and finally North American dealing) have a chance to move the market, a closing price tic is placed on the chart at 3:00 P.M. New York time. Key reversal price postings are considered to be a valid form of short term technical analysis on these charts.

GOLD EXAMPLE

Gold is a 24-hour market in physical trading. And the Comex division of the New York Mercantile Exchange has expanded the time parameters of futures trading with its "Access" electronic dealing. The trading in the following example occurred before the advent of electronic dealing in gold futures, but the principles espoused have not changed. The series of gold charts, beginning with Figure 13–6, show how the change in open interest helped in gauging the likelihood that the key reversal low would perform as expected.

Gold had been in a downtrend. The day before the key reversal, Thursday,

F I G U R E   13–6

Key Reversal Price Posting

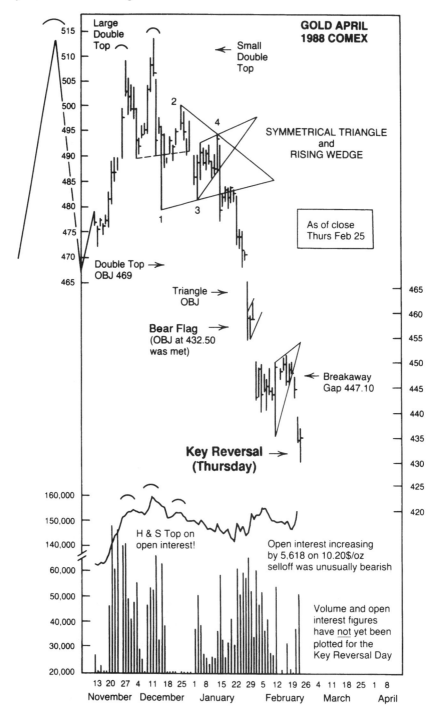

February 25, gold plunged $10.20/oz. and satisfied the minimum downside measuring objective of a bearish rising wedge pattern. Total open interest increased by 5,618 contracts on the price decline; this was an unusually bearish signal.

Gold is a commodity that the public likes to trade from the long side. The open interest increase means that the outside speculator was probably buying the price break.

A key reversal low developed on Thursday, February 25. If the key reversal was successful in purging the gold market of weak longs, open interest would decline.

Volume and Open Interest Analysis

Figure 13–7 shows the trading session immediately following the key reversal day. Friday was an inside range day. This posting on a bar chart is normally classified as a minor trend change indicator. In this case, it simply perpetuates the measuring implication of the key reversal.

It is important that plenty of time was available for the technician to check the volume and open interest of the key reversal on the prior trading session. Volume was not of blowoff proportion (only 55,964 contracts). Open interest increased by 4,504 contracts and showed no signs of liquidation.

A key reversal low should be an indication that the longs are "throwing in the towel" and the shorts are "taking profits." The technical situation would be correct for a price rally. This was not true in the gold situation where the shorts were pressing their winning positions and speculators were trying to pick a bottom. The longs were cannon fodder providing the fuel to sustain the price down move.

The Next Day

Gold gap-opened to the downside on Monday, February 29. This is shown by the opening "dot" to the left of the price plot in Figure 13–8. The opening price of 427.00 was 4.10 lower than Friday's close and 3.20 below Friday's low.

Obviously the key reversal low day on Thursday failed. *But the technician knew that the internal characteristic of open interest was not correct.* Monitoring open interest changes often allows the technical trader to sidestep a whipsaw move in prices.

Another key reversal low formed by the end of trade on Monday. Did the downside gap-open cause long liquidation? The change in open interest will tell. Figure 13–9 shows that open interest declined 1,911 contracts. Volume was 53,128 (still not ideal). Following the long liquidation, quotes rallied slightly on Tuesday. This satisfied the minimum objective of this second (and more technically proper) key reversal low.

EARLY WARNING SIGNAL

The September 1987 three-month sterling time deposit contract, traded on LIFFE (Figure 13–10), is a classic example of how open interest can act as an early warning signal. During the price uptrend in the first two months of the year, total open

F I G U R E   13–7

Trading Day after the Key Reversal

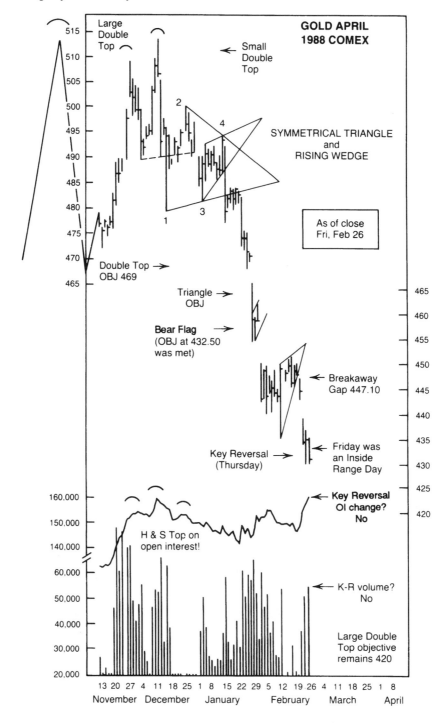

FIGURE 13-8

The Next Day

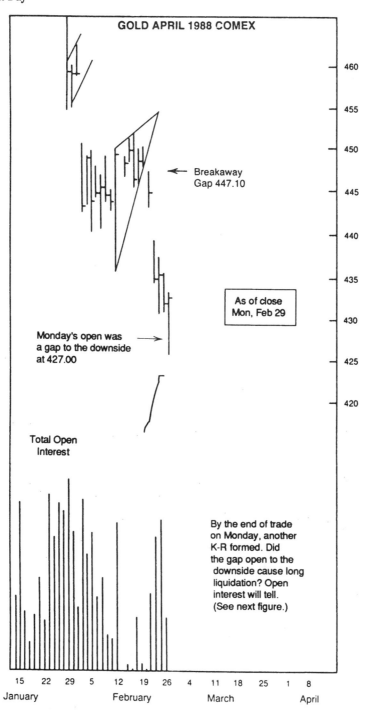

GOLD APRIL 1988 COMEX

← Breakaway
Gap 447.10

As of close
Mon, Feb 29

Monday's open was →
a gap to the downside
at 427.00

Total Open
Interest

By the end of trade
on Monday, another
K-R formed. Did
the gap open to the
downside cause long
liquidation? Open
interest will tell.
(See next figure.)

15   22   29   5   12   19   26   4   11   18   25   1   8

January   February   March   April

F I G U R E   13–9

Conclusion

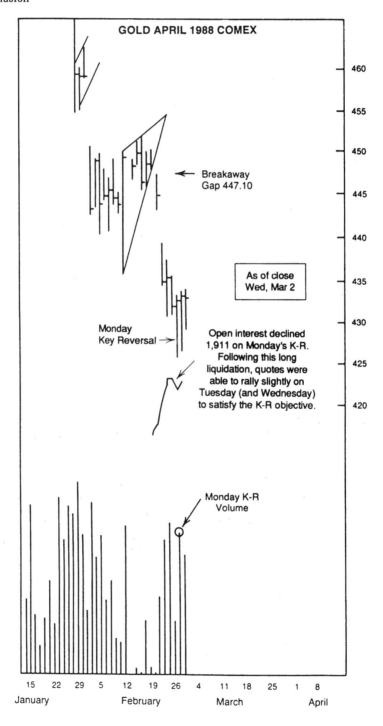

GOLD APRIL 1988 COMEX

Breakaway
Gap 447.10

As of close
Wed, Mar 2

Monday
Key Reversal →

Open interest declined
1,911 on Monday's K-R.
Following this long
liquidation, quotes were
able to rally slightly on
Tuesday (and Wednesday)
to satisfy the K-R objective.

Monday K-R
Volume

FIGURE 13–10

Early Warning Signal

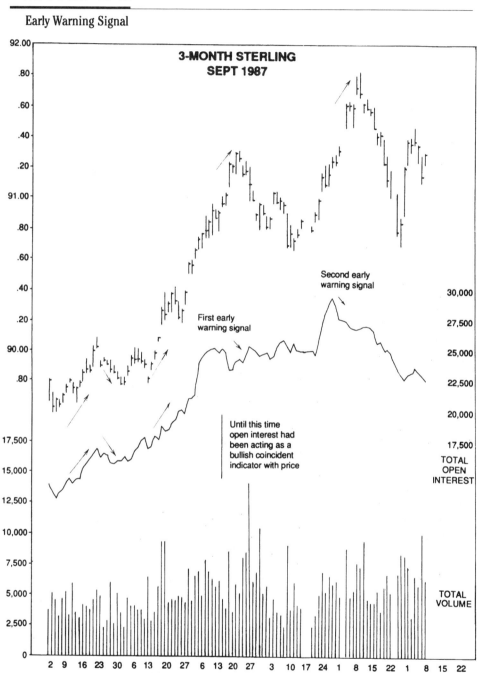

3-MONTH STERLING
SEPT 1987

First early
warning signal

Second early
warning signal

Until this time
open interest had
been acting as a
bullish coincident
indicator with price

TOTAL
OPEN
INTEREST

TOTAL
VOLUME

interest was acting as a coincident bullish indicator. As quotes moved higher, so did open interest. Note the price decline of late January. It was accompanied by declining open interest. Whoever was dealing in this contract wanted to be bullish.

A distinct departure from the coincident price/open interest interaction was first seen in early March. Price moved into new high ground; open interest did not. This open interest decline was stating the bulls (the smart money) were no longer enamored of the price rally. This led to the price correction from mid-March to mid-May.

The upward move in price at mid-April was accompanied by a strong surge in open interest. Once again the bulls were in control. An abrupt change in the internal characteristics of the rally took place on May 1st. Quotes in the sterling time deposit future rose seven basis points. In the face of this good news for the bulls, open interest declined 931 contracts. This was the start of a series of five consecutive declines in open interest as price moved higher. The early warning signal of a market ready to change direction was stronger than ever. A substantial price decline ensued, liquidating the bulls who did not heed the signal.

ASSESSING THE VALIDITY OF UPSIDE BREAKOUTS

A highly regarded principle of classical bar chart interpretation is that volume must expand on a price breakout, especially to the upside. This is necessary. Technicians must be able to ascertain that the breakout was not simply chart-followers setting off a price pattern. By themselves, this group of market participants would be unlikely to generate sufficient volume to validate a breakout. The addition of good fundamental participation (the real market-moving force) would produce the noticeable increase in turnover necessary to confirm the breakout.

As discussed in Chapter 4, the reason volume is more important on an upside breakout is due to the general public's attitude toward trading. They are always looking for reasons to buy a market rather than sell a market. They are eager to participate when they perceive a rising market.

The nonprofessional trader is usually stopped-out of a long position on the way down, rather than entering a new short. Often, this forced exit does not occur on the initial downside breakout. Several trading sessions later, it becomes painfully apparent that the trader is "long and wrong." Then the positions are sold out and volume soars.

TREASURY BOND EXAMPLE

The December 1989 T-bond chart in Figure 13–11 is a good example of using volume to validate the breakout of a symmetrical triangle price pattern. The upper boundary line of the triangle was at a price level of 99-20 on November 1. The December bonds settled at 99-22, a change of +11. This was an apparent upside breakout. The (predetermined) threshold level of total high volume was 308,000 at the time. When the actual figure of 262,671 was released, it became clear that an upside breakout on an average volume had occurred. Open interest did increase by 7,381 contracts (a bullish sign). As explained in Chapter 4, the volume interpretation should carry more weight in assessing upside breakouts.

When average volume accompanies a breakout, it does not necessarily mean that the price pattern will fail to act as expected. It does mean that a pullback (re-tracement) to the breakout is highly likely.

Figure 13–12 shows the outcome. Quotes closed five tics higher in the trading session following the "upside breakout." Volume (197,319) declined even further, falling into the low-volume category, below 244,000. The technical situation was very weak. This led to the 19-tic price drop on November 3, destroying the triangle by falling below the lower boundary line.

Figure 13–12 shows the original triangle boundary lines being redrawn using new reversals at points 3 and 4. Another apparent upside breakout took place on November 8 on a close of 99-26. Again volume was only average (266,049). Quotes dropped 13 tics the following session and the new triangle formation was eventually destroyed on Friday, November 17. To summarize.

Looking at price patterns without the confirmation of volume can lead to costly surprises.

WAS IT REALLY SHORT COVERING?

A comment from *The Wall Street Journal* on Tuesday, February 21, 1989, provides an excellent opportunity to explore several major misconceptions:

> In soybeans, last Friday's powerful closing rally ended the week on a positive technical note; one analyst attributed it to massive short-covering, or buying to offset short, or selling, positions by professional traders and commodity funds.

First, is short covering "a positive technical note?" No. This is simply poor buying. A price uptrend cannot sustain itself if the rally is due to buying by the shorts.

Second, how did the analyst (or reporter) know the price rally was short covering? The prior positions of the major buyers must first be known. If the major buyers were previously short, then the observer would be certain that the rally was really short covering. But it is difficult, if not impossible, to ascertain the prior status of the purchasers. Any statement concerning short covering made before open interest changes are released is only conjecture.

Third, how is it possible to determine what the commodity fund managers are doing? It may be possible to examine a representative moving average model (such as the Knight-Ridder CRB Electronic Futures Trend Analyzer, 30 S. Wacker Dr. Chicago, Illinois 60606) to determine if the trend-following fund managers were short. A normal technique used by these fund managers is a buy-stop-close-only order to cover shorts in a rising market.

In the soybean example, the fund managers were indeed short. Their buy-stop-close-only orders in the March 1989 soybeans were resting at the 7.81 level. But the Friday (rally) close was only 7.46. This was not high enough to activate the buy-stop-close-only orders. The buying was not from the contingent of fund managers who receive signals from models of this type.

How is any observer to know that a price rally in a futures contract was net short covering? Open interest will decline.

F I G U R E   13–11

Valid Upside Breakout?

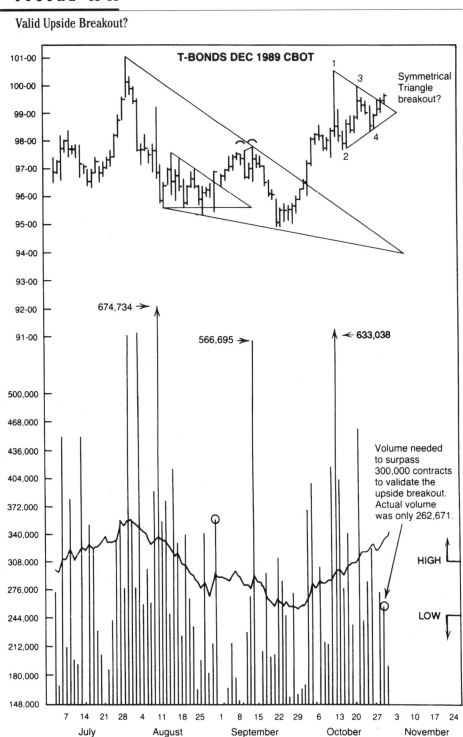

FIGURE 13–12

Outcome

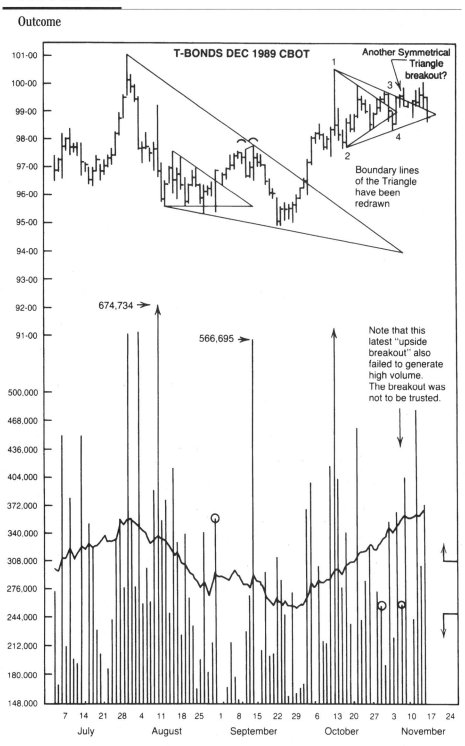

T-BONDS DEC 1989 CBOT

Another Symmetrical Triangle breakout?

Boundary lines of the Triangle have been redrawn

674,734 →

566,695 →

Note that this latest "upside breakout" also failed to generate high volume. The breakout was not to be trusted.

The first soybean indication available of preliminary volume and open interest from the CBOT Statistics Department of the change for Friday, February 17, was Tuesday, February 21. Monday, February 20, was the President's Day holiday. The point is, the reporter was not privy to the change in open interest when his comment was written. It was a guess.

One hour prior to the 9:30 A.M. opening of soybean trading on Tuesday, the CBOT Midis Touch System (code 2220#) yielded the following statistics for soybeans for Friday: volume was 65,321 contracts and open interest was 177,140 contracts. The change in open interest was an increase of 1,297 contracts. Thus, the price rally was not net short covering. An entirely different (bullish) view was the result.

To summarize the critique of this simple newspaper statement:

1. A short-covering rally may look powerful, but it really isn't.
2. Short covering cannot be identified with certainty until open interest changes are available.
3. Fund managers were not responsible for the price rally.

This scenario is played out time and time again in the financial press. Headlines proclaim that short covering was responsible for a particular price rally. However, caution is warranted.

14

24-HOUR TRADING

Cash markets involving internationally traded commodities have always been 24-hour markets. Spot interbank dealing in currencies is the prime example. Before electronic derivative dealing extended the trading hours, futures traders, typically, operating in only a single time zone, had to cope with overnight windfall gains or losses when their local markets opened each day. Exchange for physicals (EFP) did allow futures traders to offset their positions when the exchange was closed—but this was slightly more cumbersome and expensive.

THE EVOLUTION

The futures world began to change in the late 1980s when exchanges in the three major time zones of the world listed similar contracts. The Eurodollar time deposit contract became the most internationally traded future—viable on SIMEX, LIFFE, and the CME. In 1990, only a three-and-three-quarter-hour time period between Chicago's close and Singapore's open was not covered. For students of technical analysis—the three December 1989 Eurodollar charts in Figure 14–1 and the accompanying explanation should merit a smile and historic nod of the head. It shows a head & shoulders top on each of the charts—but the patterns look much different. The different shapes can be explained by *when* each of the three markets was open.

This early foray into internationalization of the futures industry has changed dramatically. In this chapter we will address the problem of what has happened since, more importantly, we will suggest a methodology of obtaining, recording, and analyzing the data on a constantly moving target.

Eurodollar Time Deposit Futures for December 1989

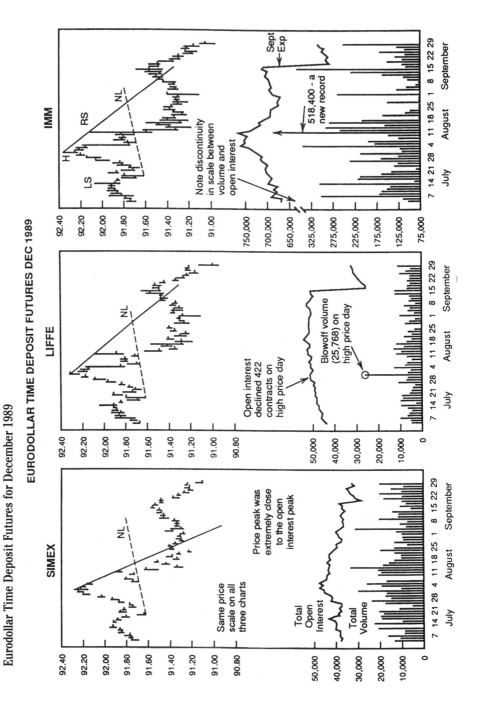

EURODOLLAR TIME DEPOSIT FUTURES DEC 1989

HISTORIC EURODOLLAR EXAMPLE

In the late 1980s, the technician's approach to monitor 24-hour dealing was to keep separate futures trading charts of all three major time zones in the world. This is shown in Figure 14–1 with three December 1989 Eurodollar charts. An examination of the charts results in these observations:

1. The open interest curves exhibit markedly different shapes. Which chart is the most important? The "home market" (the IMM) would be expected to provide the *most* relevant volume and open interest analysis. Even so, the technician should still look for nuances in volume and open interest changes on the SIMEX and LIFFE charts. For example, the highest price day (August 1) produced blowoff volume (25,768 contracts) and declining open interest (–422 contracts) on the LIFFE chart. On SIMEX, Eurodollar open interest topped with the price peak.

2. Open interest on LIFFE and SIMEX was of the same relative magnitude; but volume was much higher on SIMEX. The probable reason for this difference is the mutual offset system. It facilitates dealing on SIMEX, therefore generating volume.

3. The dominant price pattern on each chart is the same. This is the head & shoulders top, with the dashed line representing the neckline. The slope of the trendlines (drawn tangent to the high of the head and right shoulder) is different on each chart, but the direction of the major price trend is the same.

4. Many price gaps exist between daily postings on the SIMEX Eurodollar chart. The reason is that no overlap in the trading hours between SIMEX and the IMM exists. Most price-moving U.S. economic data is released during the U.S. trading hours (in the morning overlap in dealing in Chicago and London).

5. Small changes (500 or fewer contracts) in open interest are difficult to see on the LIFFE chart. The scale used in Figure 14–1 was created for an easy comparison to the SIMEX chart. In actual practice, a more responsive scale could be devised. In addition, a discontinuity between the volume and open interest scales, similar to the IMM chart, would be included in the LIFFE chart construction.

WHEN DOES THE TRADING "DAY" START—AND END?

Prior to the extensive internationalization of futures markets, the question of when a trading day starts and ends was so easy, it wasn't even asked. This was especially true for U.S.-based traders with their centric view of the world. But the use of "daily" bar charts now demands a proper and exact definition. The question can be based on several valid presumptions. Among them are:

Locally: Based on the sun.

Worldwide: Based on the international date line.

Conceptually: When a market in another time zone exerts an overwhelming influence.

Statistically: How the futures clearinghouse disseminates the data.

To students of volume and open interest, the correct answer is the fourth option. The volume bar must be plotted directly under the price activity that it represents. And the open interest figure plotted under the price bar must be the number of open contracts that existed as of the closing tic mark. This is common sense, but many new technical traders embark upon doomed voyages based upon improper alignment of price activity and the internal statistics.

To avoid the problem, many technicians simply choose to ignore this traditional form of technical analysis. However, with a little thought and then proper alignment, the price versus volume and open interest data can be made compatible and analyzed in traditional technical fashion.

EVENING TRADE ON THE CBOT

The first time a command decision had to be made concerning the organization of daily volume and open interest data was April 30, 1987. The Chicago Board of Trade introduced an evening trading session for Treasury bond futures. The opening of the evening session represented the beginning of the next official trading day. Although this seems second nature to futures traders now, it was a major benchmark in the history of the futures industry.

New terminology emerged. Trading was *suspended* at the conclusion of the evening session. A *resumption* of trade occurred the next morning and the close was registered, as usual, in the early afternoon, local Chicago time.

The answer to the question of how to handle split-session trading was contained in the availability of volume and open interest information. Having specific volume and open interest figures for each of the trading sessions would have been the most desirable. Analyzing changes in attitudes and market viewpoints by the evening session participants would be possible. But this optimal condition was nonexistent in evening CBOT trading and still is.

Many futures clearinghouses do collect trading cards during the trading session and attempt to match the trades. The complete clearing cycle occurs only once per 24-hour period. The CBOT clearinghouse, for example, does not provide open interest for the evening open outcry trade. It is possible to obtain volume figures for each separate dealing session. But it is the process of open interest dissemination that necessitates combining all the dealing sessions that have transpired since the last clearing cycle. Therefore:

Chartists have to keep the combined price range for the split-session trading on the same vertical line, directly above the combined volume figure and total open interest.

ELECTRONIC DEALING

The Sydney Futures Exchange (SFE) introduced the Sydney Computerized Overnight Market (SYCOM) in November 1989. This was the first "after-hours" screen dealing system. By 1996, average volume on SYCOM represented 10 percent of the total business transacted on the SFE.

The Sydney Futures Exchange—an Example

Figure 14–2 shows how a technician combines the two (or more) trading sessions that make up a futures trading day. The example has been simplified somewhat because the open outcry floor trading session on the Sydney Futures Exchange is actually composed of morning and afternoon trading, separated by a 1½-hour lunch break. This means, in theory, that the trading day comprises three trading sessions.

F I G U R E   14–2

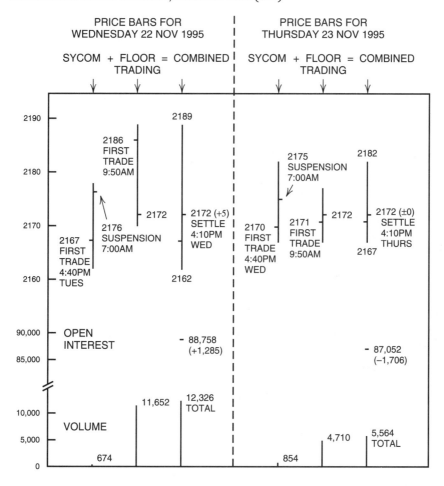

All Ordinaries Share Price Index, December 1995 (SFE)

The combining of all the trading sessions into a single price plot has become second nature to students of volume and open interest. This technique should be used on any split-session futures market. But the truism is that price is always more important than volume or open interest; the clearinghouse pays off on the settlement price, not volume or open interest! It can be instructive to examine the individual price plots before combining them. Sharp-eyed students will note in Figure 14–2 that the first trade in floor trading on Wednesday in the share price index at 2186 was above the SYCOM price high of 2178. During floor trading, quotes did move down to (and below) the SYCOM high. This concept of a gap within the trading bar will be addressed later in this chapter.

Activity on the Sydney Futures Exchange is an interesting example of *conceptually* answering the question of when the day (or week!) starts. The U.S. market exerts such a major psychological influence, even on the domestic Australian products traded, that futures traders there are often reacting to what the United States did, rather than exerting any new direction.

Each trading day on the SFE officially begins in the afternoon, with electronic dealing on SYCOM. The day closes with the conclusion of floor trading the next day. This means that electronic dealing on SYCOM is occurring while the United States is trading. Because of this, much of the activity on SYCOM occurs in early-morning Australian hours, as the U.S. markets are approaching their close.

There is an interesting ramification. "Monday's" SFE trading session begins Friday afternoon (with SYCOM), suspends *Saturday* morning, and then resumes Monday morning (with floor trading) and closes Monday afternoon. Activity Saturday morning in electronic dealing is more representative of Friday's U.S. action, rather than signaling the start of a new trading week. And Friday is often an important price-making day in the United States with the release of significant economic reports. This means that Friday's closing weekly tic mark on U.S. charts is often instrumental in activating a price pattern.

Monday's price bar starts each new trading *week* for bar chartists. Think of what this does to the look of a weekly chart of a SFE financial future versus that of a weekly bar chart of the U.S. futures. Instead of ending the week with a price breakout, Sydney will *begin* the next week with a significant price move.

The Chicago Exchanges

Electronic dealing began for the two large Chicago futures exchanges when the Global Exchange (GLOBEX) lit up on June 25, 1992. It was still not seamless trading in futures, however. There was a suspension between electronic dealing and the resumption of open outcry trading. For the first time, a Chicago Mercantile Exchange chart had the possibility of a suspension gap, and the Board of Trade chart had two possibilities. In mid-1994 the CBOT dropped out of GLOBEX to begin its own electronic futures dealing, called Project A.

Whatever an exchange names its electronic counterparts or how they tweak the opening and closing times:

An open interest analysis is dependent on the clearinghouse cycle.

SUSPENSION GAP

With the advent of split-session trading, a price gap was possible *within* the daily price bar if there was no overlap in the price ranges of the two (or more) trading sessions. Although this type of gap could occur in a market that suspends trading for lunch (typical in Asia), it was new to U.S.-based futures traders. Ken Shaleen assigned the term *suspension gap*. Serious technical traders are aware of these suspension gaps within the daily price bar. It is beyond the scope of this book to enter into a complete discussion of gap theory. But a suspension gap will often function as support or resistance, first acting as a magnet by drawing prices to close the gap and then turning prices away. This is the type of gap that initially formed between SYCOM and floor trading on the SFE share price index chart in Figure 14–2.

It is important that classical bar chartists be able to ascertain if a suspension gap is present between any of the futures trading sessions that make up the international 24-hour trading day.

The September 1995 Swiss franc chart in Figure 14–3 contains an example of a suspension gap between the suspension of GLOBEX dealing and the resumption of regular trading hours. This was a difficult gap to categorize. Because it occurred after a "rapid straight-line" price move, many technicians would refer to it as a measuring gap. This type of gap is considered a "half-way pattern" in the middle of a price move. But the gap could also be labeled a breakaway gap because prices broke and closed in new low-price ground, below the lowest point in a large symmetrical triangle price pattern.

Measuring gaps should not be filled. So, admittedly after the fact, when the September 1995 Swiss franc in Figure 14–3 rallied above classical overhead resistance (the former price low at .8250) to fill the gap, the gap was more properly labeled as a breakaway gap.

Figure 14–3 also contains an excellent example of how a classical bar charting measuring objective was met in electronic futures dealing. The .8045 measuring objective from the large symmetrical triangle on the chart was *exactly* met in GLOBEX dealing. Traders operating during regular trading hours (RTH) in the United States only, did not have a chance to take profits on any open shorts; the low during RTH on the September 1995 Swiss franc was only .8139. This leads to the following observation:

A measuring objective of any classical bar charting price pattern is considered to have been met if price trades at that level anytime during the international 24-hour trading day.

VOLUME AND OPEN INTEREST DATA

A technician desiring to organize price, volume, and open interest data in tabular form should create a data sheet akin to what is shown in Figure 14–4. Six days of Swiss franc futures statistics have been recorded on the data sheet. Each almost-24-hour international trading day comprised electronic trading hours (ETH) price

F I G U R E   14–3

Suspension Gap within the Daily Price Bar

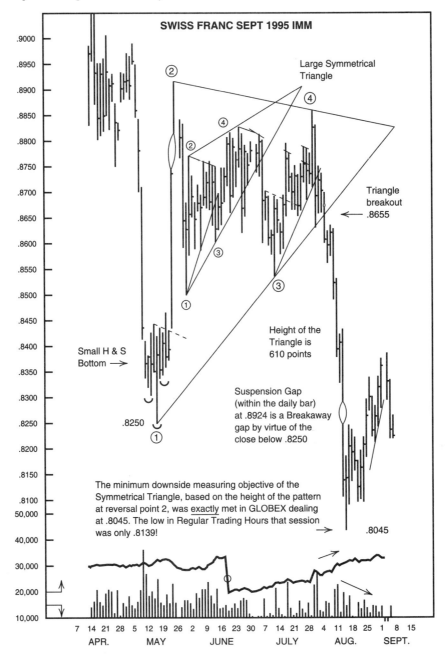

activity (this is GLOBEX dealing) and regular trading hours (RTH) price activity. The column labeled "combined" is the price activity that is actually plotted on the chart.

Space on the data sheet has been provided for the posting of both ETH and RTH volume. But electronic trading was so small in comparison to open outcry volume that only the total volume has been entered on the data sheet. The single open interest figure and, more importantly, the change has its own column.

Very important is the far-right column on the data sheet in Figure 14–4. This is where the technician refines his or her technical thoughts and formulates a trading strategy. Any relevant notes as to placement of protective stop orders, measuring objectives, or what to look for in volume or open interest can/should be distilled in this column. Note that the threshold levels for high and low volume have been entered at the top of the data sheet. The trend component of open interest increase, if the future was cash settled (refer to Chapter 8), would also be entered each week. Chapter 15 describes in detail how to obtain the data directly from the exchanges.

Diligent students may want to cross-reference the comments in the Figure 14–4 data sheet with the Swiss franc chart in Figure 14–3. The week of statistics details what was happening in the September Swiss franc when a healthy price downmove was in progress, a suspension gap formed, and a triangle measuring objective was exactly met.

The reason that technical analysis exists is to instill discipline on one's trading.

Physically writing the trading plan can be very helpful in maintaining the discipline.

PRICE DATA

The procedure to track the 24-hour day and be aware of any price gaps between the trading sessions, ideally, would utilize real-time quotes and a personal computer. PCs are becoming almost mandatory for the serious technically oriented futures trader. It is possible to get the price ranges for the various trading sessions that constitute the 24-hour trading day from the exchanges—after the fact. But the aggressive short-term trader cannot wait that long. Day traders need to know immediately if a gap is present.

With the proper software, a computer can be instructed to continually monitor and save tic data. With this data file, a 10-minute bar, always encompassing the last 24-hour period, is plotted. By visual inspection, any price gap can be spotted. An example of two "fundamentally related" 10-minute bar charts is shown in Figure 14–5. Knight-Ridder Profit Center software was used to construct the charts. Each trading session is butted up to the next with no time gap present. A time gap would be blank horizontal space on the chart when trading was closed or suspended.

The subject of time is a major subset of technical analysis. Time gaps are not material to the bar chartist. Having said this, the convention for a daily bar chart is to leave a blank line if a holiday occurs in the middle of the five-day trading week—but leave no space between the Friday and Monday price bar. This is not consistent, but it is the accepted convention.

FIGURE 14-4

Data Sheet

ChartWatch
312: 454-1130
AUGUST 1995

H 20,000+
L 14,000-

SWISS FRANC
SEPT '95
930-8282 P (ETH)-919 V (ETH)-918
P (RTH)-349 V&OI (RTH)-350
V&OI (TOTAL)-131

Date	Price			Volume	O.I.	Comments
Fri. 11	ETH OPEN ELECTRONIC TRADING HOURS	RTH RESUMPTION REGULAR TRADING HOURS	Combined 8532 8395 -138 8380	ETH RTH TOTAL 22,632	30,979 +1,539	HEIGHT OF SYMMETRICAL TRIANGLE = 610 PTS B/OUT= 8655 -610 STAY SHORT OBJ = 8045 8556 STOP
Mon. 14	O 8410 8338 -7 8330	R 8425 8336	Combined 8425 8402+7 8330	ETH RTH TOTAL 12,141	29,922 -1,057	OI+ ON FRIDAY = BEARISH HIGHER PRICE HIGH TODAY⇒ TWO CHOICES: CLOSE OR WIDE STOP. WILL USE CLOSE STOP AT 8453
Tues. 15	O 8435 8305 -96 8294	R 8250 8110	Combined 8435 8144 -25 8110	ETH RTH TOTAL 19,708	30,609 +687	OI - ON MON = SHORT COVERING RALLY △ OBJ REMAINS 8045 STAY SHORT, COVER 1/2 AT 8051 GAP AT 8294 = MEASURING OR B.A.
Wed. 16	O 8175 8167 +23 8045	R 8188 8139	Combined 8188 8147+3 8045	ETH RTH TOTAL 14,462	31,377 +768	IMPORTANCE OF GLOBEX; MEAS. OBJ EXACTLY MET. 1/2 SHORTS COVERED IF OI↓ FOR TODAY, COVER REMAINING SHORTS. 8206 STOP
Thurs. 17	O 8180 8105 -42 8095	R 8248 8105·	Combined 8248 8208+6 8095	ETH RTH TOTAL 18,324	31,539 +162	OI DID NOT↓, BUT BUY STOP AT .8206 HIT. STAY ON SIDELINES
Fri. 18	O 8240 8188 -19 8135	R 8240 8176	Combined 8240 8197 -10 8135	ETH RTH TOTAL		IF SLIGHT RALLY, TRIANGLE OR RISING WEDGE MIGHT FORM. WAIT & WATCH

Note: This time frame can be seen on the price chart in Figure 14–3.

The 10-minute T-bond chart superimposed over the S&P 500 stock index chart in Figure 14–5 is an interesting study for intermarket traders. Because the algorithm used to construct the charts leaves no time gaps between trading sessions, the vertical comparison of time on both charts is somewhat difficult. Nonetheless, a correlation between the intraday price movements can be seen. This began with the price rally in T-bonds in overnight Project A dealing. Just past midnight in New York, T-bonds moved up 8/32; GLOBEX dealers bid up the S&Ps by 100 points.

F I G U R E 14–5

Ten-Minute Bar Charts

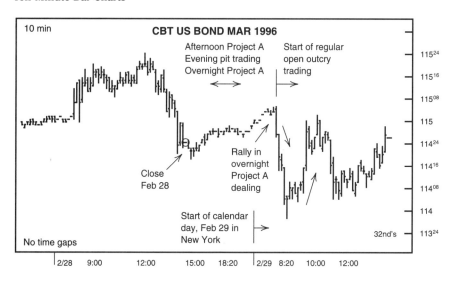

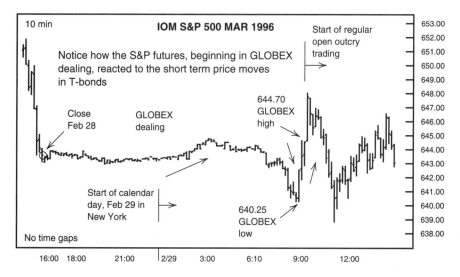

Also visible on the S&P chart is the early-morning increase in the price volatility as U.S.-based traders awake and move to their screens: the 10-minute bars become larger. When the Chicago floor traders arrive at the Chicago Mercantile Exchange, they want/need to deal in the S&P futures before the resumption of open outcry trading. The reason is the release time of the most important economic reports. They occur *during* GLOBEX S&P dealing, *before* the start of floor trading. The T-bond futures resume open outcry floor trading resumption 10 minutes *prior* to the reports. This provides a major guide for the S&P dealers.

The two 10-minute bar charts in Figure 14–5 have been vertically aligned very close to the start of the two open outcry sessions, although the resumptions are 1 hour and 10 minutes apart. The strong correlation between price moves of the S&Ps and the T-bonds continued through the entire trading session.

GLOBEX DEALING DURING U.S. HOLIDAYS

Futures traders should be able to initiate/offset positions in the internationally sensitive contracts on days when the U.S. markets would normally be closed for a holiday but Asia or Europe are open. The three U.S. holidays having these characteristics in 1996 were President's Day, Independence Day, and Labor Day. GLOBEX was open for 38½ hours between clearing cycles on those three occasions.

Here was another decision node for classical bar chartists:

1. Split up the session with two daily price bars with the open interest plotted below the close on the second day.
2. Plot a single price bar with two days of combined price and volume and the single open interest figure.

President's Day Holiday Example

An examination of both approaches was made for Monday, February 19, the President's Day holiday in 1996. The technical situation before and the two methods of showing the outcome are detailed in Figure 14–6.

A classical bar chartist would have been investigating the potential for a bearish rising wedge price pattern on the March 1996 D-mark chart. This scenario would have gained credibility if Friday's high of .6875 was not taken out to the upside on Monday. It was. A gap open to the upside occurred in GLOBEX dealing which started at 5:30 P.M. on Sunday afternoon in Chicago. This pattern gap is clearly seen when the first 20½ hours of GLOBEX dealing (up to the normal 2:00 P.M. close on Monday) is plotted as Monday's bar. The sell-off on Tuesday, again in GLOBEX dealing, closed the gap. Plotting Monday and Tuesday as a combined price session does not show the gap. In general, a technician would rather know, than not, if a gap was present on any chart. In this regard, splitting the holiday session into its normal price components is favored.

Analyzing the volume aspects of the two methods presents other problems. GLOBEX D-mark dealing generated 1,090 contracts as of the normal 2:00 P.M. Monday afternoon close. Although this was good volume for GLOBEX at the time, the 1,090 figure could not be used in a proper comparison to any of the normal volume plots. On the other hand, combining Monday and Tuesday includes 1,090 contracts of volume that might also make relative volume comparisons suspect. With electronic-dealing volume representing so small a percentage of total volume back in 1996, the combined two-day total of 1,090 + 1,208 + 31,064 was OK to use for comparative purposes.

Open interest considerations were straightforward. In both plotting methods, the total open interest was plotted on Tuesday's bar. This was the only choice.

A conclusion to this GLOBEX holiday case study is that more information is better—but more information can be confusing/overwhelming to the novice

F I G U R E   14-6

Two Methods of Plotting U.S. Holiday Trading

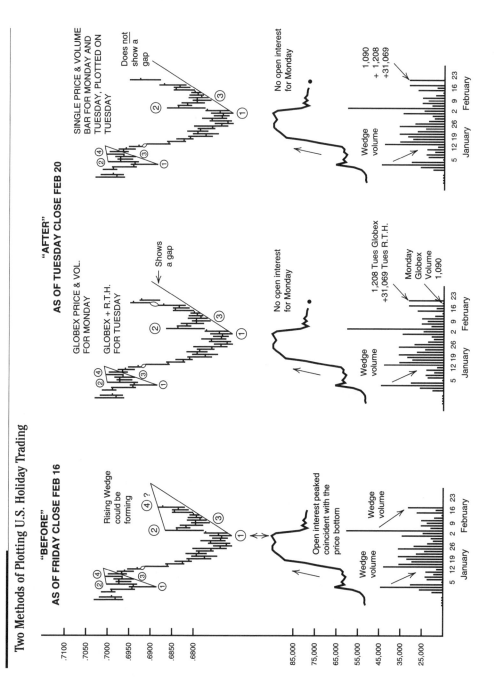

technician. The most probable solution is to use whatever plotting algorithm is already contained in the technician's computer software. Most software defaults to correspond with the normal trading day. There is no easy override function to force two daily time frames into one.

An example of the GLOBEX dealing screen can be seen in Figure 14–8 at the end of this chapter.

S&P 500 AND GLOBEX

On most futures exchanges, once a contract is listed for electronic dealing, it continues until the expiration of the contract. Not so, the S&Ps. The spot month in S&P futures is *delisted* (as of mid-1996) for dealing on GLOBEX in the last full week of trading prior to expiration.

So traders live with it. Or do they die with it? An interesting example occurred on Friday March 8, 1996. The technical overview in daily bar charting format is shown in Figure 14–7. A key reversal high (new price high with a lower close) was posted on the Dow Jones industrial index (not shown) on Wednesday, March 6, 1996. The S&P 500 future, as measured by the March 1996 contract did not post a similar key reversal. But the March S&Ps did post a minor trend change indicator in the form of an inside range day. Thus, both charts forecasted an excellent possibility of a reversal of the minor price trend, from up to down.

Indeed, on March 7 both equity indexes declined to lower daily price lows, satisfying the minimum requirement of the minor trend change indicators. What happened next is/should be of interest to all equity futures traders. GLOBEX dealing did *not* take place in the spot March 1996 S&P 500 future on Friday March 8 because it had less than one full week to expiration. Yet the March open interest going into Friday's dealing was 117,386, compared to 99,992 for the June future.

An important economic report (employment) was released on Friday morning, March 8. It was bullish for the U.S. economy and bearish for T-bond prices. Treasury bond futures plunged limit down, three full price points. June S&Ps were trading on GLOBEX and took a dive as well, down the initial permissible 1,200 point limit. But the contract with the greatest open interest, the spot March, had to wait until the open of regular open-outcry trading to react. It gapped open to the downside.

It is true that any participants caught long the spot March S&P future could protect themselves via short sale in the June contract during GLOBEX dealing, prior to the resumption of trading via open outcry in the March S&P futures. This, of course, would generate S&P spreads that would have to be offset in the pit.

The spot March S&P 500 futures gapped open to the downside, below the previous day's low of 649.50. This is shown in Figure 14–7. The highest intraday rally in the March future was up to 646.00—leaving a 350 point gap. The June future (not shown) did not post a gap because it was open for dealing during the mayhem that occurred after the report was released.

The technical-analysis observation is that the gap opening to the downside on the spot March contract was not representative. The gap is classified as a breakway gap on Figure 14–7 because price activated a double top (unsymmetri-

FIGURE 14–7

Gap Due to Delisting of Nearby Future on GLOBEX during Last Week of Trading

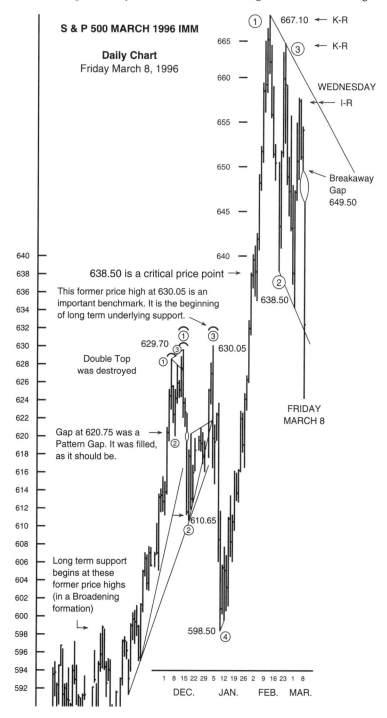

cal) on the March 1996 chart. Breakaway gaps do not have to be filled. The June 1996 chart does not contain a gap.

When bar chartists tackle the subject of gap theory, the most active futures chart is always the basis for the analysis. In most instances, the charts of the back months will contain gaps due to their lack of liquidity. Cash-settled futures contracts tend to be liquid, although maybe not the most active, up until the last day of trading. The nearby S&P 500 future not trading in GLOBEX during the last week is a definite idiosyncrasy.

The moral of the story—know the contract specification.

LOOKING AHEAD

Following the expiration of the March 1996 S&P 500 futures, considerable pressure was placed on the pit committee to change the delisting rule discussed in the previous example. The point is not whether this rule was rescinded. The march toward true 24-hour trading is invariably going to expose other idiosyncrasies. Forethought and prior planning will always be necessary to be successful. S&P traders desiring to remain with a bullish position should have rolled their positions forward into the June future to be assured of the ability to execute a trade in their open contract during GLOBEX dealing hours.

The S&P example in Figure 14–7 is important enough to merit additional introspection. Ken Shaleen, as president of CHARTWATCH and, more importantly, as someone writing technical comments on the futures markets for more than 20 years—and like all traders—is always looking ahead. One problem that long-term students of the markets face—being too early—is almost worse than being too late in climbing aboard a new, developing price trend.

What does this observation have to do with technical analysis, volume and open interest, or looking ahead? During the mega-bull market in equities from the 1987 share market crash into the mid-1990s, students of futures markets knew that an accident in another part of the world (or, in the March 1996 S&P example, a plunge in T-bond prices prior to the formal opening of the U.S. equity exchanges) could easily overwhelm GLOBEX S&P futures dealing.

Someday the general investing public would be faced with a sharply lower opening in the traditional equity markets such as the New York Stock Exchange. In the March 1995 S&P example, the idiosyncrasy that the spot futures contract could not be electronically traded exacerbated the deluge. Three limit-down circuit breakers were hit on the S&P 500 futures that day.

GLOBEX volume, all in June, the second month, of 3,461 contracts was "high"—but nowhere approaching the 144,220 contracts that changed hands in pit trading later that day. It is imperative that traders do not get complacent. Playing what-if scenarios is important. This involves staying abreast of what the world's exchanges are doing to broaden their time horizons.

Electronic trading is only going to grow. A trader always has to know the risk exposure of all open positions and where to lay it off anywhere in the world at any time.

FIGURE 14-8

GLOBEX Dealing Screen

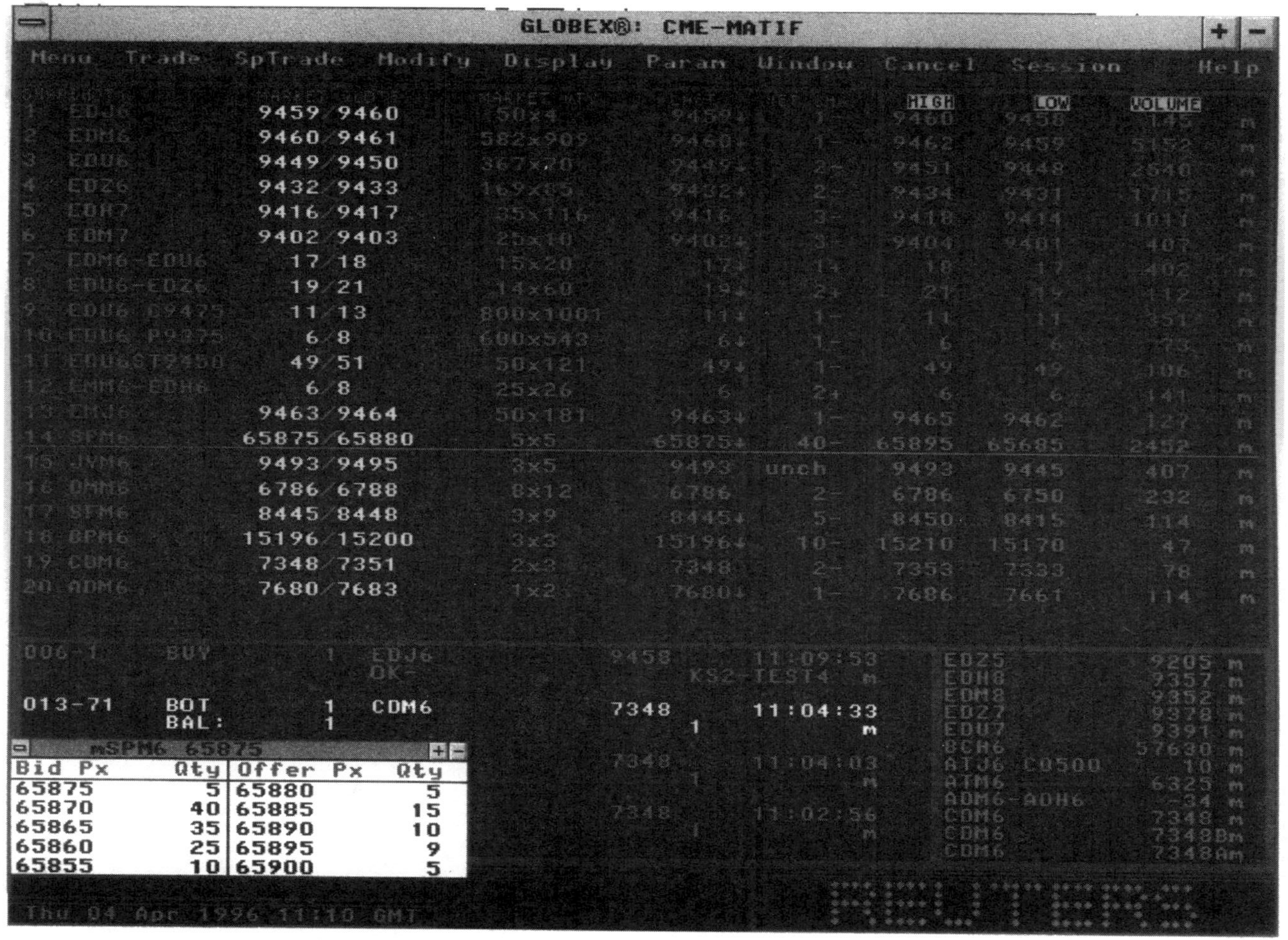

15

THE DATA

The term *clearinghouse* or *clearing corporation* is often used interchangeably by industry participants in referring to the same entity. Every trade has to be cleared/processed by a member (firm) of the exchange's clearing entity. It is this entity that is responsible to the buyer and seller as a third party guarantor. The clearinghouse generates the volume and open interest data. The figures are then distributed to the exchange statistics departments and third-party vendors such as newspapers and quote services.

The timely distribution of volume and open interest statistics varies widely by exchange. The ease of obtaining the figures also varies considerably. Waiting until the volume and open interest are published in a newspaper is too late for active futures traders. Table 15–1 contains information from a U.S. edition of *The Wall Street Journal*. Note that the actual volume and open interest results are always one day behind the price data given. And, as discussed in Chapter 14, the price activity will not show if there was a suspension gap between the trading sessions that constituted the *combined* high-low price shown. Much more timely and detailed methods of obtaining the data are available.

ESTIMATED VOLUME

Some U.S. exchanges, the Chicago Mercantile Exchange in particular, make an attempt to estimate volume during a trading session. On the CME this is a mechanical estimate. The estimate is not derived from actual order tickets. It is derived from tic volume. When the price changes by one tic, the tic volume is increased by one.

The CME extends (multiplies) the tic volume by a specific multiplier depending on whether the contract is a lead month or further back. This produces a

T A B L E   15–1

Volume and Open Interest from a Newspaper

Thursday, March 21, 1996.

Open Interest Reflects Previous Trading Day.

	Open	High	Low	Settle	Change	Lifetime High	Low	Open Interest

GRAINS AND OILSEEDS

CORN (CBT) 5,000 bu.; cents per bu.

	Open	High	Low	Settle	Change	High	Low	Open Int
May	387¼	388½	384¾	387¾	+ ¾	394¾	259½	190,138
July	376	377	374	375½	− ¾	384	254	129,729
Sept	326	327¼	325	325	− 1	335	260	37,925
Dec	313¾	315	312¼	312½	− 1¼	320	239	91,401
Mr97	320	320¼	317½	317¾	− 1¼	324¾	279¼	8,047
May	322	322½	320½	320½	− 1¼	327	306	331
July	322¼	322¼	320	320	− 1¼	327	284	2,148
Dec	290	290	288¼	289	− ¾	294	249¾	2,191

Est vol 50,000; vol Wd 66,503; open int 462,938, +95.

OATS (CBT) 5,000 bu.; cents per bu.

May	229¾	230½	227¾	229¼	− ½	248¾	153½	6,292
July	228	230¾	227¼	228½	....	244¾	165	2,622
Sept	194¼	195¼	193¾	195	+ 1	199	163	2,639
Dec	196¾	197¾	196¾	197¾	+ 1¼	200¾	160	2,329

Est vol 1,000; vol Wd 1,272; open int 13,937, −108.

SOYBEANS (CBT) 5,000 bu.; cents per bu.

May	718¾	722¾	717¼	721¾	+ 3	775	602	67,851
July	725	730¼	725	729½	+ 2½	775	599½	51,423
Aug	729	730	726	729¾	+ 2½	768	626	7,713
Sept	722	724	720	723	+ 1	752¼	623	3,658
Nov	720	723	717½	720¾	− ¼	746	585	55,844
Ja97	728½	729	723½	726½	− ½	750½	650	3,031
Mar	733	733	730½	732	....	754½	679	1,009
May	735	736½	735	736½	− 1	755½	735	175
July	737	739½	736¾	739	+ ½	761	633	838
Nov	688	688	685	685½	− 2	698	601	929

Est vol 30,000; vol Wd 32,681; open int 192,829, −2,624.

INDEX

S&P 500 INDEX (CME) $500 times index

	Open	High	Low	Settle	Chg	High	Low	Open Interest
June	656.00	657.90	653.20	654.65	− 1.50	673.20	554.25	181,258
Sept	663.00	663.25	659.00	660.30	− 1.45	677.80	589.95	4,528
Dec	668.80	669.00	664.50	665.90	− 1.40	681.80	612.70	2,513

Est vol 84,179; vol Wd 69,756; open int 188,309, +942.

Indx prelim High 651.54; Low 648.10; Close 649.20−.78

S&P MIDCAP 400 (CME) $500 times index

June	233.20	233.20	231.70	232.70	....	237.90	202.45	10,356

Est vol 694; vol Wd 809; open int 10,413, −135.

The index: High 230.67; Low 229.85; Close 229.99−.29

NIKKEI 225 STOCK AVERAGE (CME)-$5 times index

June	20860.	20890.	20810.	20880.	+ 265	21210.	14655.	25,793

Est vol 916; vol Wd 1,892 ; open int 25,841, +175.

The index: High 20745.76; Low 20470.70; Close 20727.53+284.93

GSCI (CME)-$250 times nearby index

Apr	204.00	205.50	203.50	205.50	+ 1.70	205.60	176.70	12,281
June	191.60	192.80	191.60	192.80	+ 1.50	192.80	176.40	1,467

Est vol 1,854; vol Wd 741; open int 13,748, +38.

The index: High 205.36; Low 203.18; Close 205.19+1.30

CAC-40 STOCK INDEX (MATIF)-FFr 200 per index pt.

Mar	1978.0	1990.0	1972.0	1982.0	+ 6.0	2038.0	1779.0	36,318
Apr	1981.0	1991.5	1977.5	1985.0	+ 6.0	2040.5	1779.0	6,929
May	1973.0	1974.0	1970.0	1977.0	+ 6.0	2031.5	1789.0	937
June	1955.5	1965.5	1950.5	1959.5	+ 6.0	2036.5	1777.0	9,909
Sept	1976.0	1976.0	1976.0	1971.0	+ 6.0	2019.5	1921.0	6,723

Est vol 26,955; vol Wed 17,040; open int 60,816, +2,914.

FT-SE 100 INDEX (LIFFE)-£25 per index point

June	3690.0	3708.0	3675.5	3696.0	+ 11.0	3799.0	3490.0	61,425
Sept	....	....	....	3712.0	+ 11.0	3809.5	3452.5	2,340

Est vol 8,888; vol Wed 11,140; open int 62,899, −866.

DAX-30 GERMAN STOCK INDEX (DTB)
DM 100 times index

June	2501.0	2517.5	2499.0	2513.0	+ .64	2541.0	2142.0	142,791
Sept	2522.0	2536.0	2521.0	2532.0	+ .62	2529.5	2295.5	2,746

Est vol 20,812; vol Wed 20,347; open int 149,086, +1,332.

The index: High 2507.43; Low 2491.73; Close 2505.32 +.55

ALL ORDINARIES SHARE PRICE INDEX (SFE)
A$25 times index

Mar	2239.0	2263.0	2235.0	2260.0	+ 20.0	2374.0	1950.0	101,803
June	2266.0	2287.0	2261.0	2285.0	+ 19.0	2396.0	2068.0	23,599
Sept	....	....	2306.0	+ 20.0	2369.0	2231.		584

Est vol 13,308; vol Wed 12,910; open int 125,987, +477.

The index: High 2262.9; Low 2244.9; Close 2262.9 +13.5

volume estimate in number of contracts. *This process does not consider the actual number of contracts that changed hands.* Comparison of the estimated volume versus the actual the volume total has shown that the estimated figure can be off by one volume category. This could mean the difference between an average volume and high volume or an average trading session versus a low-volume trading session. The mechanical volume estimate is seldom different enough from the actual to change the classification of the figure by two volume categories (i.e., from low to high or vice versa). But it cannot be relied upon for technical analysis.

The Chicago Board of Trade and the New York exchanges rely on volume estimates gathered from traders, pit committee members, and floor reporters. This is the figure that appears in *The Wall Street Journal* as the initial estimated volume. Extreme care must be exercised by the technician regarding these initial estimates. They too can be off enough to shift the volume one category in either direction. A better turnover estimate, during an open outcry trading session, is obtained by physically asking a pit broker for his opinion. Floor brokers, hearing the quantities traded, will possess a more accurate guesstimate.

HOW/WHEN TO OBTAIN THE DATA

Most futures exchanges realize that traders need to access the data in a manner that is both timely and efficient. To this end, many exchanges have a combination of a recorded-telephone-message system, an electronic bulletin board, or Internet World Wide Web (WWW) site. A telephone call to the statistics/marketing department of the various exchanges (to ask what is currently available) is well worth the minimal cost. In fact, it is necessary because of the proliferation of new contracts and trading sessions. Appendix H provides a partial list of exchange telephone numbers to obtain the data.

Recorded Message Systems

The Chicago Board of Trade has a recorded telephone message system that is called the Midis Touch. This acronym stands for Market Information Data Inquiry System. The Chicago Mercantile Exchange has the MercLine. Both efficiently facilitate the acquisition of voice data.

CME MercLine, 312/930-8282

It is important to determine *when* the data is made available. The Chicago Mercantile Exchange has always been far ahead of its cross-town rival in the timely release of statistics. The reason is the difference in the margining procedures. This is detailed in the discussion of omnibus accounts later in this chapter.

Final CME volume and open interest figures are always available before the market resumes dealing each weekday morning in regular trading hours (RTH). On the weekend, the information is available before GLOBEX officially begins the Monday trading day (Sunday evening in the United States). An example of how to access MercLine statistics for S&P 500 stock index futures is shown in Table 15–2.

T A B L E   15–2

Chicago Mercantile Exchange
Telephone Recorded Message System—
the MercLine, 312/930-8282

Regular Trading Hours, Available by 4:00 A.M. Chicago Time

	Price Code	Volume and Open Interest Code
Eurodollars	321	320
Deutschemark	345	346
Swiss franc	349	350
Japanese yen	347	348
British pound	341	342
S&P 500	127	126

Electronic Trading Hours (GLOBEX), Available by 7:15 A.M.

	Price Code	Volume Code
Eurodollars	955	954
Deutschemark	719	718
Swiss franc	919	918
Japanese yen	819	818
British pound	801	800
S&P 500	764	769

Combined Volume and Open Interest Available by 4:00 A.M.
(this is what is plotted on the chart)

	Volume and Open Interest Code
Currencies	131
Interest rates	132
Equity futures	133

The asterisk key (*) stops any recording and prompts user to enter new code.

The usual time availability of CME's futures volume and open interest statistics was 4:30 A.M. central standard time in 1996. The earliest release was 3:00 A.M.; the latest, 6:00 A.M. CME options data is released slightly later.

A note regarding the CME's MercLine statistics is in order. When a Saturday "out-trade session" occurs, the data is not available until later on Saturday. In 1989 there were 32 regularly scheduled Saturday out-trade sessions because of option expirations. In addition, two special Saturday out-trade sessions were dictated by hectic volume conditions on the previous Friday.

CBOT Midis Touch, 312/939-2268

The Chicago Board of Trade has preliminary volume and open interest statistics available on its Midis Touch recorded message system between 7:30 and 8:00 A.M. Chicago time the next morning. This means the trader must wait as much as

40 minutes *after* the resumption of RTH. And the final statistics are not available until approximately 12 o'clock noon that day. The good news is that the preliminary figures are not materially different from the final figures.

A example of how to access the Midis Touch statistics for T-bonds is shown in Table 15–3. This same system can also be used to access Mid-America Commodity Exchange information.

HOW ACCURATE IS THE DATA?

This entire book is predicated on the belief that informed trading decisions can be made based on the interpretation of volume and open interest data. The exchange clearinghouses do their best to process and release the information given to them by their clearing members. But just how accurate is the data—especially on a day to day basis—which is the time horizon in which the technical trader (using volume and open interest) is conducting his or her analysis? Two specific cases will be examined using a contract from both of the two Chicago exchanges.

T A B L E   15–3

Chicago Board of Trade
Telephone Recorded Message System—
the Midis Touch, 312/939-2268

Volume and/or Open Interest	Code	Release Time
Afternoon Project A		
Evening open outcry	03#	7:00 A.M. (and most often earlier)
Overnight Project A		
Preliminary volume and open interest for the *previous* trading day	08#	7:30–8:00 A.M. (depending on release from clearinghouse)
Final volume and open interest for *previous* trading day	08#	12:30 P.M.
Estimated volume for the *current* trading day, which just closed at 2:00 P.M. (Note: This is a notoriously unreliable figure.)	30#	2:30 P.M.
Current Price		
Early afternoon Project A	25#	2:30–4:30 P.M.
Evening open outcry	23#	Electronically updated during the trading session	5:20/6:20–8:05/9:05 P.M.
Overnight Project A	37#	10:30 P.M.–6:00 A.M.
Regular trading hours	20#	7:20 A.M.–2:00 P.M.

Example: The commodity code for T-bonds is 00. To access T-bond prices, the entry would be 2000# for the high, low, and last price during regular trading hours.

Chicago Board of Trade

A particular insight into accuracy of the data is available for the Chicago Board of Trade financial instrument futures when the Board is open for agricultural futures trading but the interest rate futures are not trading. This occurs on the Martin Luther King, Jr. holiday in January every year. Two sets of the final Volume and Open Interest Report (see an example of this daily report in Appendix H) can be scrutinized.

On the day of the Monday holiday in February, an exchange final Volume and Open Interest Report is released, as usual, for Friday's trade. In 1995, this report showed an increase of 6,977 contracts in total T-bond futures open interest from the previous trading session. The price change on Friday, January 13, 1995, was significant: +32/32. This report included a partial ("upstairs") resolution of Friday's out-trades, cash exchanges, give-ups, and office transfers that were conducted on Monday. But errors that necessitated talking to a floor broker or trader could not be resolved until Tuesday morning. After this out-trade checking session on the exchange floor Tuesday, a second final set of figures was released. This resulted in volume of 3,885 contracts being reported for Monday (when the T-bonds were closed)! And open interest for Friday was reported to have declined 2,265 from Thursday. It is the sign (from positive to negative) of the change in open interest that should make any student of open interest cringe. This obviously implies a 90 degree change in the interpretation of the large price rally on Friday—from bullish to bearish.

Another look was available on the same holiday in 1996. In February of 1996, at least the sign of the open interest change remained the same: from –6,672 in the first report to –10,654 in the second report. The adjustments to volume in a contract as large and liquid as the T-bonds are unlikely to be of sufficient magnitude to move the reading from one volume category to another.

The good news in this look behind the scenes is that most of the adjustments and errors are cleared up when a floor out-trade checking session is available. And this is the normal operating procedure. In fact, most of the time, only insignificant changes occur between the CBOT's preliminary volume and open interest figures and the final set of numbers. Thus, the preliminary report can be used for analytical purposes. But students of the market should always make an attempt to inquire of their floor sources or the exchange statistics departments when something highly unusual is reported.

Chicago Mercantile Exchange

Total volume in IMM British pound futures set a new record of 78,169 contracts on Monday, December 11, 1995. Price closed only 20 points higher (1.5344 versus 1.5324) on the nearest-to-expire December 1995 contract. This was a very small price change and not considered significant. Therefore, no bullish connotation should have been attached. There might have been a huge price range that trading session, creating the record volume, but this did not happen. The high to low range (including GLOBEX dealing) was only 46 points. This was actually a narrow range.

T A B L E 15–4

Breakdown of December British Pound Volume, December 11, 1995

1. Traditional volume:		
a. Regular Trading Hours	=	22,539
b. Electronic Trading Hours	=	23
c. Exchange For Physicals	=	9,059
2. Deliveries	=	0
3. Options exercise (counted in options volume only)		
4. Futures positions established by the exercise of options:		
a. Expired calls	=	1,235
b. Expired puts	=	22,173
5. Expired options (counted in options volume only)		
6. SIMEX mutual offset (British Pounds not eligible)		
Total		55,029

What created the record volume? The CME expanded the definition of volume, beginning January 3, 1994. This concept was introduced in Chapter 2. Now the problem will be examined in detail.

December 11, 1995, was the Monday following the (Friday/Saturday) quarterly currency options expiration at the CME. At the time there were fundamental (as always) considerations that influenced the willingness to hold open positions. Market participants were anticipating a U.S. interest rate cut (in fact, one had already been factored into three-month Eurodollar futures) by the U.S. Fed. Extremely important budget negotiations between the U.S. president and the political parties were also occurring.

Examine the breakdown of the December British pound volume on December 11 in Table 15–4.

Adding the 55,029 contracts of December volume to the March volume (RTH of 23,100 and ETH of 40), yields the 78,169 record turnover that was reported to the trading world. This was a ludicrous record. The problem is the 23,408 exercised options. This distorts any comparison with other volume postings. Admittedly, even without the 23,408 in-the-money options, total volume would have been regarded as high. But no strong technical signal resulted, given the small price change.

The moral of this story is that astute futures technicians will remove the expired in-the-money options that are included in CME futures, especially on the important quarterly options expirations. Figure 15–1 is the December 1995 British pound chart with the record volume indicated with a small circle. Note that the circled volume is considerably higher than the volume bar actually plotted. This produces a chart with homogeneous volume, for day-to-day comparisons. This same gyration must be used after the nearest future expires and deliveries are included in volume on the delivery day, which is also shown on Figure 15–1.

One final observation can be made, although it does not involve volume and open interest interpretation specifically. The 9,059 exchange for physicals (Table

F I G U R E   15–1

Record Volume (December 11)?

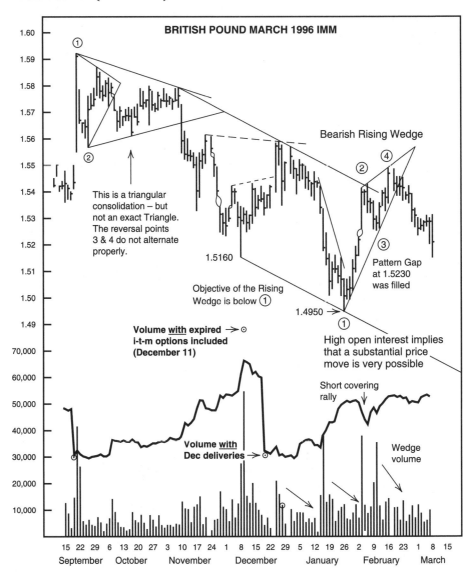

15–4) was a sizable figure, considering total British pound open interest of 66,842 contracts. This undoubtedly caused consternation with the GLOBEX promoters, who wondered why EFP volume was not moving to electronic dealing.

OMNIBUS ACCOUNTS

Most futures trading accounts cannot carry concurrent long and short positions in the same commodity and month (and strike price); omnibus accounts can. An example of this type of account may be a grain elevator that is carrying specific hedges for multiple customers. The bookkeeping is made much easier by allowing each specific hedge to be identified.

In the context of this book, the importance of reporting accurate open interest for the large-trader positions and long positions eligible for delivery is paramount. The good news here is that exchanges realize that open interest becomes increasingly important as futures contracts near delivery and relatively small errors can have a material impact. Any inaccurate reporting is a serious violation. But when we investigate how omnibus accounts can affect open interest, in particular, it is amazing to find substantial differences in the various clearinghouse procedures. Some exchanges are more strict in requiring clearing member firms to "P&L out" (profit & loss) open long and short futures in the omnibus accounts.

Chicago Mercantile Exchange

The Chicago Mercantile Exchange Clearing House uses a "gross margining" procedure, which requires that CME clearing member firms report their final gross (long and short) positions by 8:00 P.M. The clearinghouse is able to finish matching trades by approximately midnight and is thus able to release volume and open interest figures to the statistics department well before the resumption of regular trading hours the next morning. However, what does happen on occasion, is that an omnibus account does not let the clearinghouse know about some positions that should have been offset—until a day later. This results in an adjustment to the total open interest figure (and involves a cost, monetary fine, to the firm). The adjustment is not made retroactive to the actual day and the adjustment is not made public. This obviously causes a misalignment between the price change and open interest change.

There have been times when, for example, the British pound future experienced a sharp price rally just before the open outcry close in the afternoon in Chicago. The rally looked like short covering. But the open interest *increased* that trading session. Was the educated guess that the rally was short covering totally wrong? Sometimes on the *next* trading day (when price is doing nothing) the open interest takes a big plunge! Although the CME clearinghouse won't reveal what happened, adjustments do occur. When an omnibus account fails (delays) to P&L out a trade, the total open interest figure will be overstated. An error could occur in the other direction, but probably with considerably less frequency.

Chicago Board of Trade

The Chicago Board of Trade, with its "net margining" procedure, requires electronic transmission of positions from its clearing members by 5:30 A.M. the next morning. Manual adjustments can still be made as late as 6:45 A.M. This gives the omnibus accounts more time to properly report their positions. The trade-off is that the release of the preliminary volume and open interest figures does not occur until slightly after the 7:20 A.M. resumption of regular trading hours. After the 10:00 A.M. deadline for out-trades, the final volume and open interest statistics for the previous trading session are computed. The final report is available from the Board's Market Information Department by 12:30 P.M.

Sydney Futures Exchange

One exchange that appears to be somewhat lax in requiring their clearing members to offset open long and short same-month futures is the Sydney Futures Exchange. Until more stringent rules are added, more care than usual must be used when evaluating open interest changes for SFE contracts.

> *Authors note: To diligent students who have digested and understood this analysis of "How Accurate is the Data": You are well on your way to a Ph.D. in Volume and Open Interest!*

NON-U.S. EXCHANGES

Interestingly, the volume estimates from most non-U.S. futures exchanges are more accurate and released earlier than their U.S. counterparts. This is because trade matching is conducted during trading hours.

LIFFE

Estimated volume on the London International Financial Futures Exchange (LIFFE) is usually available about 20 minutes after the open outcry close the same trading day. The exchange states that the estimated volume is within .03 percent of actual volume, even on a busy day. Volume generated by after-hours electronic trading (APT) is available on the screen. The LIFFE Daily Information Bulletin (see a sample in Appendix H) details APT volume as well as basis trading volume. A unique feature of this bulletin is that the release *time* is contained in the report (e.g., 18:21). Unfortunately, LIFFE's open interest statistics are not available until approximately 5:00 P.M. the next trading day.

Simex

Trades on the Singapore International Monetary Exchange (SIMEX) are matched every hour during the trading session. Estimated volume is available about 30 minutes after the close of the last future. This is a very accurate figure because a match has been attempted for every trade. All cleared trades are counted. The actual release of cleared volume is approximately 11:00 P.M.

Actual open interest figures for SIMEX contracts are ready late in the evening of that trading day. Quote vendors generally have access to the data by 11:00 P.M. SIMEX volume and open interest data are transmitted to the CME the following morning (Singapore time). This is then transferred to the CME's Merc-Line System and easily available by 7:00 A.M. Chicago time.

INTERNET WORLD WIDE WEB SITES

The ease of electronic access to exchange data via the Internet resulted in a flurry of activity (and the usual competition) by exchanges establishing web sites in 1995. As this medium becomes more user friendly, it will be a superior method for technical traders to use to obtain the data. Selected web site addresses are located in Appendix H. A particularly useful site with links to numerous futures exchanges around the world is the U.S. Commodity Futures Trading Commission's site at http://www.cftc.gov/cftc/.

As an example of the maturity of electronic media as of mid-1996, the prior technology of the CME's MercLine's telephone update was still able to beat the CME's web site in the dissemination of the volume and open interest statistics by 1½ hours! Stay tuned.

16

PRACTICAL EXERCISES

EXERCISE ONE: SETTING VOLUME PARAMETERS

One of the first steps in analyzing any bar chart containing volume is to establish the threshold levels for low and high volume. In this exercise, the manual approach suggested at the beginning of Chapter 6 should be used.

The December 1989 T-bond chart in Figure 16–1 on the next page does show price activity. But the setting of volume parameters is independent of price.

Use the bottom of the T-bond chart in Figure 16–1, including a look at the plot of total open interest, to determine suitable levels of high, average, and low volume.

There is a text comment on an appropriate answer as well as the graphic answer in Figure 16–2.

F I G U R E   16–1

What Is Your Definition of High, Average, and Low Volume?

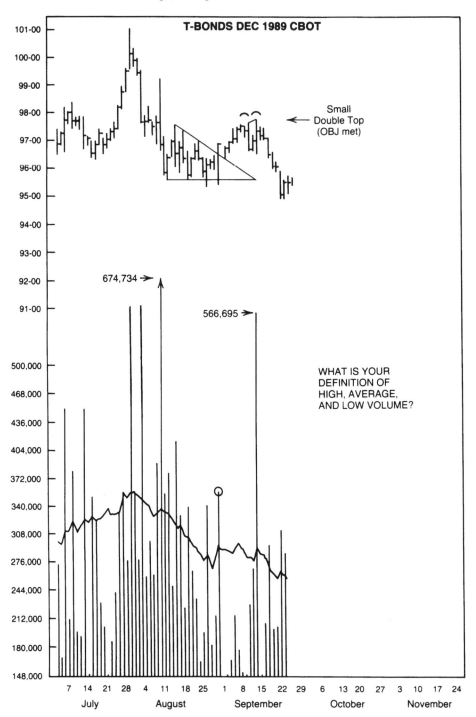

FIGURE 16–2

Graphic Answer to Exercise One*

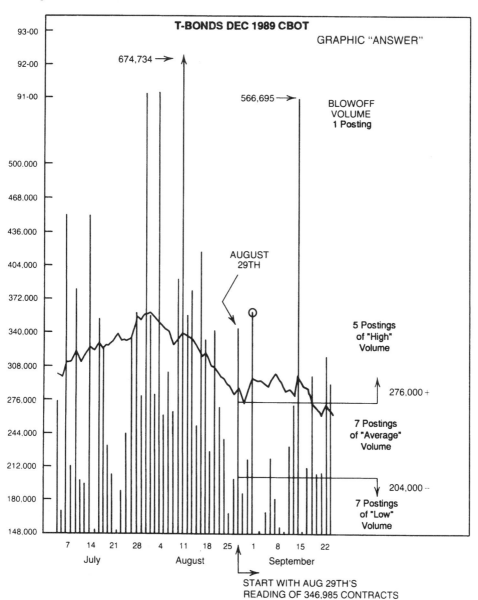

*Text answer is on next page.

EXERCISE ONE: SETTING VOLUME PARAMETERS: THE ANSWER

The analysis is started by going back an appropriate distance on the chart. Because total open interest has fallen so dramatically in August, do not go back further than August 29 to draw (imaginary) horizontal lines.

Figure 16–2 shows the suggested answer as values of 204,000– and 276,000+. Counting the postings in each category beginning with the 346,985 figure on August 29 yields the following breakdown:

One blowoff posting (566,695).

Five postings above 276,000.

Seven postings from 204,000–276,000.

Seven postings below 204,000.

This is close enough to the rule of thumb that an equal number of postings fall into each of the three main categories.

EXERCISE TWO: INTERPRETING PRICE, VOLUME, AND OPEN INTEREST INTERACTION

These questions are to be answered in the context of the ideal interaction of price, volume, and open interest. The general rule is:

Volume and open interest should increase as prices move in the direction of the major price trend.

Fill in either *UP* or *DOWN* in each of the blanks to make the statement correct.

1. The ideal situation for a healthy price downtrend is: Price _____ with volume _____ and open interest _____ . Note: This is a difficult configuration to find because of the bias by the public to avoid the short side of the market.

2. Price _____ with volume _____ and open interest _____ , uptrend doubtful.

3. Open interest _____ , price _____ , shorts are offsetting, strength of trend is weakening, and a downside reaction is likely.

4. Volume _____ with price _____ indicates selling pressure is diminishing and an upside reaction is likely.

5. Price _____ with volume and open interest _____ , uptrend valid. Note: This is the most bullish configuration.

6. Price _____ with open interest increasing indicates the underlying price _____ trend is healthy and should be expected to continue.

EXERCISE TWO: INTERPRETING PRICE, VOLUME, AND OPEN INTEREST INTERACTION: THE ANSWER

1. Price DOWN with volume UP and open interest UP represents a healthy price downtrend.

2. Price UP with volume DOWN and open interest DOWN means the uptrend is doubtful.

3. Open interest DOWN with price UP is a weak situation (short covering) and a downside reaction would be expected.

4. Volume DOWN with price DOWN is a weak situation and an upside reaction would be expected.

5. Price UP with volume and open interest UP is the most bullish situation.

6. Price UP , UP trend healthy;

Or

Price DOWN , DOWN trend healthy.

Also see Figure 16–3 to see illustrated answers to exercise.

FIGURE 16-3

Graphic Answer to Exercise Two

1) 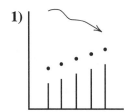 Price __DOWN__ with volume __UP__ and open interest __UP__ represents a healthy price downtrend.

2) 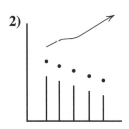 Price __UP__ with volume __DOWN__ and open interest __DOWN__ means the uptrend is doubtful.

3) 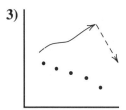 Open interest __DOWN__ with price __UP__ is a weak situation (short covering) and a downside reaction would be expected.

4) 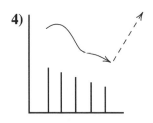 Volume __DOWN__ with price __DOWN__ is a weak situation and an upside reaction would be expected.

5) 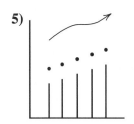 Price __UP__ with volume and open interest __UP__ is the most bullish situation.

6) 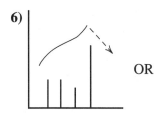 OR 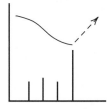 Extreme high volume (of blowoff proportion) indicates that the current price __UP/DOWN__ trend is likely to encounter a reaction to the __DOWN/UP__ side.

APPENDIX A

Glossary

APT   Automated Pit Trading, after hours electronic trading on LIFFE.

arbitrage   The purchase in one market and the simultaneous sale in another market of the same or equivalent commodity contract in order to profit from a price aberration; for example, Eurodollar futures in London versus Chicago during the overlap in trading.

back month   Any contract expiring later than the nearby contract.

backwardation   pricing structure in which a nearby contract is priced higher than a back month. The term is usually used in storable commodity markets, such as the London Metal Exchange, where a cost of carry exists. The opposite is contango.

basis   The difference between a cash and future, usually the nearby contract; basis = cash – futures.

basis point (b.p.)   1/100 of 1% or 0.01%. Most short-term interest rate futures, such as Eurodollar futures have a minimum price fluctuation of one basis point.

basis trading   equal and offsetting positions in both the cash and futures markets. Some exchanges have a "basis trading facility" that allows the easy entry into basis trades via a single order.

blowoff volume   Extraordinarily high volume. This is a warning signal that the price trend is in the process of exhausting itself, at least temporarily. Prices often move violently in the opposite direction after blowoff volume.

buying in   Covering short positions by purchasing contracts to offset the short sale.

carrying charges   The costs involved in holding physical inventory. May include storage, interest, insurance, commissions, and inspection/handling charges.

cash market   Usually an over-the-counter market that involves trading for immediate delivery. Sometimes the physical or cash securities are referred to as *actuals*.

CBOT   Chicago Board of Trade.

CME   Chicago Mercantile Exchange.

come in   To cover short positions. Traders "come in" from existing short positions and "get out" of existing longs.

Comex   Commodity Exchange Incorporated—a division of the New York Mercantile Exchange.

continuation chart   Weekly or monthly chart that posts the high, low, and close of the nearest-to-expire futures contract. A discontinuity on the chart is often encountered when plotting of the nearby contract is switched to the next expiring contract.

contango   Pricing structure in which the price for a nearby contract is at a discount to the back months. Opposite is backwardation.

daily chart   Futures chart with price, volume, and open interest data recorded daily.

EFP   Exchange For Physical. The simultaneous exchange of futures for an equal amount of the spot commodity, where the seller of the spot must have the commodity (for example, D-Marks) in his possession.

ETH   Electronic Trading Hours.

First Delivery Day   First day on which delivery can occur. On the CBOT physical-delivery contracts, this is the first business day of the expiration month.

First Notice Day   First day on which a seller's notice of intention to make delivery may be received by a long; delivery will occur the next business day. On the CBOT, First Notice Day is the last business day of the month preceding the contract expiration month.

First Position Day   Longs holding an open position at the termination of trading this day could possibly receive a notice the next business day that delivery will be taking place. An awareness of First Position Day is very important to the longs. On the CBOT, First Position Day is the second-to-last business day preceding contract expiration month.

floor broker   Order filler on an exchange floor. Traditionally, these were independent exchange members; they now may be salaried employees of a member firm.

forex   Foreign exchange.

full carry   In a storable commodity, full carry is the theoretical maximum differential that a more distant contract should trade above a nearby contract.

GLOBEX   Global Exchange. The after-regular trading hours electronic dealing system developed by the Chicago Mercantile Exchange and Reuters. GLOBEX began on June 25, 1992.

GNMA   Government National Mortgage Association. GNMA futures were the first interest rate futures contract. They began trading on the CBOT on October 20, 1975. The GNMA contract was difficult to analyze because the underlying instrument (a pool of mortgages) involved a monthly repayment of principal and interest and did not have an exact maturity. The GNMA contract was revised many times, including a "mortgage backed" contract in the early 1990s.

gap   No overlap in price on a chart from one trading session to the next. Gaps occur most frequently on a chart encompassing one time zone only. A gap would only be found on a 24-hour chart over a weekend or major worldwide holiday.

> **breakaway gap**   Occurs at the *beginning* of a new price move; associated with the penetration of a trendline; does not have to be closed. The higher the volume on the trading session that created the gap, the less likely the gap will be closed.

> **last traverse pattern gap**   Occurs on the "last traverse" across a congestion area prior to a breakout; does not have to be filled.

> **measuring gap**   Found *during* a rapid, straight-line price move; represents the midpoint of a dynamic price trend. They should not be closed.

> **pattern gap**   Occurs *within* a congestion area or trading range; quickly closed.

> **suspension gap**   Created when no overlap in price occurs between one trading session and the resumption of trading the *same* day. This gap was first possible on a futures chart when the CBOT introduced evening trading in T-bond futures. Trading was *suspended* and then resumed the following morning. The suspension gap must be classified as one of the four main types of gaps.

hedger   Market participant who holds an opposite commitment in the cash market. The motive is to transfer risk.

high-low-close bar chart   Chart with posting of high, low, and closing price data for a specified time period.

INTEX   International Futures Exchange (Bermuda) Limited.

Key Reversal High   A new contract high and a lower close; forecasts a lower price low (than the key reversal bar), usually in the next posting on the chart.

Key Reversal Low   A new contract low and a higher close; forecasts a higher high (than the key reversal bar), usually in the next posting on the chart.

lead month   Nearest to expire futures contract. This typically will be the most heavily traded contract until the rollover process is completed.

LIFFE   London International Financial Futures Exchange.

Linkage   Term used to describe a future belonging to one exchange, but traded on another; first proposed by the CBOT and LIFFE in 1995.

Liquidity Data Bank   Name the CBOT gave to the report that details the volume of trade at each price during a trading session.

local   Person who trades for his or her own account on the floor of a futures exchange. The trades must be cleared through a clearing member. Large locals may own their own clearing firms.

marked to market   Term used to describe when an open position's profit or loss is adjusted based upon a new settlement price. In a futures transaction, this results in margin flows daily. The CBOT Clearing Corporation can even demand margins from its members based upon intraday price moves.

MercLine   CME's daily telephone service for dissemination of statistics (see Appendix H for the number).

Mid-Am   Mid-America Commodity Exchange; a division of the CBOT.

MidisTouch   CBOT's daily telephone service for dissemination of statistics (see Appendix H for the number).

Mutual Offset   Transfer of an open position in a fungible contract to another exchange to close out a position on that exchange. First used between the CME and SIMEX with Eurodollar futures in September 1984.

NZFE   New Zealand Futures Exchange (a division of the Sydney Futures Exchange).

omnibus account   An account which can contain unclosed long and short positions in the same contract. Specific instructions must be given to the Exchange Clearing House to offset each individual position.

open interest   The summation of all unclosed purchases or sales at the end of the trading session. The published figure represents one side of the transaction only; long open interest = short open interest = total open interest.

options open interest   The summation of all unclosed options purchases or sales at the end of a trading session. As with futures, long open interest = short open interest.

options volume   The total volume transacted during a trading session. By definition, buy volume must equal sell volume.

perishable commodity   Futures contract in which the settlement process results in receiving delivery of a commodity that cannot be held and then redelivered into a short position in a more distant contract; for instance, live hogs.

roll (rollover)   Process that transfers an open position in a near-to-expire contract to a more distant future. Typically accomplished via a spread order.

RTH   Regular Trading Hours.

SIMEX   Singapore International Monetary Exchange.

SOFFEX   Swiss Options and Financial Futures Exchange.

speculator   Trader dealing solely to make a profit on that particular transaction; also known as a punter in some financial circles (i.e., London).

spot market   Transactions occurring for immediate delivery.

spread   (1) Overall position that contains both long and short contracts; for example, long T-bills – short Eurodollars). (2) Difference between a bid and offer price (e.g., 90.10 bid – 90.11 offered represents a one-tic spread).

storable commodity   Futures contract in which delivery results in receiving a commodity that can be held (stored) and re- delivered into a short position in a more distant contract (e.g., Corn futures).

SYCOM   Sydney Computerized Overnight Market

tic volume   Every time a price change is recorded, the tic volume is increased; recording volume in this manner is a surrogate for obtaining actual volume. This technique is often utilized on intra-day charts such as half-hour bar charts.

turnover   Another term for volume.

volume   The number of contracts traded each trading session. The published volume figure represents one side of the trade only; buy volume = sell volume = total volume.

Historical Overview

Since the organization of the Chicago Board of Trade in 1848, technical traders have been studying the interaction of price, volume, and open interest. Many of the interpretative rules used by today's technicians were derived from observation of grain futures, wheat in particular. Little change in the technical analysis of agricultural commodity futures with their physical delivery characteristics was needed until 1972.

MAY 1972

"The Great Grain Robbery," the Russian wheat buying, propelled futures into the financial spotlight. More important, financial futures were created. The Chicago Mercantile Exchange, with its new International Monetary Market Division, launched foreign exchange futures in May 1972. This required the first methodology modification in analyzing open interest. This was due to a departure in contract specification from the traditional. Physical delivery still existed; but it took place *after* the last trading day, not while the nearby contract was still trading.

OCTOBER 1975

The next revision in the traditional approach to open interest took place with the advent of interest rate futures. The Government National Mortgage Association (GNMA) contract began trading on the CBOT in October 1975. The actual commodity being traded was interest rates. But the contract was invoiced and traded in terms of *price*. A departure from typical open interest action was first noticed during the big U.S. Treasury bond price rally of early 1986; open interest declined steadily during the major price uptrend.

DECEMBER 1981

Cash-settled futures required another modification. This began with the Eurodollar time deposit contract on the IMM in December 1981. This was the first cash-settled futures contract. With no onerous delivery mechanism to avoid, the rollover process from one contract to the next created a distinct shape to the total open interest curve.

OCTOBER 1982

Options on futures began in October 1982. This produced another distortion in the typical behavior of volume and open interest. Knowledge of both futures and options contract specifications became necessary. In particular, the options expiration date emerged as an important factor in developing an expectation of futures open interest changes.

SEPTEMBER 1984

Mutual offset of futures contracts between the CME and the Singapore International Monetary Exchange (SIMEX) first took place on September 7, 1984. With one transaction, open interest was created on two exchanges. Eurodollar dealing on both exchanges soared in early 1989.

Fungible contracts between other exchanges have also emerged, but none of these links has come close to the success of the CME–SIMEX relationship.

JANUARY 1985

The earliest establishment of a purely electronic futures exchange is impossible to determine with certainty. The true definition would include both automated trading and a clearing system. An attempt was made by the International Futures Exchange (Bermuda) Limited (INTEX), but a liquid market never developed. The New Zealand Futures Exchange (NZFE) began automated trading in January 1985. In May 1988, the Swiss Options and Financial Futures Exchange (SOFFEX) opened with automated trading and clearing. In 1989, Automated Pit Trading (APT) began on LIFFE and the Sydney Computerized Overnight Market (SYCOM) started in Australia.

Of importance to the technician was the ability to obtain online actual volume information. No longer did a futures analyst endure the agonizing wait before obtaining this important technical input.

APRIL 1987

An evening session in T-bond trading on the CBOT was started April 30, 1987. Handling of volume and open interest was resolved by the CBOT Clearing Corporation. Only estimated volume from the evening session is released; no open interest statistics are made available. This required the single posting of price for the two trading sessions that constitute the day. Total volume and total open interest is plotted for the combined session.

JUNE 1992

Electronic futures dealing of selected Chicago Mercantile Exchange and Chicago Board of Trade contracts began on June 25, 1992. This really started the irreversible move toward 24-hour futures trading.

The Board of Trade dropped out of GLOBEX in May 1994 and started its own electronic trading system Project A in October 1994.

JULY 1995

Electronic dealing on GLOBEX during a normal U.S. holiday began on July 4, 1995. Since the CME Clearing House does not run a full clearing cycle on a holiday—the time between the official open and close ran more than 24 hours. Technicians once again had the challenge of determining how to record the data. The ability to compare daily price, volume, and open interest plots was the critical issue.

WHAT'S NEXT?

The creation of new contract types and their quirks are inevitable and welcomed. Regardless of what technology and financial engineers may produce, the interpretation of volume and open interest statistics remains philosophically unchanged.

It is hoped this historical look at the evolution of technical analysis will provide a trader with the momentum to tackle any contract a futures exchange may introduce.

APPENDIX C

Basis

The premise that futures represent the market as a whole needs to be examined in a more conceptual manner. What ties the two markets together is the basis. *Basis* is the difference between cash prices and futures prices, specifically:

$$\text{Basis} = \text{Cash} - \text{Futures}$$

In this case, basis is the dependent variable. The basis is determined by subtracting a futures price from a cash price. This is a simple mathematical formula. As such, the equation also can be written:

$$\text{Cash} = \text{Futures} + \text{Basis}$$
$$\text{or}$$
$$\text{Futures} = \text{Cash} - \text{Basis}$$

The conceptual question posed is: Which is the dependent variable? Which market, cash or futures, represents the dominant price-setting mechanism? There is no simple answer. It lies in the maturity and sophistication of the users of both markets.

GRAIN MARKETS

In the grain and oilseed trade, futures are the cutting edge of price determination. The world grain trade is comfortable with the term basis. Basis tables and charts have a long historical precedence. Basis is an independent variable. As a result, grain is priced at a specific differential (basis) with respect to a futures contract. Futures statistics can and should be relied upon to represent a true picture of the marketforces at work. The true functional representation in the grain trade is:

$$\text{Cash} = \text{Futures} + \text{Basis}$$

LIVESTOCK MARKETS

In the livestock sector, the terminal market has held the tradition of establishing cash market quotes. The basis is not as stable as the grain trade. Often it seems the cash price for live cattle in Omaha, Nebraska, and the price of the live cattle futures on the CME were derived independently. Basis simply being equal to the mathematical difference between the two markets. Here cash and futures quotes are two independent variables and basis is the result. Functionally, this means:

$$\text{Basis} = \text{Cash} - \text{Futures}$$

This does not mean that analysis of a futures contract cannot be used in the analysis of livestock prices. But it does mean that the basis is not as stable as in the older grain trade. At expiration, basis convergence will bring futures and cash into line. The technician does have to be aware of how much noise exists between the cash and futures.

FINANCIAL FUTURES

The financial instrument futures are a recent (and continuing) innovation. Thus, the battle between the cash market dealers and futures market traders is still observable. When a futures market starts trading, it disrupts the old boy dealer network. To many dealers, the futures market represents a group of nonprofessionals. In some financial communities, the dealers are so powerful they are able to squash fledgling futures contracts. Witness the poor success of the currency futures contracts on the London International Financial Futures Exchange (LIFFE) and in Singapore on SIMEX. It took the IMM in Chicago years to establish a critical mass in its foreign-exchange futures.

As more arbitrage between cash and futures takes place, basis trades become common. Some critics would say that these trades distort the analysis of futures volume and open interest. What actually occurs is akin to Adam Smith's "invisible hand". Arbitrageurs, by trying to profit from pricing inaccuracies, actually produce a more viable futures market. This creates environments where the financial community can substitute futures for cash, shift risk, or speculate. Whatever the motive, the internal characteristics of the market can be monitored in futures volume and open interest.

APPENDIX D

Mathematically Detrending Open Interest

As Chapter 8 presented in detail, the trending increase of open interest, in a cash-settled future, must be used to evaluate open interest changes. The actual changes in open interest need to be classified as either greater than, less than, or equal to the normal trend component.

In Figure 8–11, the trend component was determined by merely drawing a best-fit line through the open interest. A more exact determination of this trend is ascertained using standard least-squares regression to calculate the slope of this best-fit line. The slope or gradient will be expressed in contracts per trading session.

The following method outlines how this would be performed using the regression analysis program from LOTUS, a typical financial software package. Total IMM Eurodollar open interest for the first quarter of 1988 will be examined. The output from the model can then be compared to the eyeballed line in Figure 8–11.

In a blank part of a worksheet, the total open interest is entered in a column format. Periods of time very close to contract expiration should be avoided since the open interest is rather erratic before dropping sharply. The period of time analyzed in the following example is from January 4, 1988 through February 26, 1988. Other columns such as date and total volume also can be entered.

An additional column of sequential numbers is also required. This column will be the X-range for the regression analysis. This column is shown to the left of the date in the example. The date column cannot be used for the X-range since weekends and holidays cause this column not to increase in a single step-wise fashion. For the slope of this best-fit line to be calculated correctly this X-range must increase linearly. The Y-range for the regression analysis will be the open interest column.

To set these ranges, choose Data Regression from the main Lotus command menu and choose the setting of the X-range and Y-range commands. An output range must now be specified. This range should be at least nine columns wide. Finally, enter Go from the regression menu. The regression output will appear in the assigned range. This output will look like the output range in Table D–1.

The value of concern from the regression data is the X coefficient. In this example, the value is 2,015. It represents an average increase of 2,015 contracts per trading session. This figure is in close enough agreement with the eyeballed trendline with a slope of 2700 contracts shown in Figure 8–11.

Open interest increases greater than the determined trend component would be considered above average, while values below this would be considered substandard. A graphical picture of what this best-fit line represents is shown in Figure D–1.

TABLE D-1

Eurodollar Regression Analysis

X-Range	Date	Total Volume	Y-Range Total Open Interest
1	04-Jan-88	62,240	294,065
2	05-Jan-88	86,445	301,681
3	06-Jan-88	76,763	299,960
4	07-Jan-88	69,797	302,321
5	08-Jan-88	110,152	308,915
6	11-Jan-88	84,917	308,536
7	12-Jan-88	64,165	311,363
8	13-Jan-88	59,447	310,933
9	14-Jan-88	44,679	310,776
10	15-Jan-88	107,228	318,321
11	18-Jan-88	23,355	318,686
12	19-Jan-88	41,344	319,070
13	20-Jan-88	73,335	323,707
14	21-Jan-88	93,746	325,272
15	22-Jan-88	65,240	328,952
16	25-Jan-88	50,946	327,252
17	26-Jan-88	66,372	327,956
18	27-Jan-88	103,418	333,545
19	28-Jan-88	115,295	336,772
20	29-Jan-88	67,591	339,608
21	01-Feb-88	81,286	339,306
22	02-Feb-88	115,269	348,088
23	03-Feb-88	116,213	351,154
24	04-Feb-88	82,250	348,406
25	05-Feb-88	141,449	350,623
26	08-Feb-88	52,974	351,303
27	09-Feb-88	55,027	354,312
28	10-Feb-88	61,967	357,702
29	11-Feb-88	80,820	356,126
30	12-Feb-88	178,766	369,713
31	16-Feb-88	107,014	362,232
32	17-Feb-88	90,288	360,281
33	18-Feb-88	74,007	365,794
34	19-Feb-88	49,052	362,339
35	22-Feb-88	34,183	362,984
36	23-Feb-88	73,783	366,232
37	24-Feb-88	59,052	365,144
38	25-Feb-88	124,544	366,261
39	26-Feb-88	54,266	368,176

Output Range

Regression Output:

Constant		2.9697E+05
Std Err of Y Est		4075
R Squared		0.97
No. of Observations		39.00
Degrees of Freedom		37.00
X Coefficient(s)	2015*	
Std Err of Coef.	57.98	

*Slope of the least squares retression line in contracts per trading session.

FIGURE D-1

IMM Eurodollar Open Interest with Least Squares Regression Line

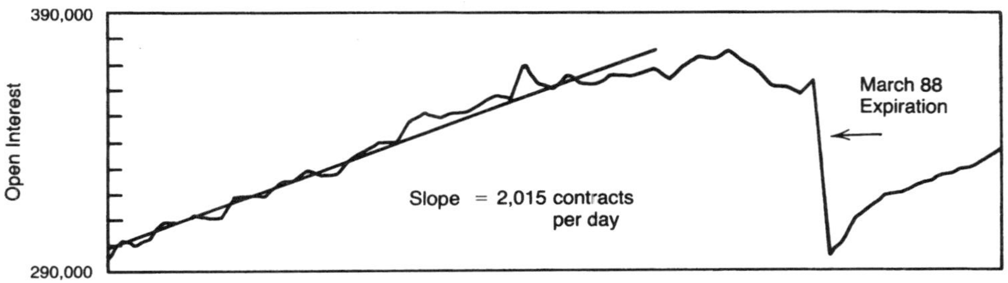

Seasonally Normal Commitments Graphs

FIGURE E–1

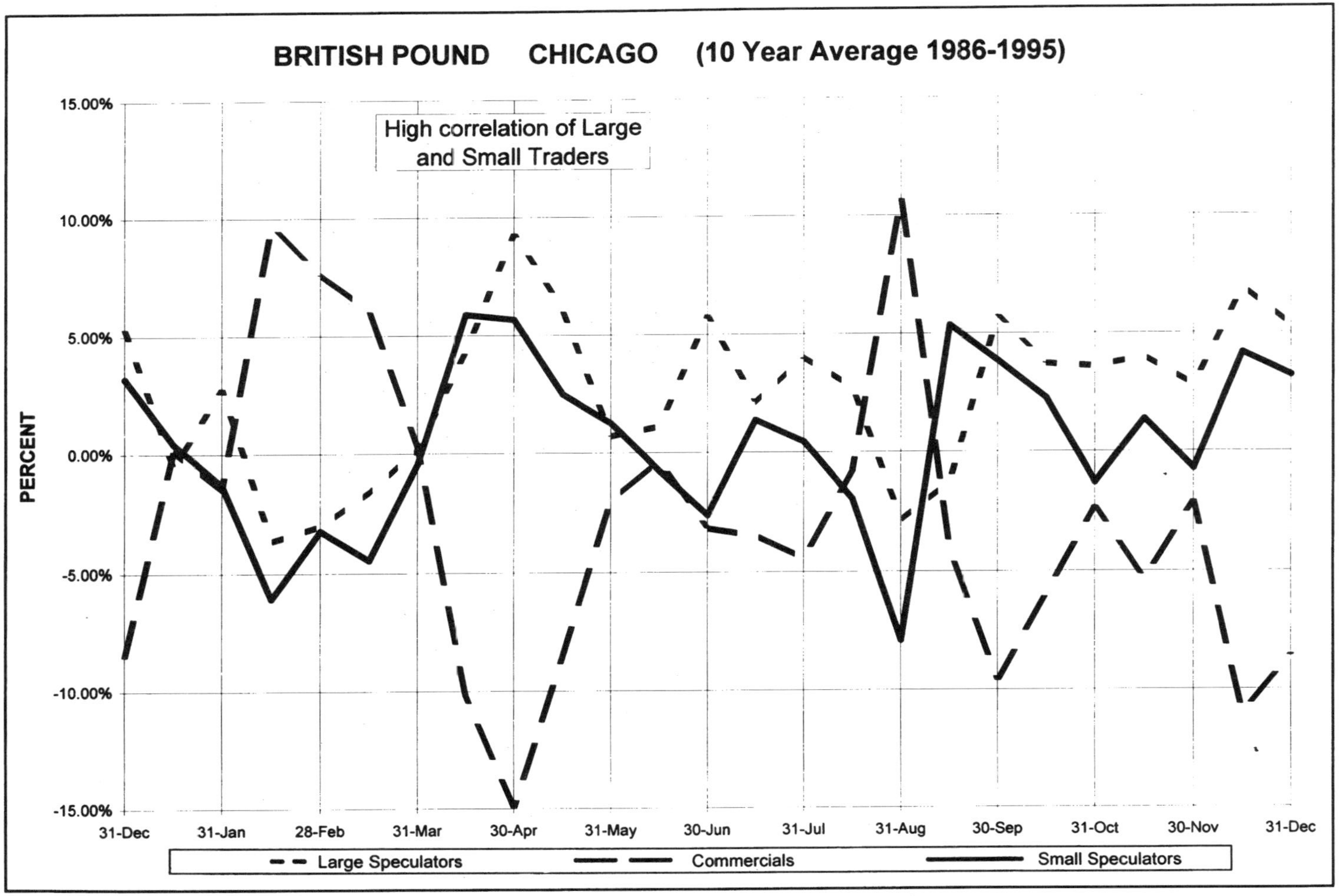
BRITISH POUND CHICAGO (10 Year Average 1986-1995)
High correlation of Large and Small Traders
PERCENT
15.00%
10.00%
5.00%
0.00%
-5.00%
-10.00%
-15.00%
31-Dec
31-Jan
28-Feb
31-Mar
30-Apr
31-May
30-Jun
31-Jul
31-Aug
30-Sep
31-Oct
30-Nov
31-Dec
Large Speculators
Commercials
Small Speculators

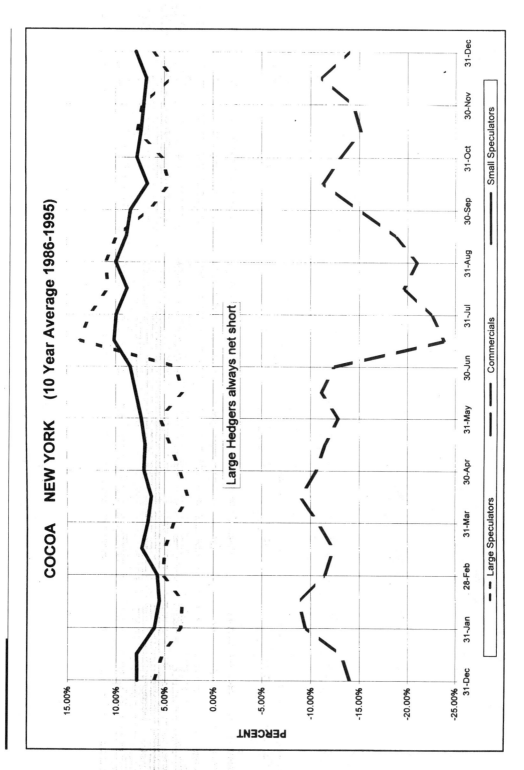

COCOA   NEW YORK   (10 Year Average 1986-1995)

Large Hedgers always net short

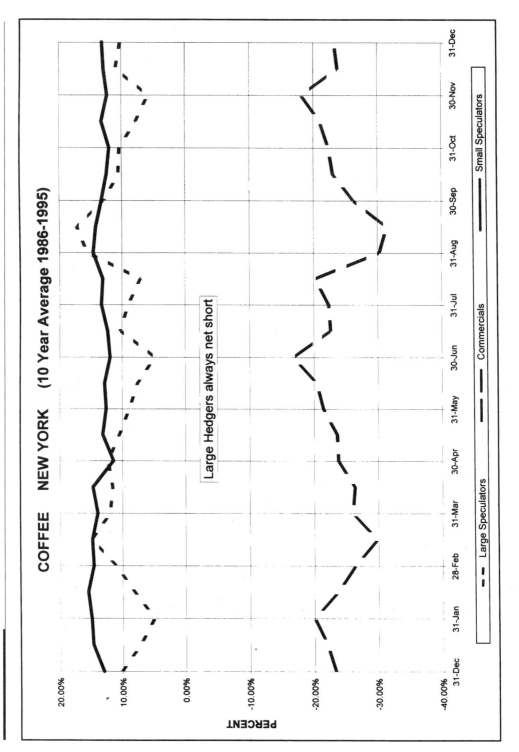

COFFEE   NEW YORK   (10 Year Average 1986-1995)

Large Hedgers always net short

- - - Large Speculators   — - — Commercials   —— Small Speculators

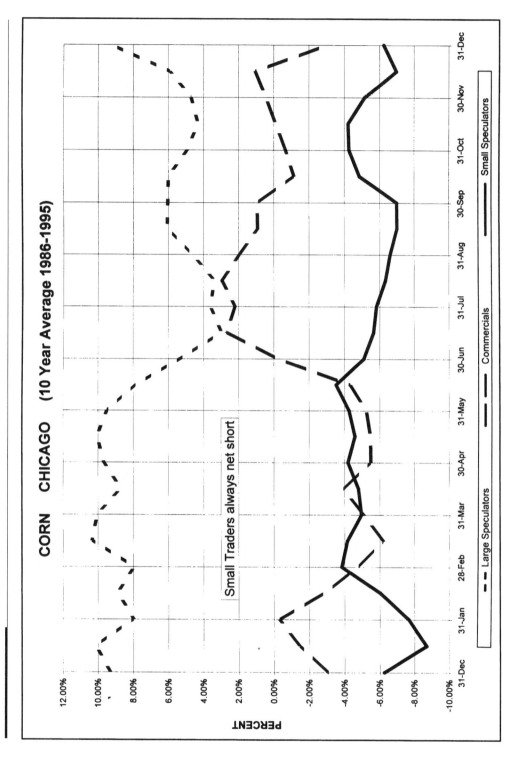

CORN   CHICAGO   (10 Year Average 1986-1995)

Small Traders always net short

Large Speculators   Commercials   Small Speculators

COTTON   NEW YORK   (10 Year Average 1986-1995)

Large Hedger moves from short to long at mid-year

- - Large Speculators   — Commercials   —— Small Speculators

FIGURE E-6

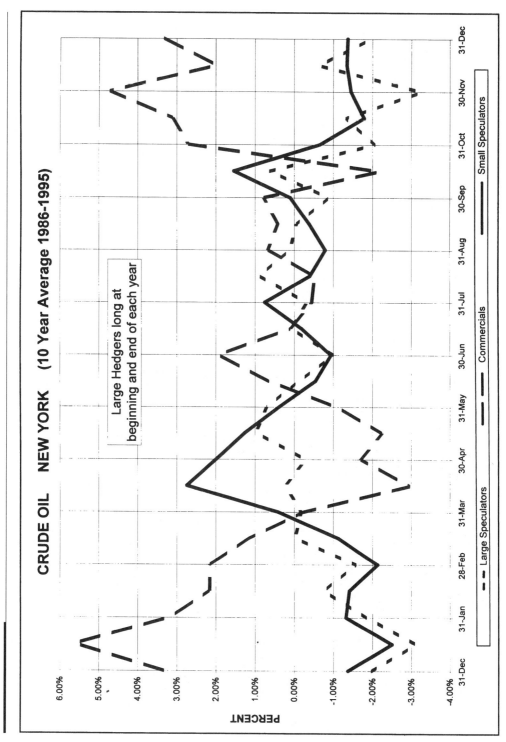

239

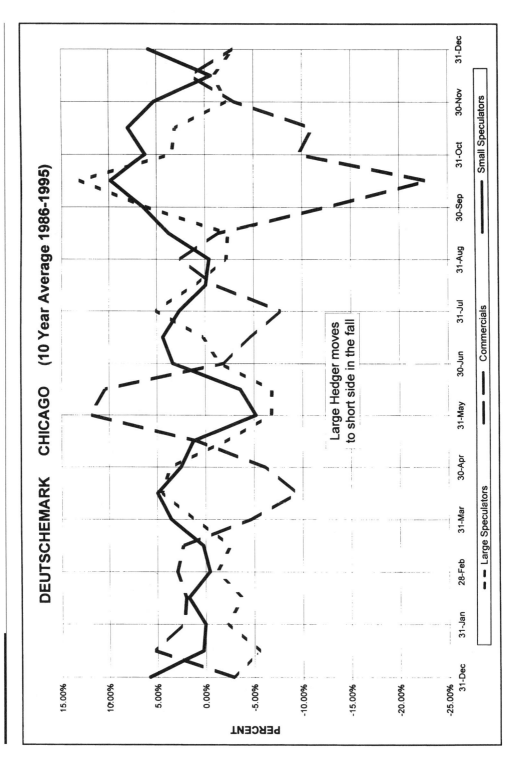

DEUTSCHEMARK   CHICAGO   (10 Year Average 1986-1995)

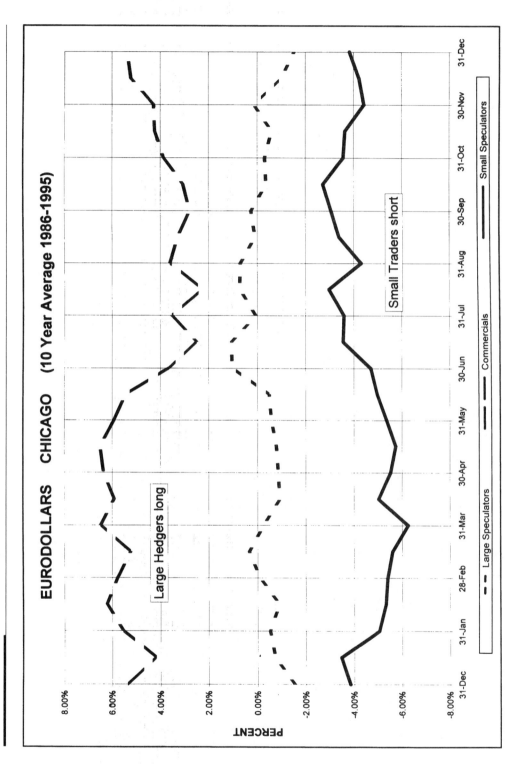

EURODOLLARS   CHICAGO   (10 Year Average 1986-1995)

GOLD   NEW YORK   (10 Year Average 1986-1995)

Small Traders tend to be long

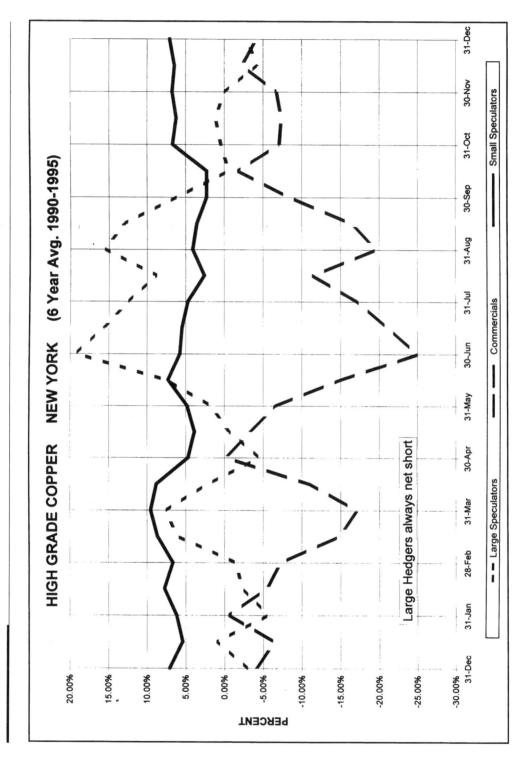

HIGH GRADE COPPER   NEW YORK   (6 Year Avg. 1990-1995)

Large Hedgers always net short

- - Large Speculators   — Commercials   — Small Speculators

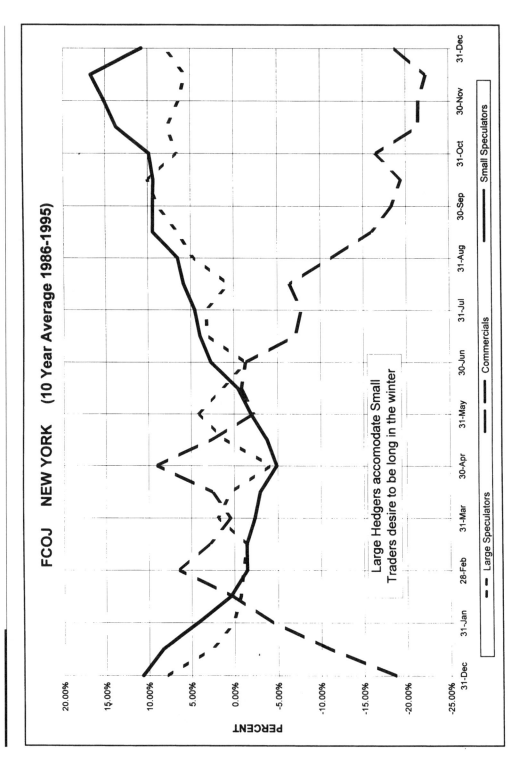

FCOJ   NEW YORK   (10 Year Average 1986-1995)

Large Hedgers accomodate Small
Traders desire to be long in the winter

- - - Large Speculators   — Commercials   Small Speculators

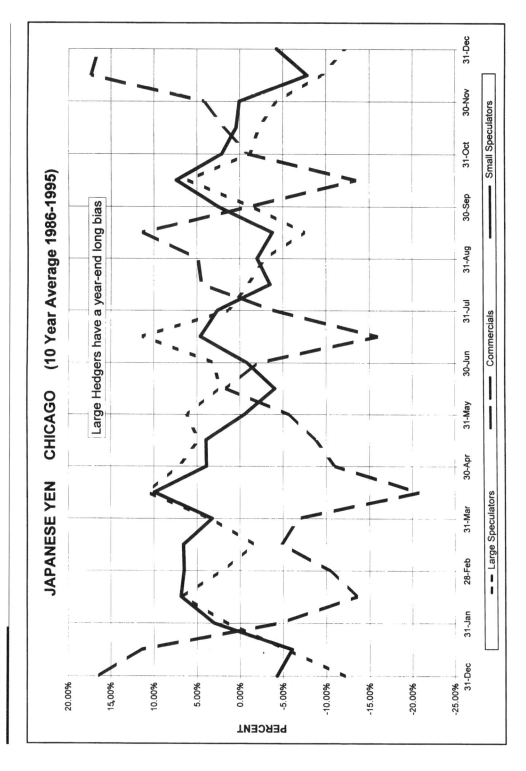

JAPANESE YEN   CHICAGO   (10 Year Average 1986-1995)

Large Hedgers have a year-end long bias

Large Speculators   Commercials   Small Speculators

245

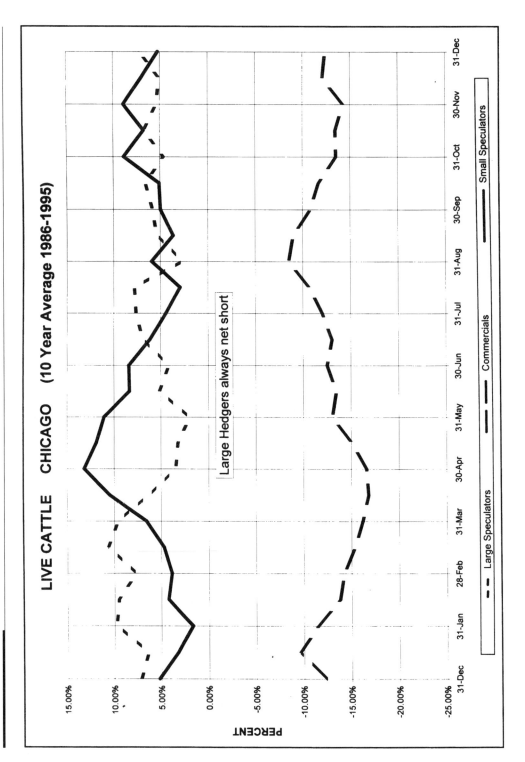

LIVE CATTLE   CHICAGO   (10 Year Average 1986-1995)

Large Hedgers always net short

Large Speculators — Commercials — Small Speculators

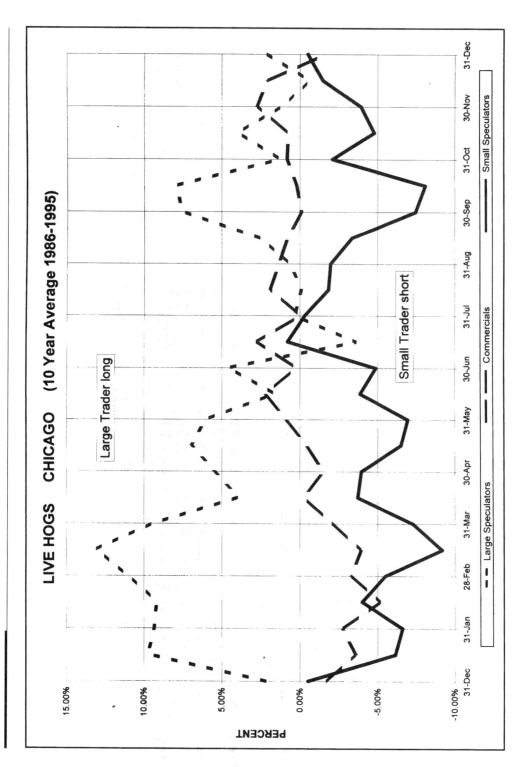

LIVE HOGS   CHICAGO   (10 Year Average 1986-1995)

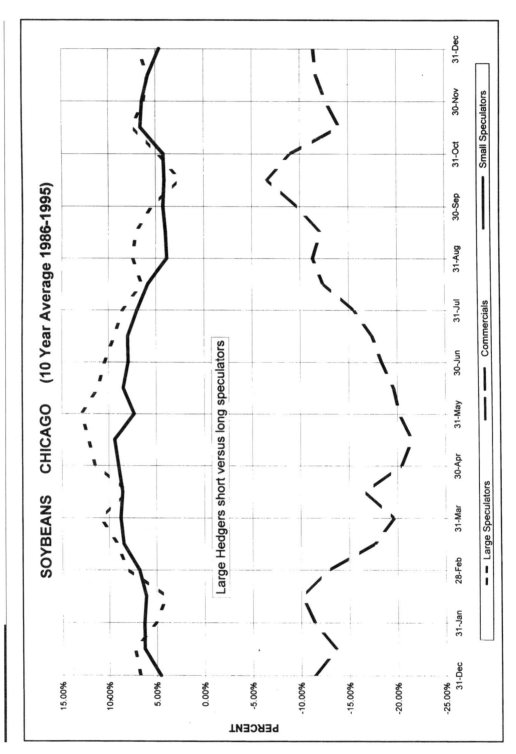

SOYBEANS   CHICAGO   (10 Year Average 1986-1995)

Large Hedgers short versus long speculators

- - - Large Speculators   — - Commercials   —— Small Speculators

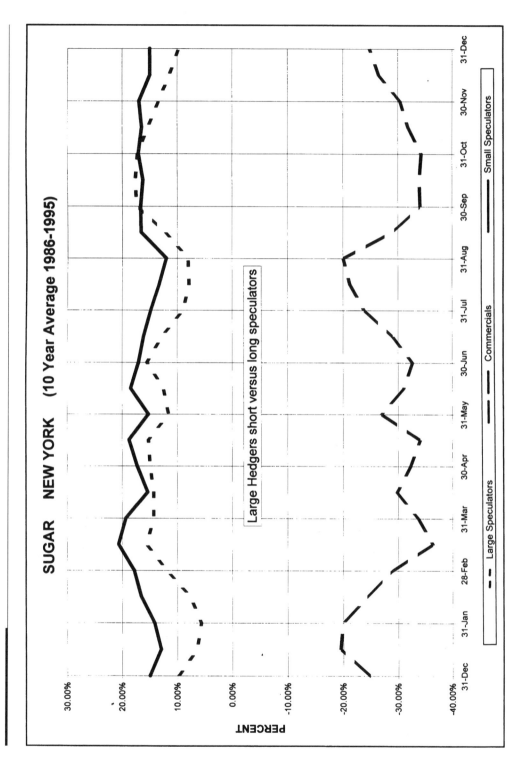

SUGAR   NEW YORK   (10 Year Average 1986-1995)

Large Hedgers short versus long speculators

- - - Large Speculators   - - - Commercials   —— Small Speculators

FIGURE E-17

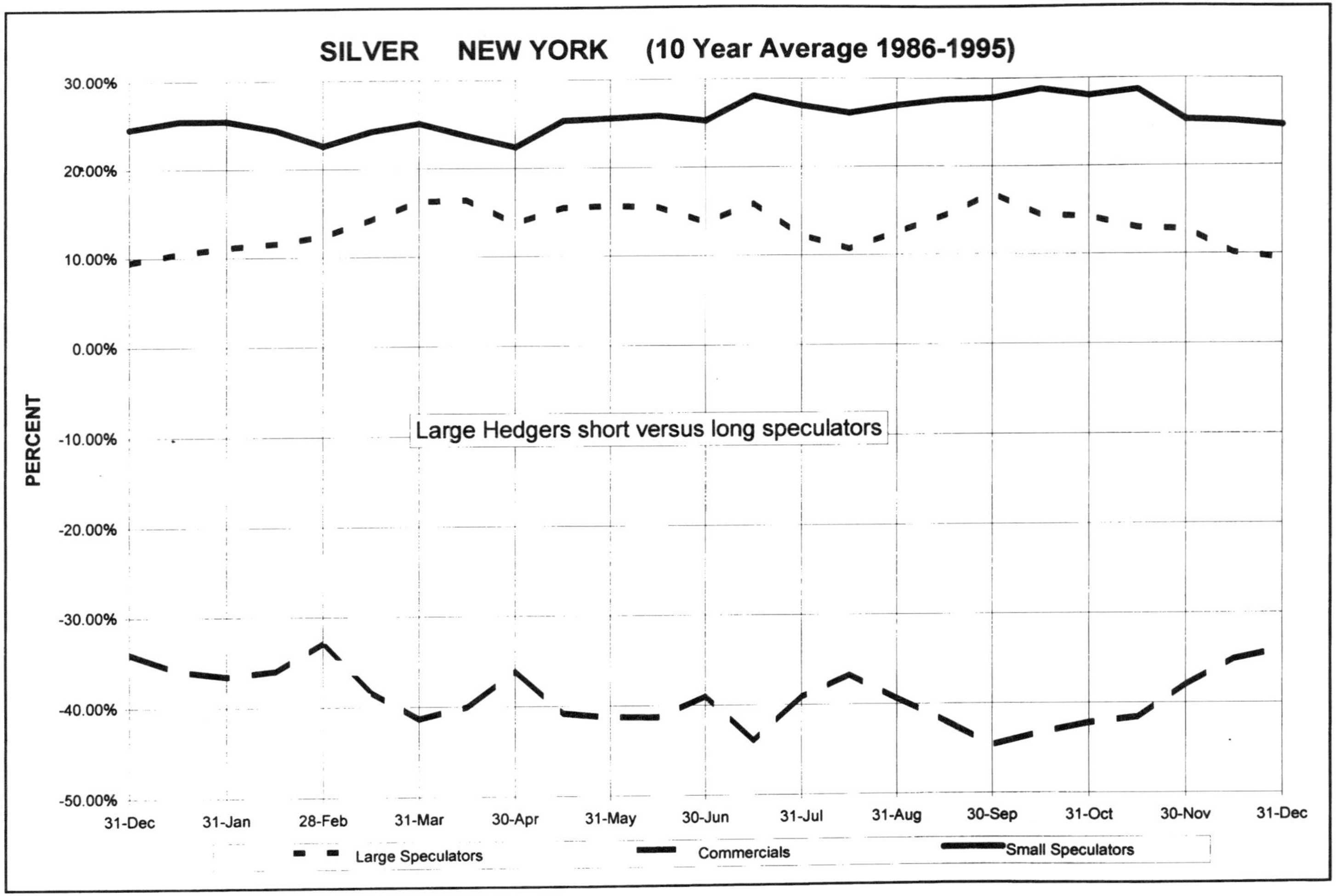

SILVER   NEW YORK   (10 Year Average 1986-1995)

Large Hedgers short versus long speculators

Small Speculators

Commercials

Large Speculators

PERCENT

30.00%
20.00%
10.00%
0.00%
-10.00%
-20.00%
-30.00%
-40.00%
-50.00%

31-Dec   31-Jan   28-Feb   31-Mar   30-Apr   31-May   30-Jun   31-Jul   31-Aug   30-Sep   31-Oct   30-Nov   31-Dec

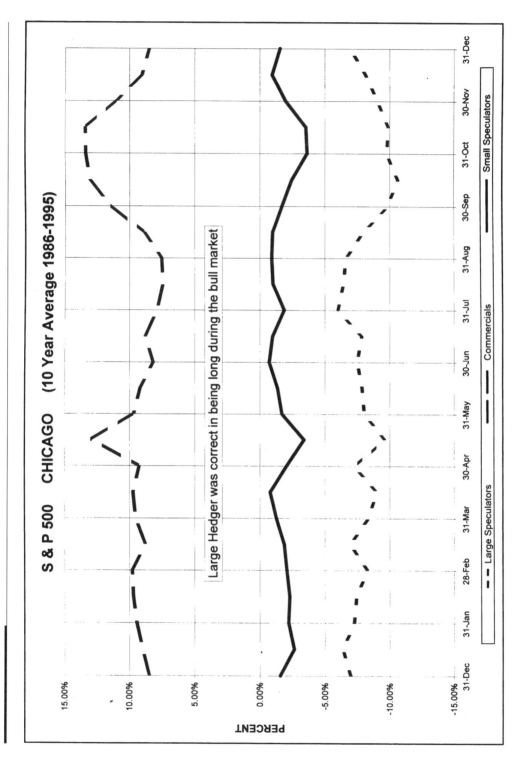

S & P 500 CHICAGO (10 Year Average 1986-1995)

Large Hedger was correct in being long during the bull market

TREASURY BONDS CHICAGO (10 Year Avg. 1986-1995)

Small traders net short early in year

- - - Large Speculators   —— Commercials   —— Small Speculators

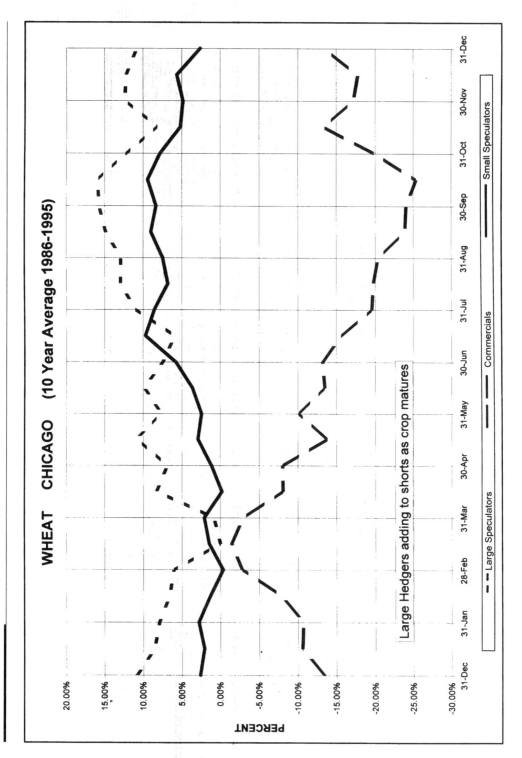

WHEAT   CHICAGO   (10 Year Average 1986-1995)

Large Hedgers adding to shorts as crop matures

– – Large Speculators   – – Commercials   —— Small Speculators

253

Reporting Levels

These are the threshold number of futures contracts for reporting Large Traders positions to the U.S. Commodity Futures Trading Commission as of June 1996.

TABLE F-1

Currently Active Contracts, 01/17/96

Exchange	Contract	CFTC ID	Report Level	Level as of
Chicago Board of Trade	Anhydrous Ammonia	253601	25	
	CBT barge freight rate index	261601	25	
	CA CAT INS LC annual index	41460A	25	09/25/1995
	CA CAT INS SC annual index	31460A	25	09/25/1995
	Canadian bonds	249601	25	
	CBT agricultural index	259601	25	
	Corn	002601	750	
	US corn yield insurance	014601	25	01/04/1996
	Iowa corn yield insurance	114601	25	04/12/1995
	Illinois corn yield insurance	214601	25	01/04/1996
	Nebraska corn yield insurance	514601	25	01/04/1996
	Ohio corn yield insurance	614601	25	01/04/1996
	Ind corn yield insurance	714601	25	01/04/1996
	Diammonium phosphate	251601	25	
	Eastern catastrophe insurance AI	10760A	25	
	Eastern catastrophe insurance QI	1076DQ	25	
	Eastern catastrophe insurance SI	10760S	25	
	Eastern catastrophe insurance LC Q	40760Q	25	09/30/1995
	Eastern catastrophe insurance SC Q	30760Q	25	09/30/1995
	ECU bonds	199601	25	
	Fosfa edible oil index	077601	25	
	Ferrous scrap metal	257601	25	
	Florida catastrophe insurance LC Quarterly	41360Q	25	09/25/1995
	Florida catastrophe insurance SC Quarterly	31360Q	25	09/25/1995
	Gold (1 kilogram)	088603	200	
	Gold, 100 troy oz	088604	200	
	Health insurance (January Pool)	10060F	25	

T A B L E F-1

Currently Active Contracts, 01/17/96

Chicago Board of Trade			
Health insurance (July Pool)	10060N	25	
Homeowners ins (Jan Pool)	10160F	25	
Homeowners insurance (July Pool)	10160N	25	
Illinois soybean yield insurance	110601	25	04/12/1995
Interest rate swaps-5 year	247601	25	
Interest rate swaps-10 year	246601	25	
International commodity index	258601	25	
Kansas winter wheat yield insurance	112601	25	04/12/1995
Long term French bonds	248601	25	
Long term German bonds	250601	25	
Municipal bond Index	121601	100	
Midwest catastrophe insurance-annual	10860A	25	
Midwest catastrophe insurance QI	10860Q	25	
Midwest catastrophe insurance SI	10860S	25	
Midwestern catastrophe insurance LC	40860Q	25	09/30/1995
Midwestern catastrophe insurance SC	30860Q	25	09/30/1995
National catastrophe insurance AI	10660A	25	
National catastrophe insurance QI	10660Q	25	
National catastrophe insurance SAI	10660S	25	
National catastrophe insurance LC Q	40660Q	25	09/30/1995
National catastrophe insurance SC Q	30660Q	25	09/30/1995
N Dakota spring wheat yield IN	113601	25	04/12/1995
Northeastern catastrophe insurance LC QTR	41040Q	25	09/30/1995
Northeastern catastrophe insurance SC QTR	31060Q	25	09/30/1995
Oats	004601	300	
Rough rice	039601	25	
Southeastern catastrophe insurance LC QTR	41160Q	25	09/25/1995
Southeastern catastrophe insurance SC QTR	31160Q	25	09/25/1995
Soybean meal	026603	175	
Soybean oil	007601	175	

Description	Code		Date
Soybeans	005601	500	
SO$_2$ emmission allowances	006601	25	
Structural plywood panel index	071604	25	
Treasury bond, zero coupon	217601	25	
Treasury note, zero-10 year	220601	25	
2 year U.S. Treasury notes CS	042602	25	
Texas catastrophe insurance LC QTR	41260Q	25	09/25/1995
Texas catastrophe insurance SC QTR	31260Q	25	09/25/1995
U.S. & Index - 5 curr	098601	50	
U.S. Treasury bonds	020601	500	
Western catastrophe insurance AI	10960A	25	
Western catastrophe insurance QI	10960Q	25	
Western catastrophe insurance SI	10960S	25	
Western catastrophe insurance LC annual	40960A	25	09/30/1995
Western catastrophe insurance SC annual	30960A	25	09/30/1995
Wheat	001601	500	
Wilshire small cap Index	263601	25	
Yield curve 10-2	512601	25	10/06/1995
Yield curve 10-5	515601	25	10/06/1995
Yield curve 10-10	531601	25	10/06/1995
Yield curve 30-2	532601	25	10/06/1995
Yield curve 30-5	535601	25	10/06/1995
Yield curve 5-2	552601	25	10/06/1995
10-year U.S. Treasury notes	043602	500	
1011 troy ounce silver	084602	150	
2-year U.S. Treasury notes	042601	200	
30-Day Federal funds	045601	100	
5-year U.S. Treasury notes	044601	300	
5000 troy ounce silver	084603	150	
Chicago Mercantile Exchange			
Fresh broilers	070642	25	
Feeder cattle	061641	50	
Lean hogs	054642	50	
Live cattle	057642	100	
Live hogs	054641	50	

TABLE F-1 (Continued)

Exchange	Contract	CFTC ID	Report Level	Level as of
Chicago Mercantile Exchange	Random length lumber	058641	25	
	Random length lumber-New	058643	25	
	Milk	052641	25	10/19/1995
	Frozen pork bellies	056641	25	
Citrus Assoc. of N Y Cotton Ex	Frzn concentrated orange juice	040701	50	
Coffee, Sugar & Cocoa Exchange	Cheddar cheese	063731	25	
	Cocoa	073732	100	
	Coffee Brazil diff	053731	25	
	Coffee C	083731	50	
	Coffee Euro-diff	003731	25	
	Non fat dry Milk	052731	25	
	Milk	052732	25	10/19/1995
	Sugar No. 11	080732	300	
	Sugar No. 14	080734	100	
	White sugar	080735	25	
Commodity Exchange Inc.	Copper-Grade #1	085692	100	
	Crude oil, sour	067691	25	
	Stock index fut. Eurotop 100	255691	25	
	Gold	088691	200	
	Gold asset participation	188691	200	
	U.S. gulf coast jet fuel	262691	25	
	Palladium	075691	25	
	Platinum	076691	50	
	Silver	084691	150	
International Monetary Market	AMEX major market index	120741	100	
	Rolling spot Australian dollar	232742	200	
	Australian dollars	232741	200	

Description	Code	Value	Date
Bpound/dmark crossrate	294742	25	
Brazilian real	102741	200	11/03/1995
Canadian dollar, forward	090743	200	
Canadian dollar, rolling spot	090742	200	
Canadian dollar	090741	200	
Cboe Mexico 3D index	152741	25	01/04/1996
Deutsche marx	094741	200	
Deutsche mark, forward	094743	200	
Deutsche mark, rolling spot	094742	200	
Dmark/Sfranc crossrate	392742	25	
French Franc	091741	200	
Forward French franc	091743	200	
Rolling spot French franc	091742	200	
FT-SE 100 stock index	254741	25	
Goldman-Sacks commodity index	256741	25	
Japanese yen	097741	200	
Japanese yen, forward	097743	200	
Japanese yen, rolling spot	097742	200	
Mark/yen crossrate	397742	25	
Mexican Peso	095741	200	
Nikkei stock average	240741	50	
Nikkei stock index 300	240742	50	
Pound sterling	095742	200	
Spot pound sterling	096744	200	
Forward pound sterling	096745	200	
Russel 2000 stock index future	239741	25	
S&P 500 Barra growth index	13874G	25	10/19/1995
S&P 500 Barra value index	13874V	25	10/19/1995
S&P 400 Midcap stock Index	338741	25	
S&P 500 stock index	138741	300	
Swiss franc	092741	200	
Swiss franc, rolling spot	092742	200	
Swiss franc, forward	092743	200	
Yen/pound crossrate	297741	25	

Exchange	Contract	CFTC ID	Report Level	Level as of
International Monetary Market	Yen/Swiss franc crossrate	497741	25	
	1-Month LIBOR rate	032741	100	
	1-year U.S. Treasury bills	041742	25	
	13-Week U.S. Treasury bills	041741	150	
	3-Mo. Euromark time deposits	394741	25	
	3-Month Eurodollars	132741	850	
	3-Mo. Euroyen time deposits	597741	25	
	30-Day Fed Fund rates	045741	25	
Kansas City Board of Trade	Natural gas	023611	100	
	Stock index future, MVL	136612	25	
	Value line stock index	136611	50	
	Wheat	001611	500	
Midamerica Commodity Exchange	Australian dollars	232631	200	
	Canadian dollar	090631	200	
	Corn	002631	750	
	Deutsche mark	094631	200	
	Gold, New York delivery	088633	200	
	Japanese yen	097631	200	
	Live cattle	057631	100	
	Live hogs	054631	50	
	Oats—old	004631	300	
	Platinum	076631	50	
	British pound sterling	096631	200	
	Silver, NY Delivery	084632	150	
	Soybean meal	026632	175	
	Soybean oil	007631	175	
	Soybeans	005631	500	
	Swiss franc	092631	200	

10/23/1995

Exchange	Instrument	Code	Value
	U.S. Treasury bonds	020631	500
	Wheat	001631	500
	13-Week U.S. Treasury bills	041631	150
	3-Month Eurodollars	132631	850
	5-year U.S. Treasury notes	044631	300
	6.5-10 year U.S. Treasury note	043631	500
Minneapolis Grain Exchange	Black tiger shrimp	059622	25
	White shrimp	059621	25
	Wheat	001621	500
	Wheat-European	001625	500
	White wheat	001624	500
New York Cotton Exchange	Cotton No. 2	033661	50
	D-Mark/Sfranc crossrate	392661	25
	French Franc/dmark crossrate	594661	25
	Ital. lira/Mark crossrate	694661	25
	Swedish Krona/dmark crossrate	494661	25
	NYCE emerging mkt debt index	265661	25
	Dmark/Pound crossrate	294661	25
	Swiss franc	092661	200
	2 year U.S. Treasury notes	042662	200
	U.S. dollar index	098662	50
	Yen/Mark crossrate	397661	25
	5 year U.S. Treasury notes	044662	300
New York Futures Exchange	Canadian dollar	090771	200
	CRB futures price index	218771	25
	W. German deutschemark	094771	200
	Stock index, NYSE CMP new	148776	50
	Japanese yen	097771	200
	British pound sterling	096771	200
	Stock index future, NYSE LCI	148775	25
	Stock index future, NYSE UTL	148772	25
	Swiss franc	092771	200
New York Mercantile Exchange	Crude oil, light "sweet"	067651	300
	Crude oil, sour	067652	25

TABLE F-1 (Concluded)

Exchange	Contract	CFTC ID	Report Level	Level as of
New York Mercantile Exchange	Unleaded gasoline, gulf coast	111655	25	
	No. 2 heating oil, N.Y. harbor	022651	250	
	Spreads, heating oil to crude	867651	25	
	Natural gas	023651	100	
	Palladium	075651	25	
	Platinum	076651	50	
	Propane gas	066651	25	
	Unleaded gasoline, N.Y. Harbor	111652	150	
Philadelphia Board of Trade	Australian dollar	232811	200	
	Canadian dollar	090811	200	
	W. German deutsche mark	094811	200	
	European currency unit	099811	25	
	French Franc	091811	200	
	Japanese yen	097811	200	
	British Pound sterling	096811	200	
	Swiss franc	092811	200	

Seasonal Trends in Volume and Open Interest

FIGURE G-1

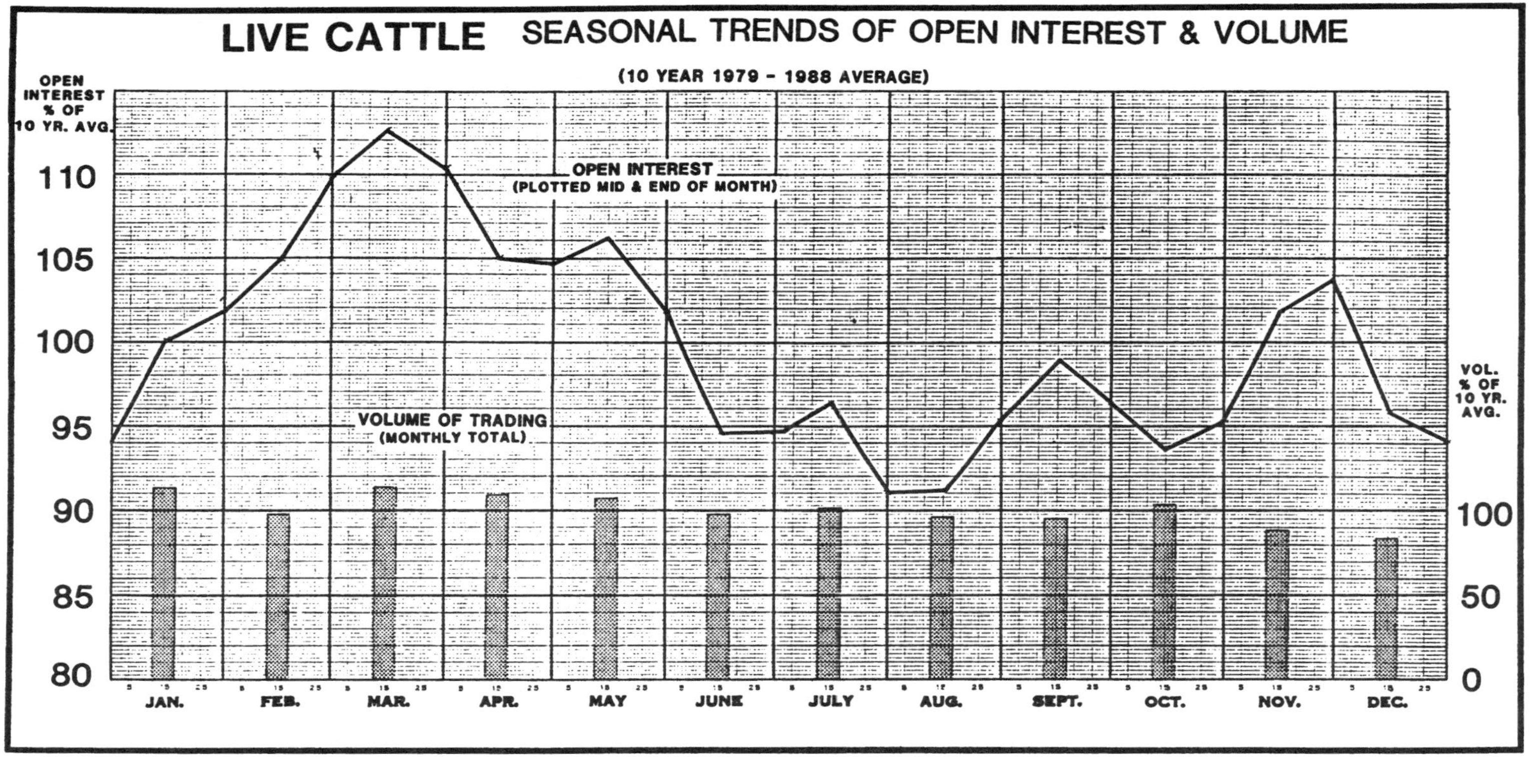

LIVE CATTLE   SEASONAL TRENDS OF OPEN INTEREST & VOLUME

(10 YEAR 1979 - 1988 AVERAGE)

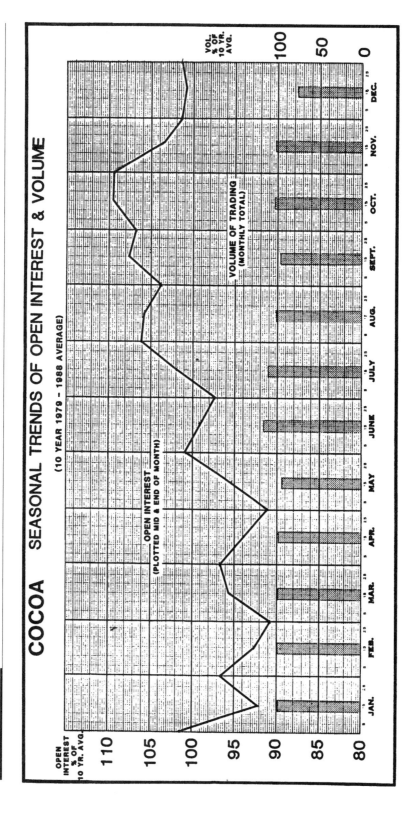

COCOA   SEASONAL TRENDS OF OPEN INTEREST & VOLUME

(10 YEAR 1979 – 1988 AVERAGE)

OPEN INTEREST
(PLOTTED MID & END OF MONTH)

VOLUME OF TRADING
(MONTHLY TOTAL)

FIGURE G-3

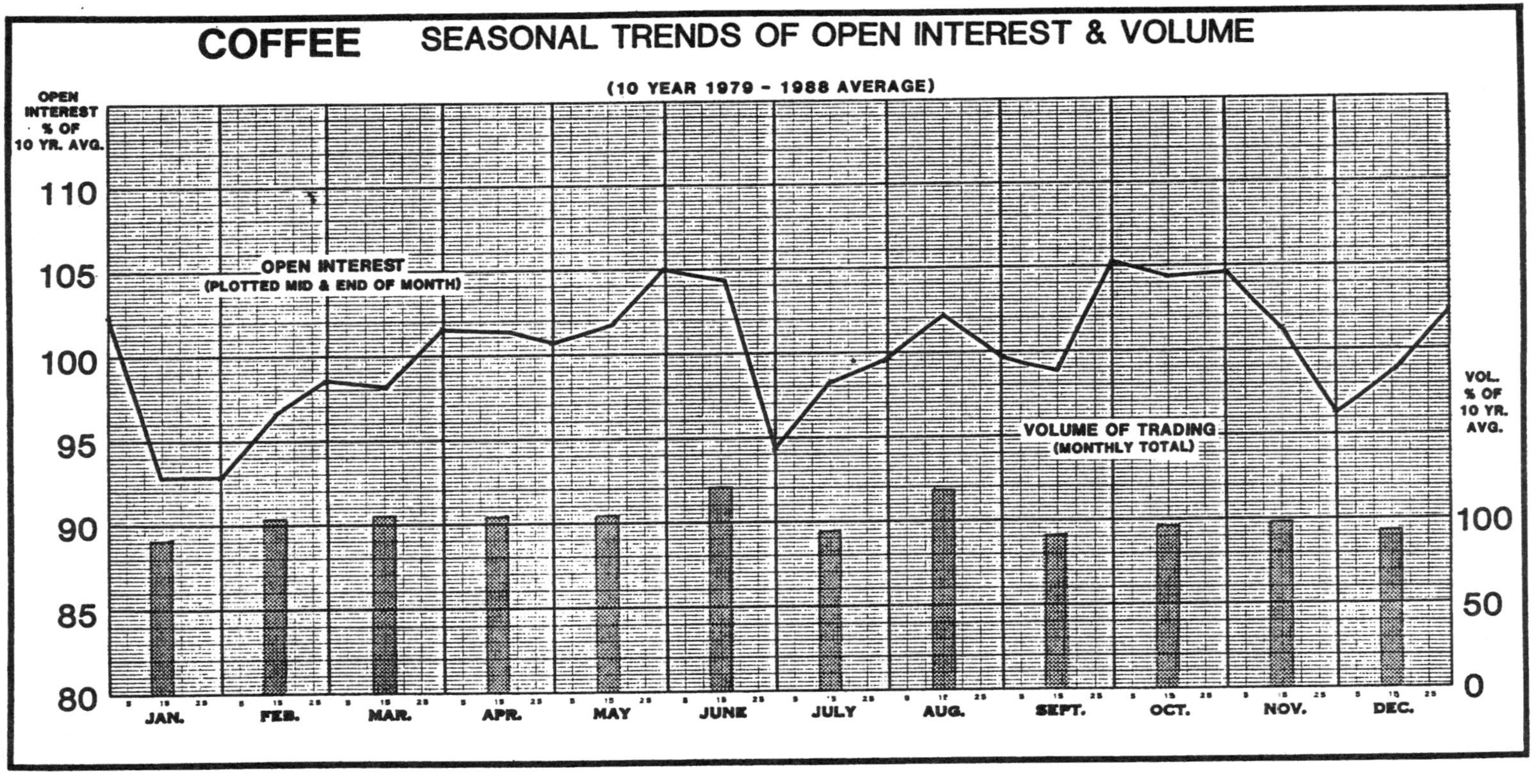

COFFEE   SEASONAL TRENDS OF OPEN INTEREST & VOLUME

(10 YEAR 1979 – 1988 AVERAGE)

266

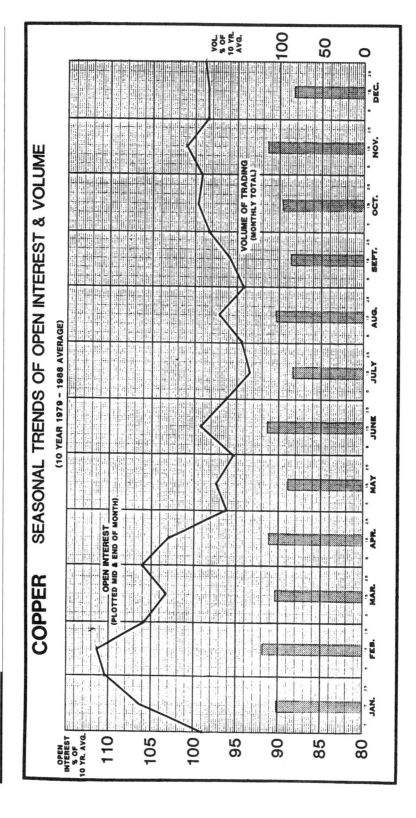

COPPER   SEASONAL TRENDS OF OPEN INTEREST & VOLUME

(10 YEAR 1979 – 1988 AVERAGE)

267

FIGURE G-5

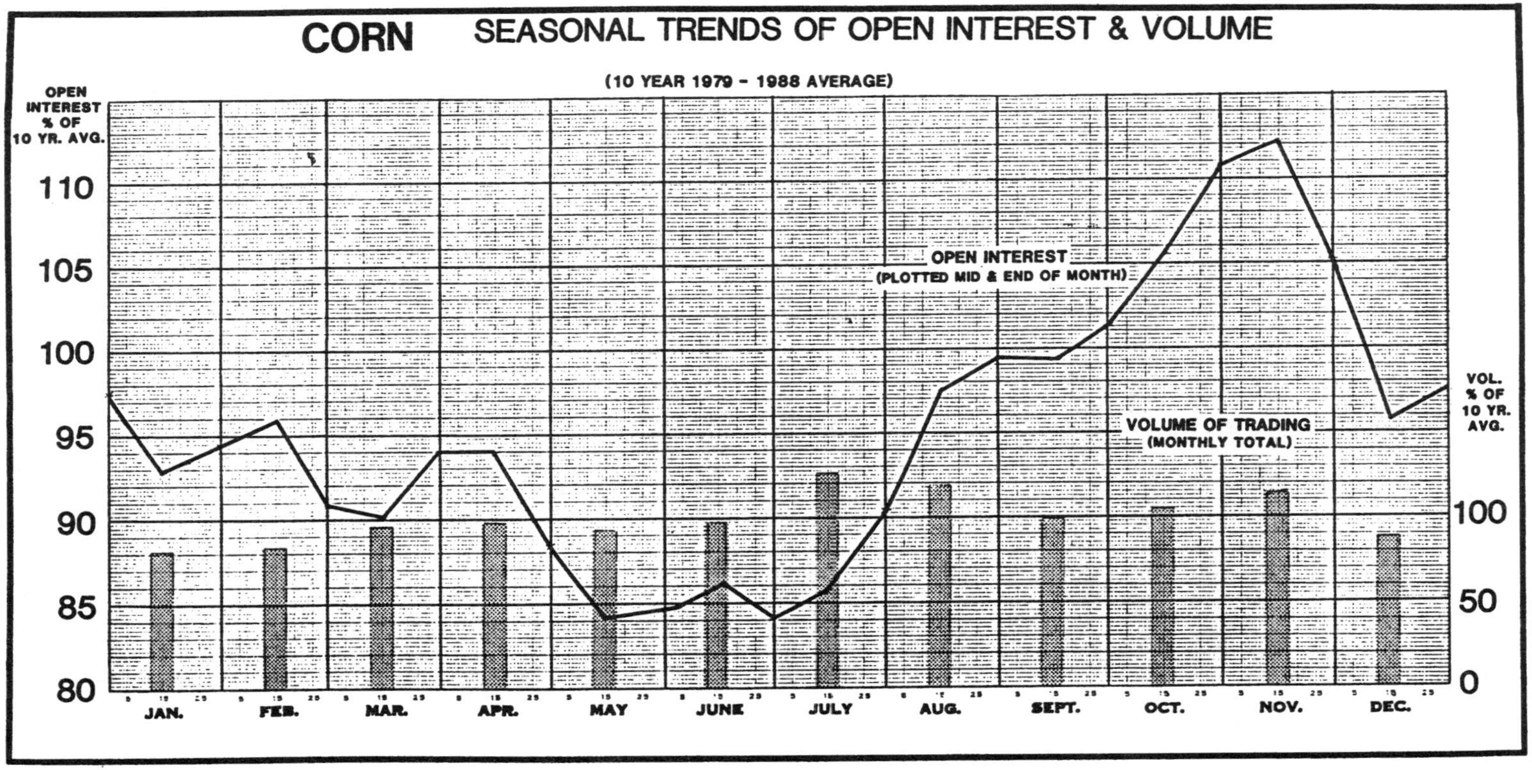

CORN   SEASONAL TRENDS OF OPEN INTEREST & VOLUME

(10 YEAR 1979 – 1988 AVERAGE)

268

FIGURE G–6

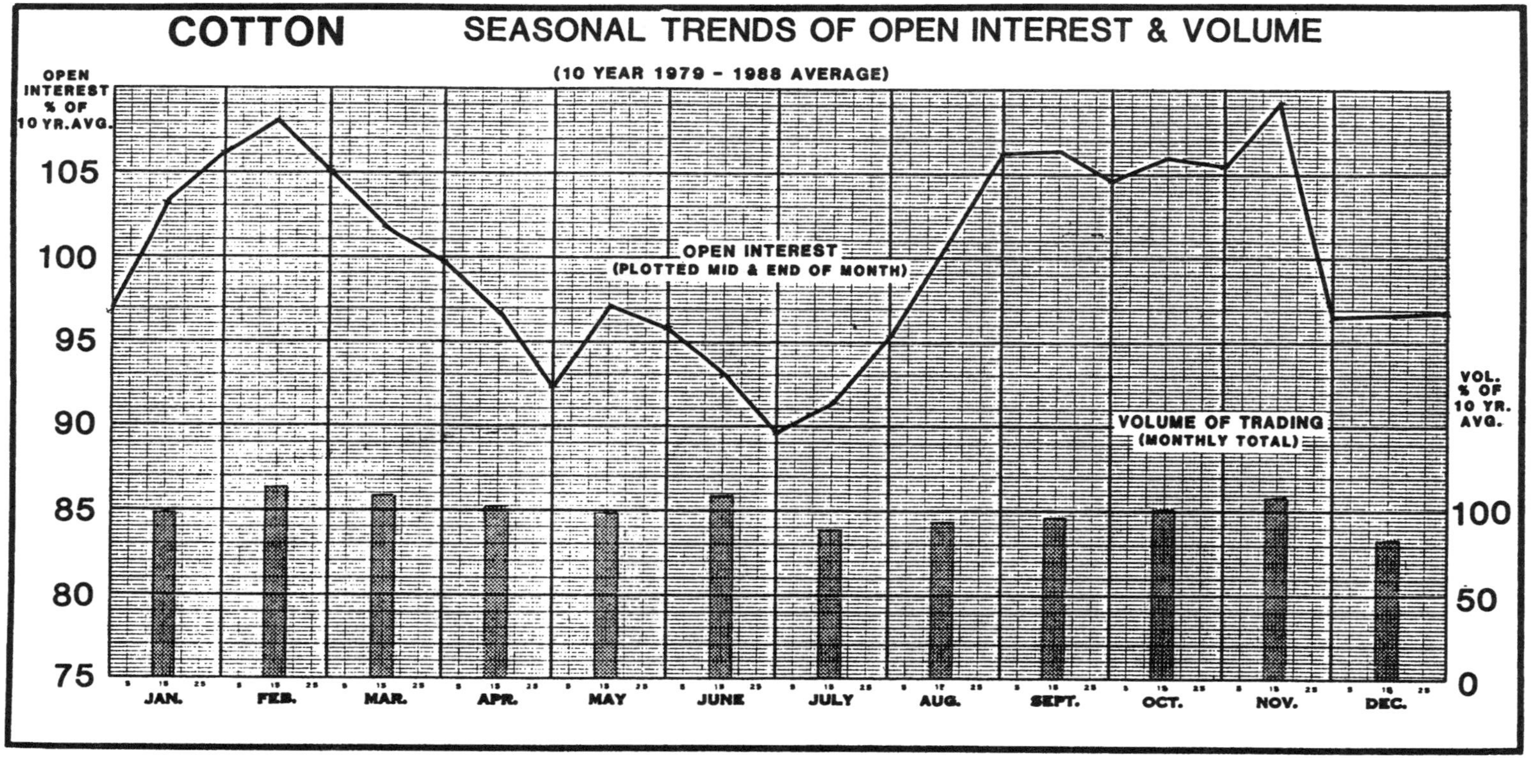
COTTON
SEASONAL TRENDS OF OPEN INTEREST & VOLUME
(10 YEAR 1979 - 1988 AVERAGE)
OPEN INTEREST % OF 10 YR.AVG.
105
100
95
90
85
80
75
OPEN INTEREST
(PLOTTED MID & END OF MONTH)
VOLUME OF TRADING
(MONTHLY TOTAL)
VOL. % OF 10 YR. AVG.
100
50
0
JAN.
FEB.
MAR.
APR.
MAY
JUNE
JULY
AUG.
SEPT.
OCT.
NOV.
DEC.

APPENDIX H

Exchange Telephone Numbers and Web Sites

CHICAGO BOARD OF TRADE & MID-AMERICA COMMODITY EXCHANGE

MIDIS-TOUCH RECORDED MESSAGE SYSTEM

(312) 939-2268

Volume and/or Open Interest example for T-Bond futures

	Code	Release Time
Afternoon project 'A', evening open outcry, overnight project 'A'	03#	7:00 a.m. (and most often earlier)
Preliminary volume and open interest for the *previous* trading day	08#	7:30–8:00 a.m. (depending on release from Clearing House)
Final volume and open interest for *previous* trading day	28#	12:30 p.m.
Estimated volume for the *current* trading day (which just closed at 2:00 p.m.) Note: This is a notoriously unreliable figure.	30#	2:30 p.m.

Price Codes (T-Bond Commodity Code = 00)

Early afternoon project 'A'	25#	2:30–4:30
Evening open outcry	23#	5:20/6:20–8:05/9:05
Overnight project "A'	37#	10:30–6:00
Regular trading hours	20#	7:20–2:00

WWW PAGE = http://www.cbot.com

TABLE H–1

Sample of the Chicago Mercantile Exchange's web site statistics

Off the Ticker: Standard & Poor's 500 Furtures   http://www.cme.com/market/quote/.Small/sp.html

Standard & Poor's 500 Futures: Settlement Prices as of 06/05/96

MTH/ STRIKE	OPEN	HIGH	LOW	LAST	SETT	PT CHGE	EST VOL	SETT	VOL	INT
		--- SESSION ---						---- PRIOR	DAY	----
SP S & P 500										
JUN96	673.30	679.70	672.75	678.85	678.75	+555	68K	673.20	66624	154525
SEP96	679.00	685.60	678.70A	684.65B	684.55	+550	8932	679.05	7910	36988
DEC96	685.50	691.55B	684.90A	690.85B	690.65	+560	166	685.05	184	4558
MAR97	697.20	698.40B	691.65A	698.00B	697.55	+580	187	691.75	1	545
TOTAL							EST.VOL		VOL	OPEN INT.
TOTAL							78251		74719	196616

T A B L E   H–2

Sample of the Chicago Board of Trade's web site statistics

Preliminary/Final Furtures Volume   http://www.cbot.com/clbfvolf.htm

FINAL FUTURES VOLUME FOR TUESDAY, JUNE 4, 1996

			TRADING VOLUME			CASH		OPEN INTEREST	
COMMODITY	MTH	YR	EVENING	PROJ A	DAYTIME	EXCHNGE	GIVEUPS	AT CLOSE	CHANGE
T-BONDS	JUN	96	126	1,891	18,115	1,923	6,517	127,671	10,204−
	SEP	96	2,860	6,235	218,487	14,412	56,973	284,396	18,388+
	DEC	96			61		10	8,711	38+
	MAR	97			445		445	1,148	5+
	JUN	97						39	
	SEP	97						4	
	DEC	97						17	
	MAR	98						1	
	JUN	98						1	
	TOTAL		2,986	8,126	237,108	16,335	63,945	421,988	8,227+

CHICAGO MERCANTILE EXCHANGE
MERCLINE RECORDED MESSAGE SYSTEM
(312) 930-8282

Regular Trading Hours (available by 4:00 a.m. CST)

	Price Code			*Vol. & O.I. Code*		
	Futures	**Calls**	**Puts**	**Futures**	**Calls**	**Puts**
Eurodollars	321	463	465	320	464	466
Deutsche mark	345	359	361	346	360	362
Swiss franc	349	363	365	350	364	366
Japanese yen	347	367	369	348	368	370
British pound	341	371	373	342	372	374
S&P 500	127	459	461	126	460	462

Electronic Trading Hours (GLOBEX) (available by 7:15 a.m. CST)

	Price Code	Volume Code
Eurodollars	955	954
Deutsche mark	719	718
Swiss franc	919	918
Japanese yen	819	818
British pound	801	800
S&P 500	764	769

Combined Volume and Open Interest (plotted on the chart)

Currencies	131
Interest rates	132
Equity futures	133

WWW page = http://www.cme.com

LONDON INTERNATIONAL FINANCIAL FUTURES EXCHANGE

WWW page = http://www.liffe.com/liffe/statdis.htm

T A B L E   H–3

Sample of the London International Financial Futures Exchange's web site Statistics

ftp://ftp.liffe.com/liffe/dfut0604.txt   ftp://ftp.liffe.com/liffe/dfut0604.txt

```
Futures

Business Day  Tue  4 Jun 1996

                                      Floor Daily    APT Daily      Lifetime       APT
              Opening Range Settle Change High   Low  High    Low  High    Low  Close

Short Term Interest Rate Products


Three Month ECU
Jun 96  95.56  95.56  95.57  +0.02  95.57  95.56  N/A   N/A   95.89  91.46  N/A
Sep 96  95.58  95.58  95.60  +0.03  95.61  95.58  N/A   N/A   95.90  91.82  N/A
Dec 96  95.46  95.46  95.49  +0.05  95.50  95.46  N/A   N/A   95.75  92.90  N/A
Mar 97  95.27  95.27  95.29  +0.04  95.30  95.27  N/A   N/A   95.47  92.70  N/A
Jun 97  94.96  94.96  94.98  +0.05  94.98  94.96  N/A   N/A   95.21  92.67  N/A
Sep 97  94.68  94.68  94.69  +0.05  94.69  94.66  N/A   N/A   94.94  93.09  N/A
Dec 97  94.31  94.31  94.32  +0.04  94.31  94.31  N/A   N/A   94.64  93.50  N/A
Mar 98  93.98  93.98  94.00  +0.05  94.00  93.98  N/A   N/A   94.16  93.23  N/A
```

COMMODITY FUTURES TRADING COMMISSION

WWW page = http://www.cftc.gov/cftc/

This is an excellent site on the INTERNET to obtain links to other sites. Particularly useful are the links to most all of the world's futures exchanges.

TABLE H–4

CFTC Web Site, with Links to Other Sites

COMMODITY FUTURES TRADING COMMISSION (CFTC)   http://www.cftc.gov/cftc/

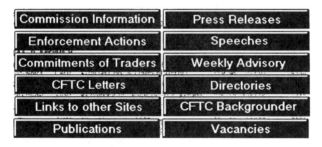

CFTC Information | Press Releases | Enforcement | Speeches | Commitments of Traders | Weekly Advisory | CFTC Letters | Directories | Links |
Backgrounder | Publications | Vacancy Announcements

INDEX

Kenneth H. Shaleen is President of CHARTWATCH, a research firm to the futures industry that he founded in 1984. Among the many services offered by CHARTWATCH are:

- A weekly technical research report *CHARTWATCH*

- Daily telephone market updates covering financial instrument futures

- Technical analysis videotapes

- Technical analysis course presentations

Please direct all inquiries concerning any of the services offered by CHARTWATCH to:

CHARTWATCH
Fulton House 1700
345 North Canal Street
Chicago, IL 60606 USA
Telephone: 312-454-1130
Fax: 312-454-1134

http://www.chartwatch.com/research